Spinoza's Authority Volume II:
Resistance and Power
in the Political Treatises

Also available from Bloomsbury

Conflict, Power, and Multitude in Machiavelli and Spinoza, Filippo Del Lucchese

Spinoza and the Specters of Modernity, Michael Mack

Between Hegel and Spinoza, edited by Hasana Sharp and Jason E. Smith

Spinoza: Ethics of an Outlaw, Ivan Segré

Spinoza's Authority Volume I, edited by A. Kiarina Kordela and Dimitris Vardoulakis

The Role of God in Spinoza's Metaphysics, Sherry Deveaux

Bloomsbury Companion to Spinoza, edited by Wiep van Bunge, Henri Krop, Piet Steenbakkers and Jeroen van de Ven

Spinoza's Authority Volume II: Resistance and Power in the Political Treatises

Edited by
A. Kiarina Kordela and Dimitris Vardoulakis

Bloomsbury Academic
An imprint of Bloomsbury Publishing Plc

BLOOMSBURY
LONDON • OXFORD • NEW YORK • NEW DELHI • SYDNEY

Bloomsbury Academic

An imprint of Bloomsbury Publishing Plc

50 Bedford Square	1385 Broadway
London	New York
WC1B 3DP	NY 10018
UK	USA

www.bloomsbury.com

BLOOMSBURY and the Diana logo are trademarks of Bloomsbury Publishing Plc

First published 2018

© A. Kiarina Kordela, Dimitris Vardoulakis and contributors, 2018

Kiarina Kordela, Dimitris Vardoulakis have asserted their right under the Copyright, Designs and Patents Act, 1988, to be identified as Editors of this work.

All rights reserved. No part of this publication may be reproduced or transmitted in any form or by any means, electronic or mechanical, including photocopying, recording, or any information storage or retrieval system, without prior permission in writing from the publishers.

No responsibility for loss caused to any individual or organization acting on or refraining from action as a result of the material in this publication can be accepted by Bloomsbury or the author.

British Library Cataloguing-in-Publication Data
A catalogue record for this book is available from the British Library.

ISBN:	HB:	978-1-3500-1106-9
	ePDF:	978-1-3500-1104-5
	ePub:	978-1-3500-1105-2

Library of Congress Cataloging-in-Publication Data
A catalog record for this book is available from the Library of Congress.

Series: Bloomsbury Studies in Continental Philosophy

Typeset by Integra Software Services Pvt. Ltd.
Printed and bound in Great Britain

Contents

Preface *A. Kiarina Kordela and Dimitris Vardoulakis*	vi
Acknowledgments	vii
Reference Guide	viii
Spinoza's Authority in the Treatises: An Introduction *Dimitris Vardoulakis*	1

1. Memory, Chance and Conflict: Machiavelli in the *Theologico-Political Treatise* Vittorio Morfino — 7
2. The Symptomatic Relationship between Law and Conflict in Spinoza: *Jura communia* as *anima imperii* Filippo Del Lucchese — 27
3. Authority and the Law: The Primacy of Justification over Legitimacy in Spinoza Dimitris Vardoulakis — 45
4. Hobbes and Spinoza on Scriptural Interpretation, the Hebrew Republic and the Deconstruction of Sovereignty James R. Martel — 67
5. Spinoza's Politics of Error Siarhei Biareishyk — 101
6. Spinoza's Immanent Sovereignty: Fantasy and the Decision of Interpretation A. Kiarina Kordela and Joseph Bermas-Dawes — 125
7. Spinoza and Signs: The Two Covenants and Authority in the *Theological-Political Treatise* Gregg Lambert — 153
8. Spinoza and the Hydraulic Discipline of Affects: From the Theologico-Political to the Economic Regime of Desire Chiara Bottici and Miguel de Beistegui — 167

Biographical Notes	193
Index	196

Preface

A. Kiarina Kordela and Dimitris Vardoulakis

Just as in the 1960s the pessimism about dialectical materialism was giving way to a new hope that Marxist dialectics can be amended or augmented by Spinoza's anti-teleological philosophy, a new, seemingly intractable problem arose. Namely, the problem that the more one opposes regimes of power, the more this opposition strengthens the structural system that makes such regimes possible. As Foucault puts this point somewhere: "Anyone who attempts to oppose the law in order to found a new order … will encounter the silent and infinitely accommodating welcome of the law. The law does not change: it subsided into the grave once and for all, and each of its forms is only a metamorphosis of that never-ending death." This problem is even more acute in neoliberal governmentality, where it becomes increasingly difficult to identify even a target to oppose or resist, given that executive government cedes a lot of its power to capital.

This may suggest that optimism of the will in the face of the pessimism of the intellect is even more urgent today—and yet such a stance is precarious for a Spinozist who would be suspicious not only of any concept of the will but also of the very idea of hope, given what Spinoza has to say about the will and about hope in his works.

The wager of the present two collections is that we may be better served by paying close attention to what Spinoza says about authority. Examining Spinoza's authority in the full range of its significations—as prophetic authority or as sovereignty, as power or as authoritative process of interpretation—we may be able to evade the dilemma between pessimism and optimism. In fact, we may be able to steer a path that shows how resistance is possible because authority is ever present as obedience or as the sad emotions that decrease our power.

Acknowledgments

We are thankful to all of our contributors as much for the final products that appear in the form of these thoughtful essays as for what came before that: their enthusiastic engagement in conference panels and workshops that have helped us all shape our ideas as we were putting them down in essay forms. These events include: the seminar on "Spinoza's Authority," organized by Dimitris Vardoulakis, which took place at the University of Western Sydney, in Sydney, Australia, in August 2012; the thematic stream on "Spinozan Politics" at the *London Conference on Critical Thought*, organized by Filippo Del Lucchese and Dimitris Vardoulakis, which took place at the Royal Holloway, University of London, in June 2013; the seminar on "Spinoza's Authority: Resistance and Power" at the conference of the *American Comparative Literature Association*, organized by Siarhei Biareishyk and A. Kiarina Kordela, which took place at the New York University in New York, in March 2014; and the workshop on "Spinoza's *Theologico-Political Treatise*," organized by Stathis Gourgouris and Dimitris Vardoulakis, which took place at Columbia University in New York, in November 2015.

Reference Guide

References to Spinoza's works

The various translations of Spinoza's works offer often significantly different interpretation of the meaning of his original Latin text. For this reason, the contributors have been free to choose their preferred translation, or to translate themselves the Latin from the established text of Spinoza's works in the Gebhardt edition of the *Opera*.

The following abbreviations of specific works have been used:

E = *Ethics* [*Ethica*]

The Roman numeral in capital following *E* indicates the part of the *Ethics*. For example, *E* I is *Ethics*, Part I, *E* II is *Ethics* Part II, and so on. The following abbreviations have been used here:

- A = Axiom
- Ap. = Appendix
- C = Corollary
- D = Definition
- L = Lemma
- P = Proposition
- Pr = Proof
- Pref = Preface
- S = Scholium

So, for instance, *E* II, P7 refer to *Ethics*, Part I, Proposition 7. And, *E* IV, P34S refers to *Ethics*, Parts IV, Scholium to Proposition 34.

Other abbreviations to Spinoza's works:

TIE (Treatise on the Emendation of the Intellect): cited by paragraph number.
Ep. (The Letters): cited by letter number.
PC (Principles of Cartesian Philosophy)
ST (Short Treatise)

TP (Tractatus Politicus): cited by chapter followed by paragraph number.
TTP (Tractatus Theologico-Politicus)

The contributors indicate in each chapter which edition of the above works they prefer to use.

Spinoza's Authority in the Treatises: An Introduction

Dimitris Vardoulakis

Any discussion of authority in Spinoza's political treatises—both the *Theological-Political Treatise* and the *Political Treatise*—needs to start by explaining what "authority" means in this context. There are at least three words in Latin which cover the semantic range of the term authority in English. They are "auctoritas," "imperium" and "summa potestas."

"Auctoritas" traditionally refers to a personal authority. Since the Roman Republic, one is understood to have "auctoritas" when his or her authority is not only unquestioned but moreover unquestionable. One can imagine here elderly wise figureheads, or figures whose office puts them in a higher and untouchable position. Spinoza's primary example of figures of auctoritas are the prophets, whose revealed knowledge cannot be questioned. One good way to understand auctoritas is to consider what it is that resists it. Traditionally, the answer to this question is laughter. Thus, the function of the court jester had been to laugh at the authority of the king—and by virtue of being the only figure who could perform that function to reinforce that authority. Maybe Spinoza's transgression, which earned him the unwanted honor of the greatest atheist in the modern philosophical tradition, was to laugh at the auctoritas of the prophets in the *Theological-Political Treatise* by showing the absurdity, for instance, of holding their laws as inviolable. The humor of the *Theological-Political Treatise* is linked to the strategy to undermine the authority of the prophets.

By contrast, one cannot laugh at "imperium." The word in Latin points to the limits of the authority's exercise of power. Thus, the imperium of a sovereign would be the territory within which the sovereign can exercise power. Synecdochically, imperium contains a legal aspect as it points out how far a legal system extends, or who is covered by certain laws. There is something less personal and more abstract in the term imperium in comparison to auctoritas.

Thus, although the word imperium has something of authority, it may be best translated in most cases as state. Imperium can be challenged by questioning how far it extends. This strategy to challenge imperium came to the fore with the Reformation by questioning the Roman Catholic Pope's *imperium in imperio* (or, state within a state), the idea being that Ecclesiastical and sovereign authorities should not overlap. Or, more simply—but no less problematically— the state becomes separate from the Church. Spinoza's political treatises and his conception and use of the various senses of authority are informed by the debates about the limits of imperium which were raging for over a century when he started writing his treatises.

If auctoritas points to a personal authority and imperium to the limits of impersonal authority, "summa potestas" points to the authority that has the greatest power within a realm. By implication, that power is the sovereign. Even if the expression "summa potestas" is an established term in Latin legal and political discourse, still it is worth pointing out that "potestas" on its own points to the power of the people. Even if summa potestas cannot be normally mistaken with the power of the people, still it retains its main characteristic, namely, the possibility that it can express itself in violent ways. Or, differently put, the exercise of violence is inherent in summa potestas. Spinoza points to an implication of this idea by noting that the most powerful violence does not actually originate from the sovereign, but rather from the people themselves. Thus, it is the multitude that is most feared, and in that sense, even in a monarchy, as he argues in the *Political Treatise*, the people ultimately hold more power than the sovereign. Hence, ultimately, it is the people who hold power—which is why Spinoza can be understood as arguing that democracy is the most primary constitution.

We have, then, three terms that denote authority: auctoritas points to personal authority, imperium to the limits of juridico-political authority, and summa potestas to the most powerful authority. Both the difficulty and the novelty in Spinoza's position consist in that the three different senses of authority are distinct and yet they overlap. Let me provide one example. The "secular" position according to which the Church should not have *imperium in imperio* is absent from Spinoza's work. Those with auctoritas are shown to be lawgivers and to yield political power and this entails that religion and politics cannot neatly demarcate their territories. In addition, Spinoza uses the same vocabulary (for instance, *Ethics* Part III) to indicate the illusion of the free will, or the illusion that humans can free themselves from natural causes. Within this context, the question of authority is transformed into a question about the power or potentia as the capacity of people to act rationally given their emotional circumstances. In other words, the three sense of authority outlined above intersect and interact in a revamped and ontologized notion of power (*potentia*) that Spinoza inherits from Machiavelli and which he develops even further.

The first chapter of this book by Vittorio Morfino explores some of the roots of Spinoza's conception of power in Machiavelli. Despite the fact that Machiavelli is not explicitly named in the *Theological-Political Treatise*, Morfino argues that his presence is felt throughout. Morfino starts tracing this influence in the way history is developed within the context of the argument about the Jews as an elected people, showing the presence of Machiavelli's use of the concept of fortune. Then, Morfino goes on to show that this conception of history is materialist since memory has been preserved and transmitted based on the operation of the aleatory. Finally, Machiavelli's insistence on the centrality of conflict for the flourishing of the state in the opening of the *Discourses* is instrumental in Spinoza's deconstruction of the authority of the lawgivers. These are not three arbitrary sites of comparison with the Florentine but rather points with far-reaching implications, for instance about the way in which the social contract and society itself are conceived.

The next chapter by Filippo Del Lucchese also takes as its point of departure Machiavelli's influence on Spinoza to argue that conflict is the productive element that leads to freedom. Drawing on Vittorio Morfino's link between freedom and Spinoza's conception of causality as connection, Del Lucchese proposes to investigate a question that has puzzled many commentators, especially those who seek in Spinoza an alternative revolutionary politics that does not rely on the dialectical materialism of the Marxist tradition. Given that both the idea of a radical break in the course of history and the idea of a cyclical movement between degenerate and good constitutions are ultimately incompatible with the Spinozan account of politics and history, how can we give an account of the revolutionary in Spinoza? Del Lucchese responds by pointing to the confluence of jus (law and right) and power and by drawing the implications that this entails for a conception of the state. Ultimately, this leads to the conclusion that the revolution is permanently unfolding in Spinoza's politics, as the relation between law and conflict and in such a way so as to mirror his rejection of the dualism between mind and body.

The idea of the law is further elaborated in Dimitris Vardoulakis' chapter. Starting with the distinction between divine and human law in Chapter 4 of the *Theological-Political Treatise*, Vardoulakis points out another Machiavellian idea that has found its way into Spinoza's work, namely, that the law is defined in terms of its utility. The figure of *auctoritas* is important in this context, as it allows Spinoza to draw inferences about history and politics. Of particular importance is the idea that the utility of the law is articulated as obedience. Given that the divine law cannot be disobeyed, as Spinoza's retelling of the narrative of the Fall avers, what does this mean about the genesis of human law? Vardoulakis shows that the radical conclusion entailed in Spinoza's analysis of Adam's action is that human law is premised on its disobedience. Furthermore, Adam as the first prophet, and hence as a paradigmatic figure of authority, also discloses that authority is generated and perpetuated by a miscognition, namely, the confusion between divine and human law.

The discussion of the law in Chapter 4 of the *Theological-Political Treatise* indicates the vital role that interpretation plays in Spinoza's adumbration of authority. By looking at interpretation, James Martel makes a surprising comparison between Spinoza and Hobbes. His argument is that they are both keen to challenge the established norms of authority. Comparing their methods of Biblical interpretation Martel arrives at the conclusion that Hobbes is more radical and democratic in the sense that he leaves the possibility of alternative—or unauthoritative—interpretations more open than Spinoza, and hence invites the demos to participate in the interpretative process. Furthermore, Martel shows that both seventeenth-century thinkers seek to undermine sovereign authority by examining the Hebrew state. In this case, it is Spinoza who appears more radical than Hobbes. But ultimately this comparison is not a matter of measuring the radicality of Spinoza and Hobbes against each other, but rather in demonstrating that resistance to authority can be inscribed in a variety of ways within their texts—and comparisons between the two may better help us see the nuances of their politics of resistance.

The process of interpretation is also linked, as Siarhei Biareishyk demonstrates, also to the way that Spinoza conceives of error. Biareishyk shows that error has both an epistemological and an ontological dimension in Spinoza, whereby it further rises to a political significance. Starting with outlining the relation between error and the three types of knowledge, Biareishyk shows that even though they are all similar in that they misunderstand the nature of cause and effect in different ways, it is nevertheless only the third kind of error, linked to the third kind of knowledge, that can also lead to truth as it has the capacity to demarcate a field of interpretation. Thus, this third kind of error retains the potential of a political realization. Or, to put it differently, the third kind of error leads to truth through its effects. This insight links Biareishyk's analysis of error to Althusser's symptomatic readings and his theory of the encounter.

How can the interpretative process in Spinoza's political treatises be accommodated within his monism? And what are the political implications of this question? These are the questions animating Kiarina Kordela and Joseph Bermas-Dawes' contribution. They are trenchant question because—to use Deleuze's vocabulary—if expression is separated from the sign, does not this lead us back to dualism? To counter this result, the authors insist that there is in Spinoza an immanent relation between expression and sign, one that replicates the relation between truth and error, as the two standards of *truth* in Spinoza's theory. This has implications in how resistance against authority can be conceived. The authors argue that authority lies in interpretation, insofar as interpretation involves decision. But at the same time, the fact that power is natural and that it cannot be confined to the potentate's authority also means that the multitude always also possesses power and hence the authority to interpret. This entails that political interpretation is not confined to the sovereign's decision, as it is in Carl Schmitt and generally decisionism. Instead, Spinoza's political interpretative decision is imbued with the fantasies and ideological processes that make it possible to recuperate truth from the errors of the multitude. Drawing on psychoanalysis the authors show that in Spinoza's work such (secondary) fantasies and ideological processes are modes of some unconscious primal fantasy (*truth*). The authors then trace the relation between the secondary and primary fantasies in Spinoza's own interpretation of the Bible, as the blueprint for similar analyses on the level of politics.

Gregg Lambert is also concerned with the relation between expression and sign. Lambert argues that there are two regions of expression, one that pertains to truth and it corresponds to philosophy, and another that pertains to interpretation that is explicated through prophetic and sovereign authority in the *Theological-Political Treatise*. Drawing attention to Spinoza's point that the sole concern of interpretation in Spinoza's *Treatise* pertains to the production of authority, Lambert outlines a typology of signs, which ultimately demonstrates that expression and expressed do not coincide. This entails that procedures of truth and interpretation are discordant. Given that interpretation is the source of authority, this insight leads to the conclusion that the production of power through the authority of the prophets as well as the sovereigns rests on misapprehension. Lambert explains how this is presented in Spinoza's interpretation of the two covenants that Spinoza outlines in Chapter 17 of the *Theological-Political Treatise*, and he links this to a concept of resistance.

At the beginning of the *Theological-Political Treatise*, Spinoza famously puzzles as to why people fight for their servitude instead of their liberation.

Chiara Bottici and Miguel de Beistegui explore what is at stake in Spinoza asking this question. They demonstrate that it has to do with how authority instils obedience. If, as Spinoza avers, obedience is most effective when it is not coercive but rather when the people willingly obey, what is it that makes us obey? Bottici and Beistegui show how Spinoza explains this through his theory of the emotions. Spinoza describes a technology of government that relies on creating desires of artificial lack that function as a void and hence resemble the operation of the siphon. Obedience is channeled through such emotions. As the authors note, the operation of the siphon of the emotion is also operative in a neoliberal governmentality where desires are siphoned off through the market. Comparing Spinoza's political analysis in the *Treatise* to the theory of the affects in Part III of the *Ethics*, the authors point out that Spinoza provides us with the tool to reverse the effect of desire, so that we can produce a plenitude of being.

1

Memory, Chance and Conflict: Machiavelli in the *Theologico-Political Treatise*

Vittorio Morfino

Machiavelli's name is never quoted in the *Theologico-Political Treatise* and nonetheless is perhaps the most important philosophical and political reference of the entire book. This is not the place to analyze thoroughly Machiavelli's subterranean presence in the *Theologico-Political Treatise*.[1] Instead, I will discuss some strategic but fundamental instances of this presence to stress the disruptive effect that they have on Spinoza's metaphysic and political theory. It is impossible to quote Machiavelli without consequences. In fact, the repetition of Machiavelli forces Spinoza to change his own philosophical position. I shall examine three passages in the *Theologico-Political Treatise* in which Machiavelli plays a crucial role: First, the ontology of history in Chapter III, based on the conceptual couple virtue and fortune; second, Chapter VII, in which the Machiavellian theory of time, memory and chance is elaborated as a materialistic theory of tradition; and, third, Chapter XVII, where Spinoza, in the wake of Machiavelli's *Discourses*, deconstructs the idea of an omnipotent legislator, showing that conflict and its aleatory effects are central to the constitution of States. The repetition of Machiavelli in *Theologico-Political Treatise*'s fundamental places allow Spinoza to deconstruct authority traditional concept both in theological and in political sense, dissolving every form of transcendence in the materiality of the relations of force, every form of eternity in a duration always contingent build by virtue in the conjuncture, catching the occasion.

Ontology of history

Chapter III, in which Spinoza seeks to demonstrate the imaginary status of the concept of election—a cornerstone of Judaism—is one of the central axes of the entire book. As usual, Spinoza sets out by defining the fundamental concepts, and in so doing he subverts the imaginary terrain of the theologico-political enemy. *Spinoza derives his own rational concept of election from the network of relations that he establishes only to transform their traditional meanings. He does so based on a specific set of terms: directio Dei, Dei auxilium externum, Dei auxilium internum and electio Dei e fortuna.*

Directio Dei, the divine government, is "the fixed and unalterable order of nature or the interconnectedness of [all] natural things [*fixum illum & immutabile naturæ ordo, sive rerum naturalium concatenatio*]."[2] The reason is that the universal laws of nature are nothing other than the eternal decrees issued by God, implying truth and necessity. Once the identity of natural and divine power (*potentia*) is established, it follows that the internal and external assistance of God is, respectively, the *conatus,* or man's aim to preserve his own being, and the spontaneous offer of the means to achieve this end by nature itself: "Whatever therefore human nature can supply from its own resources to preserve man's own being, we may rightly call the 'internal assistance of God,' and whatever proves useful to man from the power of external causes, that we may properly term the 'external assistance of God'" (*TTP* 46/45). *Directio Dei* is therefore an immutable and fixed order that includes both the human *conatus* (internal assistance) and the external causes (external assistance). Fortune, then, is nothing else than the *directio Dei* in that it *"governs human affairs through external and unforeseen causes [quatenus per causas externas & inopinatas res humanas dirigit]"* (*TTP* 46/45).

Given these definitions, the concept of election is now substantially reformulated in quite different terms with respect to the traditional ones:

> For given that nobody does anything except by the predetermined order of nature [*ex prædeterminato naturæ ordine*], that is, by the eternal decree and direction of God, it follows that no one chooses any way of life for himself nor brings anything about, except via the particular summons of God [*ex singulari Dei vocatione*], who chose this man in preference to others for this task or that way of life (*TTP* 46/45).

Starting from this definition, Spinoza begins the construction of the concept of election of an historical society. This construction is, at the same time, a genealogy of its religious form:

> But to establish and conserve a society, much intelligence and vigilance [*ingenium & vigilantia*] is required. Therefore that society will be safer, more stable and less vulnerable to fortune [*fortunæ obnoxia*], which is for the most part founded and

directed by wise and vigilant men [*prudentes & vigilantes*]. On the other hand, a society that consists of men of limited intelligence depends for the most part on fortune and is less stable. If in spite of this it has proved to be lasting, this will be due, not to its own policies, but to someone else's. Indeed, if it has overcome great dangers and its affairs have prospered, it can do no other than admire and adore God's government. ... For everything that happened to that society was beyond expectation [*præter opinionem*] and beyond belief and this can truly be considered a miracle. (*TTP* 47/46)

From this, Spinoza draws the following conclusion:

Nations are distinguished one from another only by the [form of] society and laws in which they live and under which they are governed. The Hebrew people, accordingly, was chosen by God above others not for its understanding or for its qualities of mind, but owing to the form of its society and the good fortune [*ratio societatis & leges*], over so many years, with which it shaped and preserved its state. (*TTP* 47/46)

Spinoza subverts the traditional meanings of the terms. Identifying the Hebrew concept of election with the pagan concept of *fortuna*, he neutralizes the imaginary content of both, constructing at the same time a new concept that enables him to think the history of peoples in terms of an encounter between the *ratio societatis* and the external causes.

Now, it seems to me that in so doing Spinoza appropriates for his own discourse some theoretical moves proper to Machiavelli, namely his reflections on virtue and fortune in *The Prince*, Chapter XXV:

It is not unknown to me how many men have had, and still have, the opinion that the affairs of the world are in such wise governed by fortune and by God that men with their wisdom cannot direct them and that no one can even help them; and because of this they would have us believe that it is not necessary to labour much in affairs, but to let chance govern them. This opinion has been more credited in our times because of the great changes in affairs which have been seen, and may still be seen, every day, beyond all human conjecture. Sometimes pondering over this, I am in some degree inclined to their opinion. Nevertheless, not to extinguish our free will [*libero arbitrio*], I hold it to be true that Fortune is the arbiter of one-half of our actions, but that she still leaves us to direct the other half, or perhaps a little less. I compare her to one of those raging rivers, which when in flood overflows the plains, sweeping away trees and buildings, bearing away the soil from place to place; everything flies before it, all yield to its violence, without being able in any way to withstand it; and yet, though its nature be such, it does not follow therefore that men, when the weather becomes fair, shall not make provision, both with defences and barriers, in such a manner that, rising again, the waters may pass away by canal, and their force be neither so unrestrained nor so dangerous. So it happens with fortune, who shows her power where valour has not prepared to resist her, and thither she turns her forces where she knows that barriers and defences have not been raised to constrain her.[3]

Here Machiavelli proposes a theory of history thought by means of the conceptual couple virtue and fortune, whose first term, *libero arbitrio*, is in reality nothing else than the necessary inclination of the agent, and whose second term, *fortuna*, is a "great change [*variazione*] beyond all human conjecture." On the one hand, the powerful metaphor of the river depicts fortune as a force that sometimes runs parallel to the human vicissitudes, and sometimes clashes with them violently modifying their form; on the other, virtue is nothing else than the resistance of an individual or of a people opposing these violent irruptions in order to preserve their own form. In a nature which is a-systematic and without center, singular things exist in the always open conflict between the perpetual variation of times and the effort that the individual opposes to it in order to persevere in its own being.

The encounter between these two levels renders the model of transitive causality useless to historical knowledge. As the human action unfolds in a network of constantly shifting times, and not in an empty homogeneity, the same action can lead both to success or defeat, and two opposed actions can equally lead to success, as Machiavelli writes in the "Ghiribizzi al Soderini." The only rule is to adequate one's own action to the "quality of times." Therefore, history is the conjunction of two necessities: the necessity of virtue and that of times. Because of their ever-changing character, Machiavelli likens them to the pagan divinity named *Fortuna*, whom he sets free from every anthropomorphism.

Spinoza's outline appears as a translation of Machiavelli's political theory in ontological terms. It is actually this ontological reformulation of Machiavelli that enables Spinoza to rethink the concept of election. But there's more! On this very point, Machiavelli provides a precise model: in book II of the *Discourses*, he rejects Plutarch's thesis—put forth in *On the Fortune of the Romans*—that Roman victories owed more to their fortune than to their virtue, fortune being for Plutarch a deity responsive to adulation ("since it [the Roman people] built more temples to Fortune than to any other god").[4] As Machiavelli writes:

> For if there has never been a republic that has made the profits that Rome did, this arose from there never having been a republic that has been ordered so as to be able to acquire as did Rome. For the armies' virtue made them acquire the empire; and the order of proceeding and its own mode found by its first lawgiver made them maintain what was acquired (*D* 206/126).

Machiavelli rejects, in this precise case, a conception of history that projects a transcendent plane on to the immanent relationship between fortune and virtue. Here, fortune is not the personified deity that governs mundane events, but the continual variations of times that can offers the occasion to virtue. The corollary of this materialism is that nations differ from each other due to their socio-political order, and not because of an alleged divine privilege. It follows that no definitive hierarchy between different societies exists, since this hierarchy stems from the complex and unstable relationship between the power of the material and psichic constitution of a state (its military and political organization, its laws and its habits) and the power of the external causes. Dealing with the theologico-political issue of the election—which is, in the end, the archetype of the concept of homeland—Spinoza affirms, in the wake of Machiavelli, the absolute immanence of politics and its independence from any theology, i.e. from an order that transcends and substantializes the relationships of power.

A materialistic theory of tradition

We shall now move from what we have called the foundation of an ontology of history to a materialistic theory of tradition in the *Theologico-Political Treatise*. Again, the fundamental point of reference is Machiavelli, in particular, in Chapter 5 of the second book of the *Discourses*. Here Machiavelli's conception of history takes the form of a reflection on the memories of mankind: "That the Variation of Sects and Languages, Together with the Accident of Floods or Plague, Eliminates the Memories of Things." The theory of history proposed in *Discourses*, II, 5, could legitimately appear as a philosophy of history of the humankind, were it not for the straightforward rejection of the totalization of memory's data. The beginning of the chapter is blunt, although apparently difficult to interpret:

> To those philosophers who would have it that the world is eternal, I believe that one could reply that if so much antiquity were true it would be reasonable that there be memory of more than five thousand years—if it were not seen how the memories of times are eliminated by diverse causes, of which part come from men, part from heaven (*D* 154/139).

Machiavelli says here, through a very complex syntactic construction, first, that the world is eternal, and second, that there are causes that erase the memory of things.

The power of the first philosophical thesis is evident. It fully resumes the Averroistic thesis that had flowed like an underground river from the Arab Enlightenment, crossing through the late Middle Ages and Christian Humanism, running counter to the dominant philosophy at every turn. The thesis of the eternity of the world equally opposes Platonism (*Timaeus*) and Christianity. The second thesis has the same polemical aims: it strikes at both the Platonic theory of memory understood as anamnesis and at the Holy Scriptures as the memory of human history beginning from its origin (the 5,000 years that Machiavelli mentions correspond exactly to the antiquity of the world described in Genesis).

Their combination leads to a new conception of historical knowledge. This is presented not as the conceptual double of the historical totality, but as a fragment saved from the powerful causes that destroy human memory. This fragment of memory is in no way an expression of the totality. No reason (understood as Sense) presides over its survival. It is no more than what remains of the encounters between the forces of nature and human society, and of the encounters between different societies. The error of Platonism and Christianity consists precisely in projecting the fragment onto the whole, an error that renders the world finite and establishes the alliance between memory and truth.

How, then, does Machiavelli divide up the causes of oblivion? Machiavelli begins his exposition with those that "come from men," in other words, social causes:

> For when a new sect—that is, a new religion—emerges, its first concern is to extinguish the old to give itself reputation: and when it occurs that the orderers of the new sect are of a different language, they easily eliminate it. This thing is known from considering the modes that the Christian sect took against the Gentile. It suppressed all its orders and all its ceremonies and eliminated every memory of that ancient theology. It is true that they did not succeed in eliminating entirely the knowledge of the things done by its excellent men. This arose from having maintained the Latin language, which they were forced to do since they had to write this new law with it. For if they had been able to write with a new language, considering the other persecutions they made, we would not have any record of things past. [...] It is therefore to be believed that what the Christian sect wished to do against the Gentile sect, the Gentile would have done against that which was prior to it. And because these sects vary two or three times in five or in six thousand years, the memory of the things done prior to that time is lost; and if, however, some sign of them remains, it is considered as something fabulous and is not lent faith to—as happened to the history of Diodorus Siculus, which, though it renders an account of forty or fifty thousand years, is nonetheless reputed, as I believe it to be, a mendacious thing. (*D* 154/139)

The theses advanced by Machiavelli have great philosophical value: First, the Christian religion is nothing more than one "sect" among others;[5] second, religious sects are temporal dispositives of power which naturally tend toward hegemony: the logic of the relationship between sects on the world stage is therefore a logic of war; and, third, the memory of an era's spiritual culture lies entirely in the materiality of the language that expresses it. A language does not have the expressive centrality of a subject and, therefore, cannot be submitted to absolute control.[6] Consequently, a language can be completely destroyed, but if it is not, it escapes to be totally controlled by power. Its materiality is the *de facto* guarantee of its accentricity and its structured asystematicity.

The combination of these three philosophical theses sketches the outline of a theory of history in which memory, far from being the most powerful instrument of knowledge, is what is at stake in the struggles between different sects. The winners try to destroy the memory of the losers and impose their own narrative of the world as the only true one, an attempt that can only succeed if the memory of the losers is destroyed down to its material roots, that is, its language.

We now turn to the passage in which Machiavelli sets out "the causes that come from heaven," that is, the natural causes that destroy memory:

> As to the causes that come from heaven, they are those that eliminate the human race and reduce the inhabitants of the world to a few. This comes about either through plague or through famine or through an inundation of waters. The most important is the last, both because it is more universal and because those who are saved are all mountain men and coarse, who, since they do not have knowledge of antiquity, cannot leave it to posterity. And if among them someone is saved who has knowledge of it, to make a reputation and a name for himself he conceals it and perverts it in his mode so that what he has wished to write alone, and nothing else, remains for his successors. (154–55/140)

Here are the philosophical theses that can be drawn from this passage: First, the history of mankind is deeply rooted in nature, whose power can brutally wipe out entire civilizations. As a result, the continuity that the narrative of memory provides is nothing more than the continuity of a fragment, an island that rises up in the middle of nowhere above the flood of oblivion. Second, memory does not evenly permeate society: there is a layering of memory within society that excludes the model of expressive causality and the *pars totalis*. And, third, memory is much more an instrument of power and, therefore, perversion of the truth for political ends, than an accurate knowledge of the past. The combination of these three theses constructs a theoretical position, which could be read as an *ante litteram* refutation of the great systems of idealism, founded precisely on the primacy of the logos over the matter, of history over nature, primacy which gives rise to a totalizing narration of the humankind.

Machiavelli then traces the outlines of a theory of history in which the metaphysical hendiadys Origin-End is rejected and in which a key role is played by the concept of occasion, as the encounter between virtue and fortune, in the form of a variety of material powers: the materiality of the apparatuses of religious power, the materiality of languages, hunger, diseases, natural disasters, and the cultural stratification of society. The memory of a civilization, then, is nothing but a fragile fragment of matter faced with the immense power of nature, which has no teleological respect for it. Memory can survive for a certain amount of time and imagine itself as eternal, projecting itself on the totality of time, but it is nevertheless fated for oblivion.

Spinoza's analysis fits in this theoretical framework. In fact Spinoza, in the wake of Machiavelli, considers the Bible not as the true memory of the origin and history of the world, but as the imaginary recollection of the real history:

> For many things are reported in Scripture as real, and were actually believed to be real, though they were nothing but apparitions and imaginary things [*In Scriptura enim multa, ut realia narrantur, et quæ etiam realia esse credebantur, quæ tamen non nisi repræsentationes, resque imaginariæ fuerunt*]. (*TTP* 92–93/92)

This imaginary recollection, this past imagined by means of rudimentary opinions, is not simply an erroneous knowledge of history. Actually, it plays a political role in history itself. Memory is the discipline of the body, because the rituals inscribe obedience in the everyday life of the people. The function of memory is therefore not one of truth, but it is linked up to the spontaneous teleological belief of imagination, and to the inscription of the body in a determinate set of rules that discipline the social life.

We are now in a position to consider Chapter VII of the *Theologico-Political Treatise*, where Spinoza discusses his own method of reading the Holy Scripture. Here Spinoza states the methodological rule that forever separates his reading from the traditional one:

> To formulate the matter succinctly, I hold that the method of interpreting Scripture, does not differ from the [correct] method of interpreting nature, but rather is wholly consonant with it. The [correct] method of interpreting nature consists above all in constructing a natural history, from which we derive the definitions of natural things, as from certain data. Likewise, to interpret

Scripture, we need to assemble a genuine history of it and to deduce the thinking of the Bible's authors by valid inferences from this history, as from certain data and principles. (*TTP* 98/98)

The interpretation of the Scripture must be grounded on a reconstruction of its history premised upon an exact knowledge of the nature and features of the Jewish language, upon a collection of the sentences of each book and upon their reduction to their main points. Furthermore, it has to be premised upon the careful inventory of all the obscure, ambiguous and contradictory statements, and eventually upon the collection of all the bequeathed information about the prophetical books.

It is clear that the only question that matters in the interpretation of the Scripture is not its truth, but its meaning. ("De solo enim sensu orationum, non autem de earum veritate laboramos," *TTP* 100/100). The meaning of this text is thus grasped as a complex texture of multiple durations, and is therefore irreducible to the linear model of the *Logos*. Firstly, this meaning is tied up with the materiality of a determinate language whose structure is a source of ambiguity; secondly, it is linked to the habits and customs of every single author, as well as to particular circumstances of the writing, that is, to the specific modality of the author's encounter with his own time; thirdly, it is inextricably entangled in the successive encounters, to which the temporal flux subjects all written books to other singular structures and power apparatuses.

According to Spinoza, the reconstruction of this meaning must be grounded on the material memory of language, which is to be found within the people. The meaning of the words is in fact the effect of the transindividual communicative practices of the people, and not of a decision of a subject. One must in fact be wary of interpretative traditions such as the ones proposed by the Pharisees and the Roman Church, as they have political reasons to modify the meaning of the Scripture:

> We have offered a method for interpreting Scripture and at the same time demonstrated that this is the most certain and only way to uncover its true meaning. I grant that certainty about this last is easier to find for those, if they exist, who possess a solid tradition or a true exegesis inherited from the prophets themselves, such as the Pharisees claim to have, or those who possess a Pope who cannot err in the interpretation of scripture, as Roman Catholics proclaim. Since, however, we cannot be certain either about that tradition or papal authority, nothing certain can be grounded on either of these. The latter was denied by the earliest Christians and the former by the most ancient Jewish sects; further, if we then examine the chronology (apart from any other arguments) which the

> Pharisees inherited from their rabbis by which they trace this tradition back to Moses, we shall find that it is false. ... This is why such a tradition should be altogether suspect to us. And although we are obliged, by our method, to consider one Jewish tradition as incorrupt, namely the meaning of words in the Hebrew language we have received from them, we can still fairly have doubts about the former tradition while accepting the latter. For it could never have been of any use to change a word's meaning, but it might quite often have been useful to someone to alter the meaning of a passage. In fact it is extremely difficult to alter the meaning of a word; anyone who tried it would have at the same time to interpret in his own way and manner all the authors who have written in that language using that term in its accepted sense, or else with the greatest wariness corrupt the text. Again, the learned share with the common people in preserving a language, but the learned alone preserve books and the meanings of texts. Accordingly, we can easily conceive that the learned could have altered or perverted the sense of a passage in a very rare book which they had under their control, but not the significance of words. *(TTP* 105–06/105)

Knowledge of the meaning of the Scripture requires the knowledge of Hebrew language. The knowledge grounded on the material continuity of communicative interactions rather than on the spiritual continuity of the truth, because it is impermeable to the attempt to twist and modify the meaning of words for a political aim. Such a knowledge must in fact distrust all the interpretative traditions, such as the Roman and the Pharisee, that may be interested in modifying the meaning of the words. Such an analysis corresponds to the structure of Machiavelli's argument on memory: on the one hand, we have the material memory of language belonging to the people ("Deinde vulgus linguam cum doctis servat") and capable of circumventing every practice of semantic control;[7] and on the other hand we have the political perversion of memory, which nonetheless must take into account the materiality of language itself.

Spinoza's method of interpretation of the Holy Scripture requires a perfect knowledge of the Hebrew language and of the "historia casuum omnium librorum Scripturæ" (history of each and every book of the Scripture). About the difficulty to recover these "histories" Spinoza introduces another Machiavellian topic: the one about the destruction of memory due to natural and political events. First, time has eroded the very memory of the language:

> Firstly, a major obstacle in this method is that it requires a perfect knowledge [*integra cognitio*] of the Hebrew language. But where is this to be sought? The ancient scholars of Hebrew have left nothing to posterity about the principles and structure of the language. ... The Jewish people have lost all their cultural and artistic accomplishments (no wonder, after suffering so many massacres

and persecutions [*clades & persecutiones*]) and have held on to nothing but a few fragments of their language and a few books. ... Thus the meaning of many nouns and verbs occurring in the Bible is either completely unknown or disputed. ... [W]e have no phrase-book of the language; for almost all the idioms and modes of speech peculiar to the Hebrew people have been erased from man's memory by all-devouring time [*omnes fere tempus edax ex hominum memoria abolevit*]. (*TTP* 106/107)

The meaning of the discourses could not be inferred *ex linguae usu*, and will therefore remain forever unknown. The reasons of this loss, whose theorization implies the rupture *ante litteram* with a fundamental dogma of every philosophy of history—the belief in the continuity of the Meaning, of the *Logos*—are at the same time political and natural: on the one hand the disintegration of the political unity (diaspora), the defeats, and the persecutions; on the other hand, the destructions caused by the passing of time, natural disasters. These two types of causality are summed up in a stunning expression which, retrieving the Greek myth of *Khronos*, makes visible with a powerful image the destructive power of time: *tempus edax*, "all-devouring time."

Language, being tied up to the everyday practice of the people, is the means of a transmission which cannot be totally subjected to political power. Nonetheless, it is constantly eroded by the devouring power of time, which manifests itself as the material destruction of the community that preserves the language: defeats, prosecutions and natural calamities. Spinoza sets the concept of tradition very precise material boundaries: it exceeds the linear logic of the series and is instead subjected to the complex logic of the intertwining, of the texture, which is a continual loss and transformation of the meaning whose origin is nothing more than a material genesis, an encounter whose aleatory necessity sets it free from any axiological meaning.

The second difficulty raised by the interpretation of the Scripture—the ignorance of the circumstances in which the texts have been written and their authors—stresses again the problem of material genesis:

A further problem with this method is that it requires a history of the vicissitudes of all the biblical books, and most of this is unknown to us. For either we have no knowledge whatever of the authors, or (if you prefer) the compilers, of many of the books or else we are uncertain about them. ... Also, we do not know under what circumstances [*qua occasione neque tempore*] these books whose compilers are unknown were composed or when. Nor do we know into whose hands all these books subsequently came, or in whose copies so many variant readings occur, nor whether there may not have been many additional readings in others.

> ... If we read any book that contains incredible or incomprehensible things, or is written in very obscure language, and if we do not know its author or when and under what circumstances he wrote it, our efforts to get at its true sense will be fruitless. For if all this is unknown, we cannot ascertain what the author intended or might have intended. When, on the other hand, all these things are adequately known, we determine our thoughts so as not to make prejudicial judgements or attribute to the author, or person on whose behalf he wrote, either more or less than is correct, or take anything else into consideration but what the author could have had in mind, or what the period and context demanded. (*TTP* 109/110)

The Holy Scripture is not, then, the true memory of the past tradition understood as the transmission of continual sense coming from God to the successive generations of the Hebrew people (a tradition that is identified with the totality of history). Rather, it is the imaginary memory of a fragment whose meaning is forever lost with the memory of the conjuncture that produced its emergence. It is not by chance that Spinoza here uses repeatedly the word "occasion [*occasio*]."[8] On this Machiavellian concept, he builds a materialist theory of tradition according to which the text of history, as Althusser wrote, is not a "text in which a voice (the *Logos*) speaks, but the inaudible and illegible notation of the effects of a structure of structures."[9]

Deconstruction of the omnipotent legislator and the crucial role of conflict

Let us consider now the deconstruction of the omnipotent legislator, the equivalent on the political level of the God author of the Scripture in the theological level. The fundamental point of reference is again Machiavelli. On this, it is necessary to take into account what Machiavelli says in *Discourses* I, Chapter 2, when he describes the cyclical movement regulating the historical development of the forms of power. This chapter is devoted to an exploration of the relationship between the particular form of the Roman Republic and the traditional—that is, the Platonico-Aristotelian—typology. However, after describing the six forms of government and the passional and generational dialectics which causes the transition from one form of power to another, he highlights the abstract character of this cycle once it is placed in connection with the concrete plane of historical relationships:

It is while revolving in this cycle that all republics are governed and govern themselves. But rarely do they return to the same governments, for almost no republic can have so long a life as to be able to pass many times through these changes and remain on its feet. *But indeed it happens that in its travails, a republic always lacking in counsel and forces becomes subject to a neighboring state that is ordered better than it*; assuming that this were not so, however, a republic would be capable of revolving for an infinite time in these governments. (*D* 80/13, emphasis added)

The serial temporality exhibited in the succession of forms of power appears as an abstraction of the imagination when faced with the reality of complex historical and political relations. There is no law of development governing a society's forms of power that is independent of the power relations which oppose and bind this society to other societies. Consequently, the intersection of the different cycles produces a temporality traversed by ruptures and discontinuities. Nonetheless, the distance he takes from the theory of *anacyclosis* or cyclical time is even more radical. Machiavelli does not limit himself to complicating the framework inherited from Polybius, or simply to noting that there are indeed cycles but that these interfere with each other. He does not conceive chance as the intersection of the necessary development of multiple cycles. Rather he posits chance at the origin of the form. As soon as he begins to tackle his subject—the specific form of the Roman Republic—he gets rid of all the conceptual tools that come with the theory of *anacyclosis* in order to study his object in all its real complexity. In other words, when Machiavelli approaches his subject—the history of the Roman people—the philosophy of history is abandoned in favor of a study of the laws and institutions ("leggi e ordini" in the language of Machiavelli) that allowed the state to regulate and stabilize the power relations of the society's "humors."

Before dealing with the specific object of his essay, Machiavelli offers two examples: Lycurgus, who gave Sparta a constitution assuring political stability for eight centuries, and Solon, whose laws established a precarious form of power that soon turned into tyranny:

Among those who have deserved most praise for such constitutions is Lycurgus, who in Sparta ordered his laws so as to give their roles to the kinds, the aristocrats, and the people and made a state that lasted more than eight hundred years, achieving the highest praise for himself and quiet in that city. The contrary happened to Solon, who ordered the laws in Athens: by ordering only the popular state there, he made it of such short life that before he died he saw the tyranny of Pisistratus born there. His heirs were expelled after forty years and Athens returned to freedom, yet because it took up the popular state again, according to the orders of Solon, it lasted no more than a hundred years. To maintain it, [Athens] made many constitutions that had not been considered by Solon, by which the insolence of the great and the license of the collectivity were repressed. Nonetheless, because it did not mix them with the power of the principality and with that of the aristocrats, Athens lived a very short time in respect to Sparta. (*D* 80–81/13)

There are two theoretical consequences, which actually remain implicit, that need to be noted about the two examples chosen by Machiavelli. On the one hand, the mythical character of Lycurgus—who in Machiavelli's text plays the exemplary role of the legislator "at a stroke [*ad uno tratto*]," as opposed to legislations that arise by chance—suggests that any form of first causality is in reality nothing but a form of mythology about the origin.[10] On the other hand, Athenian history invalidates the theory of *anacyclosis*, since the "Athenian cycle" passes from a democracy into a tyranny, then back into a democracy, and finally into an oligarchy after the defeat suffered at the hands of Sparta in 404 BC.

In other words, Machiavelli suggests that the history of Rome must be analyzed rejecting on the one hand the belief in the omnipotence of a legislator and on the other a predetermined historical development. History is the locus of aleatory encounters between forces internal and external to the State, and it is the continuous regulation of these forces that make it possible for a State to endure. Here is the long passage that closes the chapter:

> But let us come to Rome. Notwithstanding that it did not have a Lycurgus to order it in the beginning in a mode that would enable it to live free a long time, nonetheless so many accidents arose in it through the disunion between the plebs and the Senate that what an orderer had not done, chance did. For if the first fortune did not fall to Rome, the second fell to it; for if its first orders were defective, nonetheless they did not deviate from the right way that could lead them to perfection. For Romulus and all the other kinds made many and good laws confirming also to a free way of life; but because their end was to found a kingdom and not a republic, when that city was left free, many things that were necessary to order in favor of freedom were lacking, not having been ordered by those kinds. Even though its kings lost their empire by the causes and modes discoursed of, nonetheless those who expelled them expelled from Rome the name and not the kingly power, having at once ordered two consuls and the Senate in that republic, it came to be mixed only of two qualities out of the three written of above—that is the principality and the aristocrats. It remained only to give a place to the popular government; hence, when the Roman nobility became insolent for the causes that will be told below, the people rose up against it; so as

not to lose the whole, it was constrained to yield to the people its part, and on the other side the Senate and the consuls remained with so much authority that they could keep their rank in that republic. Thus arose the creation of the tribunes of the plebs, after which the state of that republic came to be more stabilized, since all three kinds of government there had their part. (D 81/14)

The denial of the first cause embodied by the legislator-founder—who in the political space occupies the place that God has in the Christian cosmology—brings with it the same theoretical move, the denial of the series of transitive causes resulting from it: "so many accidents arose in it through the disunion between the plebs and the Senate that what an orderer had not done, chance did." Of course, Machiavellian conflict is not to be interpreted on the wake of the great power of the negative, as this would equate it to the Hegelo-Marxist contradiction, whose outcome is always already decided in advance. Rather, conflict in Machiavelli must be thought in its complex and aleatory positivity, occasion for the emergence of new institutions. So, the essence of the Roman State does not lie in a form of power—the mixed form, evoked by Polybius apropos of Rome—imposed to a formless matter, the Roman people, but rather in the relationship of forces between fundamental elements of the people. It is their conflictual encounter that occasioned—occasion being the implicit deconstruction of every form of teleology—the creation of new institutions and laws that allow a regulation without which the State wouldn't endure. Therefore, the study of the specific logic of the specific object leads Machiavelli to renounce the services of the idea of a legislator "at a stroke," who establishes the order for the whole people, and of the philosophy of history premised upon the idea of a cycle of forms of power. In this sense, Machiavelli puts forward a theory of the individual—of the individuality *in fieri* of the Roman people—as an anti-philosophy of history. In other words, he refuses to inscribe the Roman society in a totalizing narrative.

We find this very refusal of a totalizing narrative in Spinoza's history of the Hebrew people. To deny an original meaning, the divine *Logos* bequeathed from one generation to another (Abraham's Isaac and Jakob's God, etc.), is in fact also to deny, on a political level, the existence of the first mythical cause represented by a God-inspired legislator that establishes the eternal order of a determinate society and, symmetrically, to denounce the pact as being adequate to account for the complex historical texture that constitutes a society. The point is that Spinoza, through the analysis of the singular history of the Hebrew people, wants to deconstruct the idea of a God-Legislator. Such a history in fact allows him to show the imaginary status of a God that gives laws to the people. After the exodus, being now free from the laws of another nation, the Hebrews had the opportunity to occupy new lands and to forge new laws. In such conditions, they opted for a pact with God:

> Being in this natural state, they resolved, on the advice of Moses in whom they all had the greatest trust, to transfer their right to no mortal man but rather to God alone. Without hesitation, all equally with one shout promised [*omnes æque uno clamore promiserunt*] to obey God absolutely in all his commands, and to recognize no other law but that which He himself conferred as law by prophetic revelation. (*TTP* 205/213)

The Hebrew State was therefore a theocracy, in which God was the unique monarch. But Spinoza immediately adds that "the fact of the matter is that all these things were more opinion than reality [*Verum enimvero haec omnia opinione magis, quam re constabant*]" (*TTP* 206/214).

So the transmission of the divine law to the people is as imaginary as the idea of a legislator "at a stroke," of which in reality the pact between the people and God is the symmetric form. In fact Spinoza, in his reconstruction of the Hebrew State, shows how the constitution of this state eschews the classical typology:

> Moses ... chose no such successor, but rather left a form of state to his successors that could not be called democratic, aristocratic or monarchical, but rather theocratic. For the right to interpret the laws and communicate God's responses was assigned to one man while the right and power of administering government according to the laws interpreted by the first and the responses he communicated was given to another. (*TTP* 207–8/215)

Such a constitution does not correspond to the plan initially conceived by Moses; it is instead the consequence of the adoration of the golden calf by the people, a fact that led Moses to exclude the first-born from the holy ministry in favor of the Levitical tribe. The Biblical passage shows that the new constitution, far from being the result of a rational plan, was the outcome of a terrible violence that established a new balance of forces within society:

> Then Moses stood in the gate of the camp, and said, Who is on the LORD's side? let him come unto me. And all the sons of Levi gathered themselves together unto him. And he said unto them, Thus saith the LORD God of Israel, Put every man his sword by his side, and go in and out from gate to gate throughout the camp, and slay every man his brother, and every man his companion, and every man his neighbour. And the children of Levi did according to the word of Moses: and there fell of the people that day about three thousand men. For Moses had said, Consecrate yourselves to day to the LORD, even every man upon his son, and upon his brother; that he may bestow upon you a blessing this day.[11]

Spinoza deconstructs here the myth of the omnipotent legislator, showing that the legislator's action is embedded in the relationship of forces in the conjuncture. Moses was not a disarmed prophet as underlined by Machiavelli: "Whoever reads the Bible judiciously [*sensatamente*] will see that since he wished his laws and his orders go forward, Moses was forced to kill infinite men who, moved by nothing other than envy, were opposed to his plans" (*D* 236/280). So the structure of the Hebrew State did not arise from Moses' prophecy, was not a simple matter of faith, but the effect of an intervention in a field of forces through the materiality of the arms and the materiality of the ceremonies that introduced religion—that is, obedience—in the everyday practices of the Jewish.

Like Machiavelli apropos of Roman history, here Spinoza, approaching the singular object of his study, leaves behind the idea of a first cause from which a linear time would spring, and analyzes it in its own singularity, in the conflictual intertwining that produced its political form not "at a stroke," but "by chance and at many different times, and according to accidents [*a caso, ed in più volte, e secondo li accidenti*]" (*D* 79/10).

Conclusion

This subterranean repetition of Machiavelli in crucial moments of the *Theologico-Political Treatise* is not without consequences on a theoretical level. It contributes to shaking some tenets of Spinoza's philosophy and opens up new solutions:

1. On the ontological level, the model of serial causality deriving from God, still present in the *Treatise on the Emendation of the Intellect*, undergoes a crisis. In the *Ethics*, with the introduction of immanent causality, Spinoza will think of the *res singulares* not as elements of a series, but as *connexiones*, intertwinings. In this perspective, the concept of natural law will have to be thought anew by means of the concept of immanence. It cannot be the transcendent *lex seriei* but the necessity of the complexity of the intertwining.
2. The crisis manifests itself also on the political level. Here, two aspects undergo a transformation: the model of the pact, conceived as an effect of a calculus by single individuals, as well as the idea of democracy understood as a transitive cause of the State (still at the center of the Chapter XVI of the *Theologico-Political Treatise*). In the *Political Treatise* the term *pactum* will disappear,[12] and the political power [*Imperium*] will be grounded in the

power [*potentia*] of the multitude, which is not to be conceived as subject but as a interweaving of relations, and hence as immanent, not transitive, causality. It is in this sense, I think, that we can agree with Caporali's interpretation, according to which the political theory expressed in Chapter XVI of the *Theologico-Political Treatise* is not fully consistent with Spinoza's metaphysics of *causa sui*; this metaphysics would be consistent, instead, with the political theory proposed in the *Political Treatise*.[13]

Therefore, if one could include Hobbes, as acutely suggested by Matheron, among the utopian thinkers of the first paragraph of the *Political Treatise*,[14] one can also list with them the Spinoza of Chapter XVI, according to whom society was born from a calculus of the individuals that takes the form of a pact. The utopia does not lie so much in the pact, as Spinoza already criticizes the philosophy of natural law by anchoring the respect of the pact to its utility for the single individuals. Rather, the utopia lies in the idea of an individual that ponders the pros and cons of staying in society, moment by moment. Furthering Machiavelli's reflections through his own metaphysics, Spinoza thinks of human society as an intertwining of fortune and virtue, memory and oblivion, power and language, violence and resistance, conflicts and relations of force always piercing through the individual, a concept whose etymological meaning the *Ethics* will soon have blown up. In this sense, freedom cannot be thought according to the Hegelo-Marxist tradition as a conceptual double of the transitive cause—democracy as the origin of society, lost and then found according to the famous couple alienation-disalienation. The critic of authority concept both in theological and in political sense is not carry out through the concept of alienation, it is not re-appropriation of a transcendence in an immanence 'human, all to human'. It is on the contrary that genealogy so far does not look for an *Ursprung* but an *Entstehung* of the authority in the relation of forces, in the conflict, in chance, in the materiality of the language and of the memory. And in this context freedom must be thought as an immanent and conjunctural intervention, on the side of reason, to transform the conflict in political freedom.

Notes

1 For a detailed reconstruction of the presence of Machiavelli in the entire work of Spinoza, see my *Le temps et l'occasion. La rencontre Spinoza Machiavelli* (Paris: Garnier, 2012). See also Filippo Del Lucchese, *Tumult and Indignation: Conflict, Power and Multitude in Machiavelli and Spinoza* (London: Continuum, 2009).

2 Baruch Spinoza, *Tractatus Theologico-Politicus*, *Opera*, ed. by Carl Gebhardt (Heidelberg: Carl Windters Universitätsbuchhandlung, 1924), Volume 3, 45, 46; *Theologico-Political Treatise*, trans. by Jonathan Israel (Cambridge: Cambridge University Press, 2007), 44, 45.

3 Niccolò Machiavelli, *Il Principe*, in *Tutte le opere*, ed. by M. Martelli (Milano: Sansoni, 1993), 295; *The Prince*, trans. by J. B. Atkinson (Indianapolis: Hackett, 2008), 361–63.

4 Niccolò Machiavelli, *Discorsi, in Tutte le opere*, 206; *Discourses*, trans. by Harvey C. Mansfield and Nathan Tarcov (Chicago: University of Chicago Press, 1996), 125. Hereafter cited as *D* in the text.

5 On this see Spinoza to Burgh, cf. Epistola VXXVI in *Opera*, Volume IV, 316–24.

6 On the conatus of language of the multitude as a form of resistance against the mystificating attempt by power, see Filippo Del Lucchese and Vittorio Morfino, "Parole mostruose. Natura umana e politica in Spinoza," *Forme di vita* 4 (2005), 50–64.

7 The Hobbesian utopia relies precisely in the belief that is possible a political control of words meaning through a semantic police. See G. Lebrun, "Hobbes et l'institution de la vérité," *Manuscrito* 6 (1983), 105–31.

8 The computer-generated index attests sixteen occurrences of the term "occasio." See G. Totaro and M. Veneziani, "Indici e concordanze del *Tractatus Theologico-politicus* di Spinoza," *Lexicon Philosophicum* 6 (1993), 51–204. In Chapter 7 Spinoza uses it five times, always together with the term "tempus" (*Opera*, Volume III, 101, 102, 109, 110)

9 Louis Althusser, *Reading Capital* (London: Verso, 2007), 17.

10 In Chapter VI, Machiavelli puts the virtue of the founders Moises, Cyrus, Romulus Theseus in relation to the occasion. Foundation is not the action of a first cause, but the action of virtue in a conjuncture which offers the occasion. And the irony about Moses' teacher, God, the first cause par excellence strengthens the hypothesis that every first cause is, by definition, mythological.

11 *Exodus*, 32, 26–29 (KJB).

12 The only occurrence of the term *contractus* is in the plural, as Cristofolini has showed. See Cristfolini, "Piccolo lessico ragionato," ed. by B. Spinoza, *Trattato politico* (Pisa: ETS, 1999), 242.

13 See R. Caporali, *La* fabbrica dell'*imperium* (Napoli: Liguori, 2000).

14 A. Matheron, "Spinoza et la décomposition de la politique thomiste: Machiavélisme et Utopie," *Archivio di filosofia* (*Lo spinozismo ieri e oggi*) 46 (1978), 1, 59.

Bibliography

Althusser, Louis. *Reading Capital*. London: Verso, 2007.

Caporali, Riccardo. *La* fabbrica dell'*imperium*. Napoli: Liguori, 2000.

Cristfolini, Paolo. "Piccolo lessico ragionato," in ed. by B. Spinoza, *Trattato politico*. Pisa: ETS, 1999, 241–46.

Del Lucchese, Filippo. *Tumult and Indignation: Conflict, Power and Multitude in Machiavelli and Spinoza*. London: Continuum, 2009.

Del Lucchese, Filippo and Morfino, Vittorio. "Parole mostruose. Natura umana e politica in Spinoza," *Forme di vita* 4 (2005), 50–64.

Lebrun, Gérard. "Hobbes et l'institution de la vérité," *Manuscrito* 6 (1983), 105–31.

Machiavelli, Niccolò. *Discourses*, trans. by Harvey C. Mansfield and Nathan Tarcov. Chicago: University of Chicago Press, 1996.

Machiavelli, Niccolò. *The Prince*, trans. by J. B. Atkinson. Indianapolis: Hackett, 2008.

Machiavelli, Niccolò. *Tutte le opere*, ed. by M. Martelli. Milano: Sansoni, 1993, volume 1.

Matheron, Alexandre. "Spinoza et la décomposition de la politique thomiste: Machiavélisme et Utopie," *Archivio di filosofia* (*Lo spinozismo ieri e oggi*), 46 (1978), 1, 29–60.

Morfino, Vittorio. *Le temps et l'occasion. La rencontre Spinoza Machiavelli*. Paris: Garnier, 2012.

Spinoza, Baruch. *Opera*, ed. by Carl Gebhardt. Heidelberg: Carl Windters Universitätsbuchhandlung, 1924, 5 volumes.

Spinoza, Baruch. *Theologico-Political Treatise*, trans. by Jonathan Israel. Cambridge, Cambridge University Press, 2007.

Totaro, Giuseppina. and Veneziani, Marcello. "Indici e concordanze del *Tractatus Theologico-politicus* di Spinoza," *Lexicon Philosophicum* 6 (1993), 51–204.

2

The Symptomatic Relationship between Law and Conflict in Spinoza: *Jura communia* as *anima imperii*

Filippo Del Lucchese

Spinoza is often praised by modern scholars as a revolutionary author, providing a metaphysics which can complement or even replace a Marxian political framework. Yet Spinoza does not seem to endorse in his politics any idea of radical change, or even to express a preference for social transformation. A theory of revolution thus seems to be the blind spot of Spinozism. In this chapter, I will argue that a traditional theory of revolution is actually impossible within Spinoza's philosophy. In fact, the idea of radical change is alien to Spinozism insofar as this philosophy involves an unorthodox concept of the causal relationship between law and politics, and in particular between law and conflict.

We can start by approaching the traditional theories of revolution through Hannah Arendt. In her influential book *On Revolution*, Arendt maintains that "revolutions are the only political events which confront us directly and inevitably with the problem of beginning. For revolutions [...] are not mere changes."[1] Neither a change in itself nor violence as a means of changing belong to the very essence of revolution. Revolution is a much more complex historical phenomenon, ontologically linked with the idea of a radical transformation of the existing state of things. The actors of revolutions express this idea and feel the movement of history, and this makes possible for Arendt to say that "only where this pathos of novelty is present and where novelty is connected with the idea of freedom are we entitled to speak of revolution."[2]

Arendt's intention is to separate the noble concept of revolution from the ignoble phenomenon of violence, and to separate the political question from the social question, according to a thesis that has become very influential since her book was published. In order to do so, she does not hesitate to embrace the classic historiographical opposition between a cyclical conception of history, typical of the ancients (insofar as they were concerned with the problem of changes taking place within a natural circle of forms of government) and a linear conception of history (typical of the modern mentality and connected to the "notion that the course of history suddenly begins anew, that an entirely new story, a story never known or told before, is about to unfold"[3]). Although classical scholars have pointed out the limits of such a thesis concerning the concept of time and history in the ancient world, and have questioned the dichotomy between the linear time of the modern and the cyclical time of the ancient, the distinction continues to be influential and still functions today as a paradigm.[4]

My aim in this chapter is to show that such a model of Revolution is incompatible with Spinoza's philosophy. Both the cyclical and linear conceptions of time clash with Spinoza's idea of history. We do not and cannot find, within Spinozism, either the supposedly classical idea of eternal return of forms of government, or the supposedly modern idea of a revolutionary break that determines an entirely new beginning, a permanent deviation in the line of time that moves history in a completely new direction.

Both notions are impossible within Spinoza's philosophy because Spinozism involves an idea of *permanent* revolution that can only be grasped by understanding the peculiar and original relationship that Spinoza conceives between law and conflict.

In *Conflict, Power, and Multitude*, I called this relationship "recursive," a term I largely borrowed from Laurent Bove.[5] We should recall here that "recursion" has a variety of meanings specific to different disciplines, and it has been successfully introduced in computer sciences over the last decades to indicate "a repeated procedure such that the required result at each step is defined in terms of the results of previous step," or, in other words, "a rule which can be reapplied to a form or construction that is itself [...] derived by that rule."[6] But the term itself has a much longer genealogy, and can be found for example in Robert Boyle, who speaks of "the Recursions of the Pendulum," referring to the Latin root *recurro*, used of heavenly bodies in their course to indicate their returning to the starting point.[7] I found then the term "recursive" useful in overcoming a conception of *linear* causality between law and conflict, usually summarized by the idea that virtuous and moderate conflicts produce good laws, or, in Arendt's terms, the notion that the "political" question produces American freedom and the good revolution, while the "social" question produces the French and the Soviet tragedies, and the bad revolution.

Yet I think now that a better word, and consequently a better idea, must be found to describe this relationship. The idea of recursivity is helpful in moving beyond the concept of circular history. It is, however, too indebted to and dependent on the idea that one must choose between circularity and linearity, a paradigm that is historically inaccurate and theoretically unfruitful for describing Spinoza's idea of revolution. In this chapter I will try to propose a new definition of the relationship between law and conflict. What is at stake in it for Spinozism as a political philosophy? How is the very same idea of revolution influenced by the answer to this question?

Of the two conceptions, that is, the radical interruption of history and the absolute new beginning on the one hand, and the circular motion and eternal return of the same on the other—the former seems the most alien to Spinoza's philosophy. He plainly shows that human history is rich enough and wide enough to include already every major change that one could possibly imagine. History has already shown everything that can happen. No absolute beginning is thus to be expected: "I am fully convinced," he writes in the *Political Treatise*, "that experience has revealed every conceivable form of City where men may live in harmony, and also the means whereby a multitude may be governed or restrained within fixed bounds. I do not believe that our researches in this field can lead us to anything not at variance with experience and practice that has not already been discovered and tried" (*TP* 1.3).[8] Thus the question is not about saying or doing something new, but about better understanding what men have not yet understood and that, although self-evident, is too often neglected.[9]

Moreover, following Spinoza's metaphysics, the very idea of a new beginning is alien to his system, insofar as Nature, the unique substance, is characterized by a constancy and a consistency that reflect God's perfection: "Nature is always the same, and its force and power of acting is everywhere one and the same; that is, the laws and rules of Nature according to which all things happen and change for one form to another are everywhere and always the same" (*E* III, Preface). Human societies are no exception, precisely because the substance is one and only one. This idea of a strong constancy and consistency must therefore be extended to the world of human events as well, because man is not an *imperium in imperio*. There is no void in political history, a void that could be filled with a new political idea, in the same way that there is no void in nature, a void that could be filled with a body created out of nothing.

The idea of circularity might seem to be less alien to Spinoza's philosophy. In fact, within this absolute constancy and consistency of Nature and its laws, things—both human and non-human—are constantly in motion, varying between higher and lower levels, between a maximum and a minimum, mutually influencing each other, for example, in the cycles of affects developed and described in Part III of the *Ethics*.[10] Even the classical circle of the forms of government (monarchy, aristocracy and democracy), in this sense, could be interpreted as a repetition of conflicts and laws, sequentially produced under new forms of governments, and connected to each other in a circular motion, following a rigid chain of causes and effects.

A further element seems to suggest the possibility of inscribing Spinoza's conception within the ancient idea of circularity. For the classical philosophers, like Aristotle and Polybius, the problem was to figure out how to slow down and possibly interrupt this cyclical movement, by fixing it in a virtuous form of government, a mixed government that could prevent the periodic corruption and degeneration of one form of government into another. Spinoza seems to go in the same direction, for example when he argues for the conservation of the form of government in order to prevent corruption, and seems to develop a conservative role for politics: "by the means required to preserve the state I understand those that are necessary to preserve the form of the state without any notable change" (*TP* 4.2).

In fact, through his apparently conservative approach, Spinoza develops a completely new, original and revolutionary doctrine, developed through a non-linear relationship of causality between law and conflicts, a relationship that, as mentioned, I previously called "recursive." In recent years, Vittorio Morfino has explored Spinoza's concept of causality, explaining the passage from a linear model in the early works to a "connective" causality in his more mature works.[11] Morfino claims that Spinoza is led toward a new idea of causality by the encounter with Niccolò Machiavelli's political philosophy and theory of temporality, and in particular with his theory of history as intersection and relation, as well as—borrowing Althusser's language—an *aleatory* composition of virtue and fortune. In the early writings such as the *Tractatus de Intellectus Emendatione*, Spinoza maintains an idea of causality grounded on the concept of series, which represents the necessary and essential order of a chain of singular events. While existence only implies accidental relations that cannot be adequately known, essence represents the principle of a necessary order that emanates from the series of fixed and eternal relations.

As Morfino explains, the encounter with Machiavelli's philosophy produces an amazingly interesting new conception of causality, in which the idea of the series of events is replaced by that of a *connection* of events. The essence of something is not an absolutely independent and unrelated monad. Rather it is located within and exists through the relations and the circumstances that have produced that specific thing. The *ordo sive series* is replaced by the *ordo sive connexio*, an idea of order that obliterates the simple linear relationship between causes by revealing the dynamic multidimensionality of their structure. In this way, an "ontology of relation" stands against every possible theology and teleology of causal relations.

Following Morfino's suggestion, we should ask if this evolution in Spinoza's ontology also has consequences for political philosophy, and in particular for the relationship between law and conflict: what is—if any—their causal relationship? This question is justified—and it seems to me fundamentally important—in view of the close relationship Spinoza had with Machiavelli, one of the few authors explicitly praised by Spinoza in his *Political Treatise*.

Machiavelli's theory of conflict is relevant here, particularly the specific relationship that he establishes between law and conflict:

> In every republic there are two different humours [*umori*], that of the people and that of the great and [...] all the laws that are made in favor of freedom arise from their disunion. [No one can] in any mode, with reason, call a republic disordered where there are so many examples of virtue; for good examples arise from good education, good education from good laws, and good laws from those tumults that many inconsiderately damn.¹²

Machiavelli poses a causal relationship that links together, via several mediations, conflicts and law. But this conclusion can in fact be expanded, given the metaphysical dimension that this problem has in Spinoza. It can include, in particular, the broader relationship between law and politics itself, given the striking theory of Spinoza for whom (1) *jus* is defined as *potentia* and (2) the *jus* (and therefore the *potentia*) of every particular thing is the same *jus* (and therefore the same *potentia*) of god itself. My thesis is that the relationship between law and politics must be interpreted within a new scheme of causality.

"Good examples," says Machiavelli, come from "good education," as a result of "good laws" that emerge from conflict. That is to say, they emerge from something that the whole philosophical tradition has always refused to recognize and has tried to expunge from political philosophy (and from real politics itself), namely conflict. With a very suggestive expression, Althusser, speaks of a "political primitive accumulation," arguing that, in his philosophy, Machiavelli predominantly uses the language of force and not of law.¹³ Althusser's metaphor does not fully take into account that Machiavelli is not only suggesting that law rests on force. He is in fact suggesting something much more complex, a conception in which the two elements are linked together inseparably in a spiral that rules out every peaceful solution.

The idea of a connection comes to the forefront once again. But this *connexio* must be explained further. It must be clarified, in particular, vis-à-vis a kind of relationship that is not based on any idea of circularity, not even the one involved in the idea of recursion. While it captures the dynamism of the relationship between law and politics, recursion fails to grasp the irregular, aleatory, and multifarious character of that dynamics: no matter how tight the loops of the spiral are, the recursive relationship has still the form of a circle, and is therefore unsuitable, in my view, to describe Spinoza's thought.

My thesis consists of two parts. The first part of my thesis is that (1) the relationship between law and conflict must be considered through and explained by the same kind of relationship that Spinoza imagines for the mind and the body: in the same way that the mind is defined as the idea of the body (*E* II, 13), the *jus*, following the analogy, must be considered as *the idea of conflict*; and that (2) this is true of *jus* both in the subjective and the objective sense. We can thus dissolve the Latin word *jus* into its two English equivalents of right and law. The second part of my thesis follows from the first and is that (a) subjective rights are *the idea* of conflicts, and also that (b) the law is *the idea* of conflict or, in other words, of the necessarily conflictual life of the multitude.

I will now turn to Spinoza's conception of *jus sive potentia* in Chapter 16 of the *Theological-Political Treatise* and the qualification of *jura* as *anima imperii* in Chapter 10, paragraph 9 of the *Political Treatise*. I refrain from translating these expressions for the time being, as translation itself refers to a major problem at stake in this discussion.

The first and most important theoretical element here is the definition of *jus sive potentia*. We know that the English translation of *potentia* presents some interesting theoretical problems. Let's use power, as translators typically do.[14] The translation of the term *jus* also presents theoretical problems. The subjective idea of individual rights is definitely implied by Spinoza's definition. We will see, however, that the objective idea of law is also involved by this original and revolutionary definition.

Some scholars have interpreted this passage as evincing the primacy/priority/superiority of power (*potentia*) over right (*jus*).[15] I think, however, that, if we want to closely follow what Spinoza says, we should instead acknowledge a strict identity and therefore full interchangeability of *jus* and *potentia*, which means that they must therefore be considered on the same ontological level. Power cannot be considered as ontologically prior or superior to law. Spinoza himself clearly suggests this conclusion, by making a fairly sharp yet somehow paradoxical distinction between natural laws and human laws in Chapter 4 of the *Theological-Political Treatise*: Saying that some laws depend on the human decision does not mean that they do not depend on the necessity of nature. The human mind, and the human decisions are in fact themselves part of the very same power (*potentia*) of Nature. Therefore, the sanction of a law surely depends on human decision, that is to say on the power of the human mind (not to mention the power of the human bodies, i.e., the effective power of sanctioning them).

Spinoza adds, however, an important restriction. He states that the human mind *can* be conceived without the laws that depend on decisions, but it *cannot* be conceived without the laws that depend on natural necessity. It is true that there is here a *kind* of equivalence, insofar as this primacy of natural laws over human laws is only due to our ignorance and not to a real ontological difference: in fact, Spinoza argues, we say that human laws depend on the human decision because we must define things through their proximate causes and we do not know the whole chain of causes. It is thus better for us, as a practical rule of life, to consider them as contingent and possible rather than necessary.

The difference, then, can only play in one direction: we *must* obey any kind of law, both natural and civil, but we *can* only disobey the latter, whereas we *can not* disobey the former. In any case, though, we need to acknowledge that the faculty that men have of disobeying some laws (civil ones) and not some others (natural ones) does not depend on the different *nature* of the laws, but only on the *relationship* between ourselves and the laws or, in other words, between our own *potentia/jus* and the *potentia/jus* of the individuals, modes, and situations with which we interact, as well as with the phenomena that we are part of: this relationship, this relational field of multiple interactions *is* the law, understood in its natural dimension, or in its civil dimension, or in both dimensions, depending on the circumstances.

Whereas the idealist would say that we *have* laws or that we are *given* laws, the Spinozist will always say that we *are* part of the law, and an active part, despite some pre-existing piece of ink-stained paper that commands or forbids something to us. It seems easier to disobey a piece of paper rather than a physical law, such as for example the law of gravitation. We are embodied, and our bodies must obey it. Yet we are also *part* of it, in the sense that we jump, we climb and we fly with airplanes and other devices, and in that sense we constantly reshape our relationship with the environment in and through the law of gravitation. We exist *in and through* laws, both natural and civil, and laws, both natural and civil, exist in and through us.

In this light, the *jus sive potentia* clarifies my interpretation of right as the *idea* of conflict. Here we can translate *jus* as "right," insofar as we consider it in a subjective sense. A right, or power, is always a conflictual field of interactions. In fact, it is the idea of these physical interactions in both the legal *and* the natural sphere at once. We are accustomed, by centuries of morally inspired legal thought, to separate the two questions: "what do I have the right to do?" and "what do I have the power to do?" But through Spinoza, these two questions must be understood to be one and the same. "What is my *jus sive potentia*?" can be taken to mean: What is the relationship between what *I am*, what *I can do*, and the way I *affect and am affected* by the environment in which I find myself in a given moment? Natural laws will describe the physical structure of this system composed by myself and other individual and things; legal laws will describe the juridical aspect of it, but they are all describing *one and the same* phenomenon, which is conflictually produced by the multiple tensions between the rights/powers that "I am" (rather than that "I have").

My thesis, though, is that even *jus* in the objective sense, that is to say the law, is the idea of conflict. Or, to make it clearer, that law and conflict are two different *modalities* of the same reality. The use of the language of modality should clarify why I have abandoned the idea of recursion and prefer to borrow a conceptual tool belonging to the heart of Spinozism, that is to say the idea of parallelism, and in particular that seen in the relationship between mind and body.

As we know, Spinoza ascribes great importance to the Cartesian philosophical revolution. And yet he thinks that Descartes himself has not been fully Cartesian, precisely because he excluded the specific relationship between mind and body from his strictly mechanical conception of nature, by maintaining (1) the primacy and superiority of the mind over the body; (2) that the mind is active when the body is passive (and vice-versa); and, (3) that the mind's aim must be to govern the body.

Spinoza strongly rejects the Cartesian solution. He considers it an absurdity guided by moral and religious principles rather than by a serious study and interpretation of nature. He maintains, contrary to Descartes, that both mind and body are *together* either active or passive, and that the former can in no way conduct the latter. The mind, in fact, is nothing else than the "idea" of the body, or *idea corporis*. For Spinoza, any ontological primacy of the mind over the body is excluded, as well as every ontological primacy of a human individual (intended as a mind *and* a body) over a nonhuman individual; this creates a new and revolutionary image of man as well as a different role for man within nature.[16]

If we now move to the relationship between politics and law, Spinoza's originality appears even more clearly. Spinoza is not the first one to think about the concept of law (or at least of sovereignty) in terms of the mind (or at least in terms of something close to the mind).[17] Thomas Hobbes, for example, explicitly discusses this idea in at least two key passages. The first is in the *Leviathan*, in which he explores the ecclesiastical power and Pope Innocent the Third's political position, following the Fourth Council of the Lateran. The pope's error, Hobbes claims, "is, that he says, the members of every commonwealth, as of a natural body, depend one of another [and] cohere together, but they depend only on the sovereign, which is the soul of the commonwealth (*anima reipublicae*); which failing, the commonwealth is dissolved into a civil war, no one man so much as cohering to another, for want of a common dependence on a known sovereign; just as the members of the natural body dissolve into earth, for want of a soul to hold them together."[18] The soul keeps the body together. The soul is the principle of the body politic, insofar as the latter would decay and dissolve if it was not for the former's action.

Hobbes had touched already the point in an even more striking way in the *Philosophical Rudimentes Concerning Government and Society*:

> they who compare a city and its citizens with a man and his members, almost all say, that he who hath the supreme power [...] is [...] such as the head is to the whole man. But it appears [...] that he who is endued with such a power [...] hath a relation to the city, not as that of the head, but of the soul to the body. For it is the soul by which a man hath a will, that is, can either will or nill; so by him who hath the supreme power, and no otherwise, the city hath a will, and can either will or nill [because] the soul's [office] is to command.[19]

The sovereign, for Hobbes, is not the head, but the soul of the body politic, which alone can provide the same body with a political will. A political body without a sovereign/soul is nothing but a corpse. Spinoza directly opposes Hobbes on this point. Through his striking definition of the *mens* as *idea corporis*, he is able to reject Hobbes' claim regarding the ontological superiority of the sovereign. This, in turn, opens up the possibility of redefining the relationship between law and politics, and in particular between law and conflict. Implicitly but clearly, Spinoza suggests the possibility of applying his notion of the mind/body relationship to the political ground, thus overcoming the rigidity of Hobbes' politics, in the same way that he had overcome the rigidity of Descartes' psychology.

The second passage we must consider is as famous and as fundamentally important as the previous one. Strangely enough, though, scholars do not agree on its meaning, as its different translations prove. Spinoza uses the following striking expression: *jura sunt anima imperii* (TP 10.9). If any *imperium* can be said to be "eternal," it is the one whose *jura* remains preserved.[20] We need to go back to the Latin, here, and the *jura*, as translators have been puzzled by several aspects of this passage. The most influential solutions over the last decades propose the following translations:

> Nagelate Shriften (1677): de wetten zijn de ziel van de Heerschappy[21]
> Ewald (1785): die Gesetze sind die Seele des Staats[22]
> Maccall (1854): rights are the soul of a government[23]
> Prat (1860): l'Ame d'un empire [...] ce sont [les] droits[24]
> Appuhn (1929): les lois sont l'âme de l'Etat[25]
> Francès (1954): la législation est l'âme de l'Etat[26]
> Droetto (1958): le leggi sono l'anima dello Stato[27]
> Wernham (1958): the constitution is the soul of a State[28]
> Moreau (1979): le Droit est l'âme de l'Etat[29]
> Dominguez (1986): el alma del Estado son los derechos[30]
> Cristofolini (1999): le leggi sono l'anima dello stato[31]
> Shirley (2002): the constitution is the soul of the state[32]
> Bove (2002): le Droit est l'âme d'un Etat[33]
> Ramond (2005): Les règles de droit sont l'âme de l'État[34]
> Proietti (2007): le leggi sono l'anima dello Stato[35]
> Pautrat (2013): les droits sont l'âme de l'*imperium*[36]
> Curley (2016): the laws are the soul of the state[37]

The diverse nature of the solutions is striking, given what is at stake for the interpretation of Spinoza's political and legal philosophy as a whole. All the translations point out, either implicitly or explicitly, the problem I have been discussing. The first word of the passage is problematic: Is it laws? Rules of law? The law? The second one is also controversial: is 'the soul' what Spinoza is thinking about?

The choice regarding *anima* is particularly relevant for my thesis. In the footnote of his recent edition, Charles Ramond points out that this is the only time in which the term appears in the *Political Treatise*, and that it must be connected with the *mens* (see TP 4.1), and therefore translated with "mind" rather than with "soul". I agree that Spinoza steadily moves away, in his works, from the use of "soul" toward that of "mind." Yet precisely for this reason, we need to pay attention to his unusual choice: as an unusual choice it deserves more attention and the lowest possible degree of approximation and interpretation.

If Spinoza moves away from *anima* in favor of *mens*, it is to suggest, following Descartes, that the mind performs first and foremost an intellectual function, of rational knowledge of nature, gods, and itself. It is also to suggest, against Descartes this time, the impossibility of separating it from the body: *modus cogitationis* (Spinoza) vs. *substantia cogitans* (Descartes). Mind and body are on the same ontological level; they share the same reality, respond to the same causes, and produce the same effects. This is, once again, where the *connexio* reveals itself: *ordo et connexio rerum idem est ac ordo et connexio idearum*.

With this in mind, an original interpretation of the relationship between politics and law becomes possible, perhaps even necessary. To arrive at it, we must first ask what Spinoza suggests by saying that the *jura* are the *anima imperii*? I claim that, first, Spinoza is bringing the problem of the relationship between law and politics to the same level of the one between mind and body. Second, he is suggesting that, without being an *imperium in imperio*, the political realm has at least one specificity, which means that it is indeed possible in one way to think about this particular kind of political *anima* as being separable from its political body. But in which way then?

My suggestion is that it is separable only in an imaginative way, that is, according to a faculty that is in fact incapable of grasping the real nature of this relationship, in the same way that it is incapable of understanding the difference between natural laws and civil laws encountered above. Our imagination can and in fact does, most of the time, take them as distinguishable, and this supports a recursive reading of their relationship: one element is imagined as ahead of the other, recursively producing effects onto the other. The law produces effects: sometimes obedience, sometimes resistance and conflicts that lead, possibly, to a revolution. This, in turns, produces new laws, a new legal order, new individual rights, a new constitution, and so on. This dynamic is grasped by humans imaginatively, that is, inadequately, and this brings forth the classic concept of revolution, whether it is described as following a cyclical or a linear historical development, to recall Arendt's categories. To be adequate, however, the relationship between law and conflict should be seen as an ontological identity: they function like the mind and the body of the "individual politic": not a Cartesian nor a Hobbesian individual, but a Spinozist individual.

This problem also throws light on a different question, much discussed in scholarship but with no less diversity of interpretations than the one we have just seen. I am referring to the Spinoza's phrase *una veluti mente ducitur* (*TP* 3.2, 3.7 and 2.16–17). A State has more power than its subjects insofar as *they are guided as by one single mind*. Scholars have recently pointed out that this expression pushes Spinoza away from his anti-Cartesian position, precisely because in his system the mind does not *guide* the body.[38] Once again, this interpretation grasps the general movement of Spinoza's philosophy, but it undermines the striking specificity of this expression.

As above, I suggest a different reading: instead of saying that, in this passage, Spinoza is not suitably Spinozist, I prefer to consider that the mind *does* in fact imagine that it guides the body, and that the multitude *does* in fact imagine itself to be guided by one single mind (or, as Deleuze says by stretching the translation, "guided by one single thought").[39] The multitude can be guided by one single mind in the same way that law can determine conflict. Imaginatively as a circular or recursive relationship, while in fact, according to a non circular/non-recursive relationship, a relationship that is a real identity like the one characterizing the attributes, all of which stand on the same ontological level of immanence.

We now need to find a name for this relationship. A good candidate might be the term *sign*, where the law is intended as the sign of the conflict, namely, that which reflects the present state of the multitude and the actual relationships of force existing in it. But in fact, on closer look, this solution points to a crude revolutionary conception: if the constitutional structure of a State does not reflect the economic structure of a society, then the legal system collapses, conflict explodes until a new economic and political balance is redefined and then reflected in the law through a new constitution.

Besides being excessively simplistic, the major problem with the concept of the sign is that it does not fit with the strict idea of parallelism I am employing here. If the law can be called the sign of conflict, it is difficult to see how the opposite could be true, that is, that the conflict be intended as the sign of the law. Or rather, one could say that this would only be *inadequately* possible, that is to say, insofar as law is intended as a moral command or a moral prohibition and not as an ethical expression of the composition of forces, to follow Deleuze's language. The sign, as Deleuze has suggested, is always inadequate insofar as it is the idea of an effect grasped under conditions that separate it from its causes, or under conditions whose nature we do not understand (in the same way that Adam did not understand God's prohibition, in Spinoza's reading of the Bible—see letter to Blyenbergh, *Ep.* XIX).

My suggestion is therefore to shift to the concept of *symptom* or, in other words, to the idea of a *symptomatic* relationship between law and conflict. Law can be intended as the *symptom* of conflict, and of course, closely following Spinoza, vice versa as well. I do not use the term symptom in its current sense;

instead I go back to its classic etymology and roots in ancient medicine. The Greek etymology is interesting: *symptôma* (σύμ-πτωμα) comes from *syn* (together) and *piptein* (falling down). It thus refers to things being joined together, things happening together, or elements meeting each other, connecting each other with no gap or delay or interval, whether ontological or chronological, between them. A thing's symptom is intended not as its effect or consequence, but rather as another aspect, another face of it, revealing a different side of the event.

Interestingly enough, the term symptom was introduced into the medical vocabulary fairly late. It cannot be found in Hippocrates (fourth century BC), but it exists in Erasistratus (third century BC) and Galen (second century AD).[40] And Galen himself, in *De symptomatum differentiis*, has a wonderful and poetical expression when he says that symptoms are like the "shadows" of the disease. This image may of course suggest the idea of the primacy of the object to its own shadow, which would not exist without the object itself.[41] We need, however, to polish the concept of symptom and avoid this idea of subordination: if it is true the shadow is the consequence of the body intercepting light, it is also true that every body intercepting light must necessarily have a shadow, so they can only exist together: they "fall" together into existence. What is left is the perfect and absolute coincidence of the object *and* its shadow, that is to say its *symptom*. In this sense, I would like to think about law as the shadow of conflict, or the symptom of conflict, and of course, the other way around as well: conflict as the shadow or the symptom of law.

This symptomatic coincidence between law and conflict thus reveals the revolutionary character of Spinoza's philosophy at the dawn of early modernity. It is a political philosophy that eludes the choice between a cyclical or a linear conception of historical time or, rather, a political philosophy that points to the possibility of an alternative way of apprehending revolutions within the one and unique substance, that is nature and its history. Spinoza's legacy offers us the invaluable theoretical tool of a notion of revolution that eludes both the fatalist conception of closed circular history and the idealist conception of an absolute break in the linear movement of history: a theoretical tool whose potentialities, in my view, have not been fully explored by contemporary political thought.

Notes

1 Hannah Arendt, *On Revolution* (London: Penguin Books, 1990), 21.
2 Arendt, *On Revolution*, 34.

3   Arendt, *On Revolution*, 28.
4   See especially the seminal work of Arnaldo Momigliano, "Time in Ancient Historiography," *History and Theory* 6 (1966), 1–23.
5   Filippo Del Lucchese, *Conflict, Power, and Multitude in Machiavelli and Spinoza: Tumult and Indignation* (London: Continuum Press, 2009). See Laurent Bove, *La stratégie du conatus: affirmation et résistence chez Spinoza* (Paris: Librairie Philosophique J. Vrin, 1996).
6   See the Oxford English Dictionary, www.oed.com (accessed on December 22, 2014).
7   See Robert Boyle, *Works* (London: Printed for J. and F. Rivington et al, 1772), 61, experiment XXVI. The most fascinating illustration of this concept, though, is a visual one, found in Dutch painter Maurits Cornelis Escher's works, in which the paradoxical possibilities of the recursion are explored in fantastic and unconventional ways, such as in the lithograph *Relativity*. See Maurice Cornelius Escher, *The Graphic Work* (Köln: Benedikt Taschen Verlag, 2008). See also Douglas R. Hofstadter, *Gödel, Escher, Bach: An Eternal Golden Braid* (New York: Basic Books, 1979).
8   For Spinoza's works, I use the *Complete Works*, ed. by M. L. Morgan and trans. by S. Shirley (Indianapolis: Hackett, 2002). Translation is sometimes modified, as it is in this case.
9   See François Zourabichvili, *Le conservatisme paradoxal de Spinoza* (Paris: Presses Universitaires de France, 2002).
10 In his seminal work, Alexandre Matheron has very well described these cyclical form of the affective life of men, and the consequences that it has on the field of politics. See Alexandre Matheron, *Individu et communauté chez Spinoza* (Paris: Minuit, 1969). See also Alexandre Matheron, *Etudes sur Spinoza et les philosophies de l'âge classique* (Lyon: ENS Editions, 2011).
11 Vittorio Morfino, *Plural Temporality: Transindividuality and the Aleatory between Spinoza and Althusser* (Leiden: Brill, 2014).
12 Niccolò Machiavelli, *Discourses on Livy*, trans. by Harvey C. Mansfield and Nathan Tarcov (Chicago: The University of Chicago Press, 1996), I.4, 16–17.
13 Louis Althusser, *Machiavelli and Us*, ed. by François Matheron and trans. by G. M. Goshgarian (London: Verso, 1999), 125–26.
14 See Antonio Negri, *Savage Anomaly: The Power of Spinoza's Metaphysics*, trans. by Michael Hardt (Minneapolis: University of Minnesota Press, 1999), Translator's Foreword, 11–12: "Whereas the Latin terms used by Spinoza, potestas and potentia, have distinct correlates in most European languages (potere and potenza in Italian, pouvoir and puissance in French, Macht and Vermögen in German), English provides only a single term, power. To address this difficulty, we have considered several words that might serve for one of the terms, such as potency, authority, might, strength, and force, but each of these introduces asignificant distortion that only masks the real problem. Therefore, we have chosen to leave the translation issue

unresolved in this work: We make the distinction nominally through capitalization, rendering potestas as 'Power' and potentia as 'power' and including the Latin terms in brackets where there might be confusion."

15 Negri, *Savage Anomaly*. On these aspects, see Mariana de Gainza, *Espinosa: Uma Filosofia Materialista do Infinito Positivo* (São Paulo: Editora de Universidade de São Paulo, 2011).

16 E II,13 and schol. See Hasana Sharp, *Spinoza and the Politics of Renaturalization* (Chicago and London: The University of Chicago Press, 2011).

17 On Spinoza's concept of sovereignty, see Dimitris Vardoulakis, *Sovereignty and Its Other: Toward the Dejustification of Violence* (New York: Fordham University Press, 2013).

18 Thomas Hobbes, *Leviathan* (Oxford: Clarendon Press, 2012), XLII, 125.

19 *Philosophical Rudiments Concerning Government and Society*, in *English Work*, ed. by William Molesworth, VI, 89.

20 On the complexity of the translation of *imperium*, see B. Pautrat, Introduction to B. Spinoza, *Traité politique*, traduit du latin, présenté et annoté par Bernard Pautrat (Paris: Editions Allia, 2013). As we know, "eternal" does not mean for Spinoza having an infinite duration, for "eternity [cannot] be defined by time, or be in any way related to time" (*E* V, P23S).

21 *De Nagelate Schriften van B.d.S. Als Zedekunst, Staatkunde, Verbetering van't Verstant, Breiven en Antwoorden*, uit verscheide Talen in de Nederlandsche gebragt (1677), 399.

22 Benedikt von Spinoza *Zwey Abhandlungen über die Kultur des menschlichen Verstandes und über die Aristokratie und Demokratie*. Herausgegeben und mit einer Vorrede begleitet von S.H. Ewald, Leipzig, in der von Schönfeldschen Handlung (1785), 244

23 Baruch Spinoza, *A Treatise on Politics*, translated from the Latin of B. Spinoza by W. Maccall (London: 1854), 111.

24 Baruch Spinoza, *Traité politique de B. de Spinoza*, traduit en français pour la première fois, annoté, suivi d'un index analytique et accompagné de trois plans des trois différentes formes de gouvernement, par J.-G. Prat (Paris: Tous les libraires, 1860).

25 Baruch Spinoza, *Oeuvres*, IV, traduction et notes par C. Appuhn (Paris: Librairie Garnier Frèes, 1929), 104.

26 Baruch Spinoza, *Oeuvres complètes*, texte nouvellement traduit ou revu, présenté et annoté par R. Caillois, M. Francès et R. Misrahi (Paris: Gallimard, 1954), 1095.

27 Baruch Spinoza, *Trattato politico*, a cura di A. Droetto (Torino: Ramella, 1958), 360.

28 Benedict de Spinoza, *The Political Works*, edited and translated with an introduction and notes by A. G. Wernham (Oxford: Clarendon Press, 1958), 437.

29 Baruch Spinoza, *Tractatus politicus/Traité politique*, texte latin, traduction par P.-F. Moreau, index informatique par P.-F. Moreau et R. Bouveresse (Paris: Editions Réplique, 1979), 179.

30 Baruch Spinoza, *Tratado politico*, Traducción, introducción, indice analítico y notas de A. Dominguez (Madrid: Alianza Editorial, 1986), 217.
31 Baruch Spinoza, *Trattato politico*, testo e traduzione a cura di Cristofolini (Pisa: ETS, 1999), 231.
32 Baruch Spinoza, *Complete Works*, with the translation of S. Shirley, ed. by M. L. Morgan (Indianapolis and Cambridge: Hackett Publishing Company, 2002), 750.
33 Baruch Spinoza, *Traité politique*, traduction d'Emile Saisset révisée par Laurent Bove, introduction et notes par Laurent Bove (Paris: Librairie Générale Française, 2002), 261.
34 Baruch Spinoza, *Oeuvres, V, Traité politique*, texte établi par Omero Proietti, traduction, introduction, notes, glossaire, index et bibliographie par Charles Ramond, avec une notice de Pierre-François Moreau et des notes d'Alexandre Matheron (Paris: Presses Universitaires de France, 2005), 265.
35 Baruch Spinoza, *Opere*, a cura e con un saggio introduttivo di Filippo Mignini, traduzioni e note di Filippo Mignini e Omero Proietti (Milano: Mondadori, 2007), 1213.
36 Spinoza, *Traité politique*, 138.
37 Spinoza, Baruch, *The Collected Works of Spinoza*, Volume II, ed. and trans. by Edwin Curley (Princeton and Oxford: Princeton University Press, 2016), 600.
38 See Charles Ramond's footnote, in Baruch Spinoza, *Oeuvres V, Tractatus Politicus/ Traité politique*, trans. by C. Ramond (Paris: Presses Universitaires de France, 2005), 309.
39 Gilles Deleuze, *Spinoza et le problème de l'expression* (Paris: Minuit, 1968), 245.
40 See Daniela Fausti, "Il segno e la prognosi nel *Corpus Hippocraticum* (*Prognostico* e *Prorretico* I e II)," *I quaderni del Ramo d'Oro on-line* 1 (2008), 258–78; Maria Antonietta Salemme Haas, Anna Maria Celani Inesi, "Dal sintomo al segno: una nuova dimensione dell'esperienza medica," *Medicina nei secoli* n.s. 17.1 (2005), 135–50.
41 And Galen himself intends them as signs of affections that cannot yet be called malady, but that precede the malady itself.

Bibliography

Althusser, Louis. *Machiavelli and Us*, ed. by François Matheron and trans. by G. M. Goshgarian. London: Verso, 1999.
Arendt, Hannah. *On Revolution*. London: Penguin Books, 1990.
Bove, Laurent. *La stratégie du conatus: affirmation et résistance chez Spinoza*. Paris: Librairie Philosophique J. Vrin, 1996.
Boyle, Robert. *Works*. London: Printed for J. and F. Rivington et al, 1772.

Del Lucchese. Filippo. *Conflict, Power, and Multitude in Machiavelli and Spinoza: Tumult and Indignation*. London: Continuum Press, 2009.

Deleuze, Gilles. *Spinoza et le problème de l'expression*. Paris: Minuit, 1968.

Escher, Maurice Cornelius. *The Graphic Work*. Köln: Benedikt Taschen Verlag, 2008.

Fausti, Daniela. "Il segno e la prognosi nel *Corpus Hippocraticum* (*Prognostico e Prorretico* I e II)," *I quaderni del Ramo d'Oro on-line* 1 (2008), 258–78.

Gainza, Mariana de. *Espinosa: Uma Filosofia Materialista do Infinito Positivo*. São Paulo: Editora de Universidade de São Paulo, 2011.

Hobbes, Thomas. *Leviathan*. Oxford: Clarendon Press, 2012.

Hofstadter, Douglas R. *Gödel, Escher, Bach: An Eternal Golden Braid*. New York: Basic Books, 1979.

Machiavelli, Niccolò. *Discourses on Livy*, trans. by Harvey C. Mansfield and Nathan Tarcov. Chicago: The University of Chicago Press, 1996.

Matheron, Alexandre. *Individu et communauté chez Spinoza*. Paris: Minuit, 1969.

Matheron, Alexandre. *Etudes sur Spinoza et les philosophies de l'âge classique*. Lyon: ENS Editions, 2011.

Momigliano, Arnaldo. "Time in Ancient Historiography," *History and Theory* 6 (1966), 1–23.

Morfino, Vittorio. *Plural Temporality: Transindividuality and the Aleatory between Spinoza and Althusser*. Leiden: Brill, 2014.

Negri, Antonio. *Savage Anomaly: The Power of Spinoza's Metaphysics*, trans. by Michael Hardt. Minneapolis: University of Minnesota Press, 1999.

Pautrat, Bernard. Introduction to B. Spinoza, *Traité politique*, traduit du latin, présenté et annoté par Bernard Pautrat. Paris: Editions Allia, 2013.

Salemme Haas, Maria Antonietta and Celani Inesi, Anna Maria. "Dal sintomo al segno: una nuova dimensione dell'esperienza medica," *Medicina nei secoli* n.s. 17.1 (2005), 135–50.

Sharp, Hasana. *Spinoza and the Politics of Renaturalization*. Chicago and London: The University of Chicago Press, 2011.

Spinoza, Baruch. *Complete Works*, ed. by M. L. Morgan and trans. by S. Shirley. Indianapolis: Hackett, 2002.

Spinoza, Baruch. *De Nagelate Schriften van B.d.S. Als Zedekunst, Staatkunde, Verbetering van't Verstant, Breiven en Antwoorden*, uit verscheide Talen in de Nederlandsche gebragt, 1677.

Spinoza, Baruch. *Zwey Abhandlungen über die Kultur des menschlichen Verstandes und über die Aristokratie und Demokratie*. Herausgegeben und mit einer Vorrede begleitet von S. H. Ewald, Leipzig, in der von Schönfeldschen Handlung. 1785.

Spinoza, Baruch. *A Treatise on Politics*, translated from the Latin of B. Spinoza by W. Maccall. London: 1854.

Spinoza, Baruch. *Traité politique de B. de Spinoza*, traduit en français pour la première fois, annoté, suivi d'un index analytique et accompagné de trois plans des trois différentes formes de gouvernement, par J.-G. Prat. Paris: Tous les libraires, 1860.

Spinoza, Baruch. *Oeuvres*, IV, traduction et notes par C. Appuhn. Paris: Librairie Garnier Frèes, 1929.

Spinoza, Baruch. *Oeuvres complètes*, texte nouvellement traduit ou revu, présenté et annoté par R. Caillois, M. Francès et R. Misrahi. Paris: Gallimard, 1954.

Spinoza, Baruch. *Trattato politico*, a cura di A. Droetto. Torino: Ramella, 1958.

Spinoza, Baruch. *The Political Works*, ed. and trans. with an introduction and notes by A.G. Wernham. Oxford: Clarendon Press, 1958.

Spinoza, Baruch. *Tractatus politicus/Traité politique*, texte latin, traduction par P.-F. Moreau, index informatique par P.-F. Moreau et R. Bouveresse. Paris: Editions Réplique, 1979.

Spinoza, Baruch. *Tratado politico*, Traducción, introducción, indice analítico y notas de A. Dominguez. Madrid: Alianza Editorial, 1986.

Spinoza, Baruch. *Trattato politico*, testo e traduzione a cura di Cristofolini. Pisa: ETS, 1999.

Spinoza, Baruch. *Complete Works*, with the translation of S. Shirley, edited by M. L. Morgan. Indianapolis/Cambridge: Hackett Publishing Company, 2002.

Spinoza, Baruch. *Traité politique*, traduction d'Emile Saisset révisée par Laurent Bove, introduction et notes par Laurent Bove. Paris: Librairie Générale Française, 2002.

Spinoza, Baruch. *Oeuvres, V, Traité politique*, texte établi par Omero Proietti, traduction, introduction, notes, glossaire, index et bibliographie par Charles Ramond, avec une notice de Pierre-François Moreau et des notes d'Alexandre Matheron. Paris, Presses Universitaires de France, 2005.

Spinoza, Baruch. *Opere*, a cura e con un saggio introduttivo di Filippo Mignini, traduzioni e note di Filippo Mignini e Omero Proietti. Milano: Mondadori, 2007.

Spinoza, Baruch. *The Collected Works of Spinoza*. Volume II, ed. and trans. by Edwin Curley. Princeton and Oxford: Princeton University Press, 2016

Vardoulakis, Dimitris. *Sovereignity and Its Other: Toward the Dejustification of Violence*. New York: Fordham University Press, 2013.

Zourabichvili, François. *Le conservatisme paradoxal de Spinoza*. Paris: Presses Universitaires de France, 2002.

3

Authority and the Law: The Primacy of Justification over Legitimacy in Spinoza

Dimitris Vardoulakis

Obedience, legality and history

The concept of authority runs through the *Theological-Political Treatise*, working through all its important concepts.[1] To grasp what is at stake with the concept of authority, as it is used by Spinoza, we can start by noting a peculiar resonance with the concept of divine law.[2] Specifically, both are excessive of human law. According to Chapter 4 of the *Treatise*, the divine law has no outside—unlike the human law. And according to the first three chapters of the *Treatise*, Moses is a lawgiver because of his prophetic authority. What are we to make of this excessive quality of both divine law and authority in relation to human law? We should start with the observation that what links the law—in both its senses—and authority is power. Only then we will be able to discover the peculiar way in which Spinoza constructs the concept of authority in such a way as to no longer lead to an authoritarian politics, but rather to a democratic politics.

Linking law and authority through power entails at least three important aspects within the context of the *Theological-Political Treatise*:

The first aspect pertains to the production of authority. Human relations are always subject to "laws" of power, even if these laws are not written down. In human relations, the fact that there is no "outside" power means also that there is no "outside" the law. The reason that authority is always subject to power relations rests on its link to obedience. Authority is present as soon as there is obedience. Or, differently put, authority *is produced* by obedience. Spinoza seems to echo in this understanding the way authority has been conceived within the tradition.[3] (I say that he *seems* to, since the first three chapters of the *Theological-Political*

Treatise agree with this traditional understanding, even though this point is complicated later by Spinoza, as I will show.) But this creates a problem, given the antidemocratic implications of this way in which obedience generates power relations, as this essentially means that disputation and persuasion are absent from the political stage. Thus, Spinoza asserts that "the authority of a prophet does not permit of argumentation [*prophetae auctoritas ratiocinari non patitur*]" (*TTP* 139/152). Authority, then, as it is produced by obedience introduces a challenge to the political from the very beginning: This is the challenge of how to evade the despotic—the *authoritarian*—construction of the political. This is a challenge Spinoza takes seriously, and in fact—even counterintuitively—uses "authority" precisely to bolster his democratic credentials.

Let me express this point in another way, so as to capture a related strand of the argumentation in the *Theological-Political Treatise*. The predominance of obedience in how authority is produced places authority in a problematic relation to philosophy. Thus, Spinoza frames the discussion of authority as a conflict between knowledge by revelation and natural knowledge or philosophical knowledge. This line of argumentation culminates in Chapter 15 where Spinoza asserts the separation between the two kinds of knowledge. We can understand, then, this first aspect of authority as linking law and power through obedience, while at the same time positioning authority in a problematic relation both with democratic forms of politics and with philosophy.

Second, authority plays also a particularly significant role in generating the human laws of constituted power. Authority *produces* legality. The figures of authority are the paradigmatic lawgivers. In the first six chapters of the *Theological-Political Treatise*, Spinoza identifies the prophets as figures of authority precisely because of their political function: they are the lawgivers par excellence. Even if the figure that occupies most of Spinoza's attention is Moses as the founder of the Hebrew state, still we will see the critical role that Adam—as the first prophet—plays in conceptualizing lawgiving.

This second aspect entails that legality, when coupled with authority, is not conceived as a static condition, as if it is possible to have a legal framework that is just there, in front of us, for us to use whenever we want to but which we leave otherwise untouched. Rather, it points to the fluidity and mutability of the law. Legality relies on the specific conditions of its possibility, which are given, inter alia, through the intervention of figures of authority. It is at this juncture where Spinoza's position is unique and important. For Spinoza, the conditions that function as the means to justify the production of legality never lead to stable forms of legitimation. Justification is primary and legitimation is its aftereffect.

Thirdly, the two aspects identified above—to wit, the fact that authority is produced by obedience and that it in turn produces legality—are intimately tied up through Spinoza's conceptions of history. Spinoza starts the *Theological-Political Treatise* with the observation about the absence of authority from the present. Spinoza asserts categorically at the beginning of the *Theological-Political Treatise* that "there are no prophets among us today [*hodie nullos ... habemus Prophetas*]" (*TTP* 10). The figure of authority, according to Spinoza, has evacuated the present. The now is structured by a loss.

The production and loss of authority link Spinoza's conceptions of history to his conception of politics. Essentially, this entails the recognition that when political activity is tied up to structures of obedience, whereby authority is operative, then it has a religious aspect. The interlinking between religion and politics is clear to any reader of Spinoza's *Theological-Political Treatise*—as the title itself announces. But the specific link between politics and the loss of authority in the "now" is addressed explicitly only after the first publication of the *Treatise*.[4] The important second note to Chapter 1 of the *Theological-Political Treatise* explains that authority is not completely absent but is rather transformed in the present. Spinoza explains that the prophets received knowledge through revelation, whose interpretation was "solely in reliance on the prophet's authority [*sola prophetae autoritate*]" (*TTP* 231/251). In other words, no one could argue with the revealed knowledge they possessed and disseminated. The prophets held *autoritatem* because their knowledge was protected from being subject to disputation. This is the first aspect of authority as outlined above. The note continues: "Similarly [*sic*], sovereign powers [*summae potestates*] are the interpreters of their own laws [*juris*], since the laws that they enact are upheld only by their own sole sovereign authority [*sola ipsarum summarum potestatum autoritate*], and are supported only by their sole testimony [*solo testimonio*]" (*TTP* 231/251). What is striking in this note is the insistent repetition of the adjective "solus" to determine both the authority and hence the kind of knowledge that the prophets and the sovereigns enjoy.

The sovereigns, in all their historical specificity, are the inheritors of the authority enjoyed by the prophets, namely, the kind of personal authority that relies solely on their interpretations of the laws. This is possible because they enjoy obedience. So, we may live in a "now" which is characterized by the lack of prophets because God no longer imparts revealed knowledge—the gods have left us, as the Romantics, good students of Spinoza, would say. And yet the politically decisive property of personal *autoritas*, namely, that it is *sola*, unchallenged and beyond dispute, is manifest through the figure of the kind of sovereign whose interpretations of the law is not subject to disputation.

To delve deeper into what is at stake in the political, legal and historical implications of Spinoza's use of the concept of authority, we need to recall the starting point, namely, that authority, just like divine law is in excess of human law. This shows the complex relation between authority and the law in Spinoza. To tackle this relation, we need to turn to a close reading of Chapter 4 of the *Theological-Political Treatise*.

Adam, the disobedient prophet: On the genesis of human law

The first six chapters of the *Theological-Political Treatise* concentrate on authority as represented by the figure of the prophet. Authority is constructed as a concept that provides both a religious and a political account of power. Spinoza provides an important clue about the *auctoritas* of the prophet in Chapter 2 of the *Treatise*—a point which is repeated throughout with rigor and consistency. As it is argued there, all the prophets, including Moses "did not completely comprehend that God was omniscient [*omniscium*] and that all human actions [*actiones omnes*] are governed solely by God's decree [*ex solo decreto dirigi*]" (*TTP* 28/38).[5] This observation allows Spinoza to give a political account of prophesy. The cognitive fault of the prophets is crucial for Spinoza's account of the contingency of their power. This is the argument familiar to all readers of the *Theological-Political Treatise*: the prophets received the message of God in a limited way, depending on their own personal idiosyncrasies, errors and deficiencies. And they further communicated that revelation in an even more distorted way, trying to account for the particular limitations of the people they were addressing.

In Chapter 2 of the *Treatise*, at the point Spinoza argues that Moses and all the other prophets misunderstood God's omniscience, and hence the divine law, Adam is also designated as a prophet (*TTP* 28). It is indeed true that in some traditions Adam is referred to as a prophet—for instance, in the Qur'an. But the use of Adam in the *Theological-Political Treatise* is much more than simply following a certain tradition. Adam becomes in Chapter 4 of the *Theological-Political Treatise* the first prophet, and by virtue of this fact, he is also the first figure of *auctoritas*. Spinoza's Adam is linked to the opening up of history and to the opening up of the political—and even questioning as to whether there is a fundamental difference at all between them. Spinoza's retelling of the story of the Fall is transformed into an account of the genesis of what the second note to Chapter 1 refers to as *sola auctoritas*—that is, of the political power of the prophet no less than the justification for the legitimacy of sovereign power.

Even though Spinoza does not combine the insights of Chapters 2 and 4 explicitly, it is important to do so to present his conception of authority. The figure of authority is used to provide a justification of political action. A lawgiver or a sovereign is justified to act in a particular way because they are obeyed. As I mentioned earlier, obedience produces authority—which politically means that authority relies on the justification arising from the fact that a figure of authority is obeyed. However, in his retelling of the story of the Fall and in the course of determining the genesis of human law, Spinoza spectacularly subverts this traditional conception which he has used earlier in his account of the function of the prophets as lawgivers. What becomes obvious with Adam is that his misunderstanding of God's omniscience and the divine law leads to an act of *dis*obedience as the "first" moment of the production of authority and legality. This shift from obedience to disobedience destabilizes the entire structure of power that relies on authority. For instance, this shift entails that the power structure the figures of authority institute never achieves legitimacy. More succinctly, justification never entails legitimacy. We need to read carefully Chapter 4 of the *Theological-Political Treatise*, paying particular attention to his reversal of the production of authority.

The title of Chapter 4, "Of the Divine Law," may be misleading, as the notion of divine law Spinoza has in mind is far removed from doctrinal accounts of divine law. The most glaring difference is that Spinoza insistently denies the existence of divine will, or relatedly the idea that God is lawgiver. Spinoza's God is radically impersonal, to the point of being identified with nature. To frame this in terms of a rigid naturalism is misleading, since this move allows Spinoza to develop a series of radical positions that are not usually associated with "naturalization," neither in the epistemological nor in the political sense.[6] In any case, the point is that the notion of the divine law developed here would have been foreign to Spinoza's contemporaries who had any familiarity with the message of the Church, be that Papal or Reformed. And this is intentional: Spinoza is using the notion of the law with the aim to interrogate the notion of authority, exemplified by the prophets, especially Moses as the paradigmatic prophet who is also a state-founder. We should keep in mind that in typical seventeenth-century fashion, the Biblical example of the Hebrew state becomes the subterfuge for discussing contemporary political questions. It is within this context that Spinoza distinguishes between divine and human law.[7]

In the chapter itself, the concept of the divine law is introduced in the first paragraph. The definition Spinoza provides here is reminiscent of the discussion of God at the beginning of the *Ethics*, where God is described as an absolute necessity and as a cause of itself. However, in the *Theological-Political Treatise*, Spinoza largely avoids the metaphysical vocabulary that dominates Part I of the *Ethics*, and seeks to sharpen his definition by contrasting divine law to human law:

> The word law, taken in its absolute sense [*Legis nomen absolute*], means that according to which each individual thing—either all in general or those of the same kind—act in one and the same fixed and determinate manner, this manner depending either on Nature's necessity or on human will. A law which depends on Nature's necessity is one which necessarily follows from the very nature of the thing, that is, its definition; a law which depends on human will, and which could more properly be termed a statute [*jus*], is one which men ordain for themselves and for others with view to making life more secure and more convenient [*ad tutius, et commodius vivendum*], or for other reasons. (*TTP* 48/57)

Law in this first paragraph is defined in terms of necessity. Spinoza identifies two kinds of necessity, one arising from nature, and the other from the free will of humans. But only the determination of a natural law is properly speaking necessary, whereas a human law is a statute or a written law—the kind of law that humans devise for a certain purpose. This purposiveness of the law is indicated by the preposition "ad" in the Latin text. This prepositional construction already inflects the main characteristic of the law, namely, its necessity. We will soon see how this becomes crucial.

Immediately after this opening, Spinoza elaborates the law "in the absolute sense" by further discussing the two laws, divine and human, in terms of their necessity. For instance, he is happy to concede that from a certain perspective, there is not much of a difference between them: so long as the human is part of nature, one acts under the law of nature. But, he also adds, humans do not have a complete knowledge of the law of nature, and so "for practical purposes, it is better, indeed, it is necessary, to consider things as possible [*ad usum vitae melius, imo necesse est, res ut possibiles considerare*]" (*TTP* 49/58). Next to the absolute necessity of nature, then, Spinoza introduces a necessity that is coupled with whatever is possible in one's particular circumstances. Or, differently put, and recalling the discussion of prophesy and the prophets from the previous chapters, human law couples necessity with contingency. Human law points to the limits of the power of the lawgivers and the state—powers which are contingently determined by how they can come into use (*ad usum*). A sense of utility is already coupled to legality—a move of immense importance, as we will see forthwith.

At this point, Spinoza raises a possible objection to this distinction between divine and human law. He notes that it appears as if we are using the word "law" as it applies to nature "*per translationem*," as a figure of speech or as a translation, of what is commonly understood by law, namely, human command. Differently put, if we approach the law through the concept of necessity, the distinction between divine and human law remains rhetorical. From the perspective of necessity, the distinction is begging the question. The suggestion is that a more rigorous definition of the law is required. Spinoza continues: "Therefore, law should be defined more precisely [*ideo lex particularius definienda videtur*], that is, as a rule of life [*ratio vivendi*] which man prescribes for himself or for others for some purpose [*finem*]" (*TTP* 49/58). It is hard to overestimate the importance of this redefinition of the law. The law is no longer defined in terms of necessity. Instead, the law is defined in terms of its end (*finem*). The law is the means toward a certain end. Law indicates an instrumental "logic of living" (*ratio vivendi*). Or, in yet another formulation, law is utility.

Contained in this redefinition of the law, there is an equivocation for Spinoza. It is contained in the word "particularius." Spinoza introduces the new definition of the law as more "particular." Does this mean narrower in the logical sense? That seems to be the meaning, as he is adducing here a definition of the human law, that is, of the kind of law that humans prescribe for themselves. And the implication seems to be that the divine law has no purpose. But if that is all that is contained in this new definition, the imaginary objection introduced by Spinoza later would persist. Instead of the divine and the human law being defined in terms of absolute and contingent necessity, respectively, they are now defined in terms of a lack of telos and instrumentality, respectively. The redefinition would still rely on a *petitio pricipii*. There is, however, a different way of understanding "particularius." It could mean that we define law from the perspective of "particularity." This is the perspective of the modes in the *Ethics*. Thus, law is material. It is, in other words, Spinoza's attempt to define the law from the opposite direction to the one he adopts in the opening of the *Ethics*. The definition of the law is carried out from the finite. The "particularius" must indicate here this latter sense of particularity.

Nonetheless, the definition of law as utility still pushes Spinoza to a precarious problematic. The instrumentality of the law may be for the sake of a logic of living, and yet Spinoza concedes that this true utility of the law "is usually apparent only to the few and is generally incomprehensible by the great majority" (*TTP* 49). As a consequence, obedience needs to be obtained through different means, namely, through promises for the law-abiding citizens, and, more importantly, through threats to those who break the law. It is, as Spinoza concedes, ultimately through the "fear of the gallows" (*TTP* 49), that is, through the sovereign prerogative of life and death, that obedience is safeguarded. Differently put, understanding the law in instrumental terms inevitably inscribes within the law the possibility of violence. Authority not only produces, but also *protects* and *preserves* the law with the use of violence.

The link between utility and violence would not have been a particularly original idea in the seventeenth century. In fact, Machiavelli—whose influence can be felt throughout the *Theological-Political Treatise*—famously argues that a lawgiver, and especially a founder of a state, is justified to use violence in order to achieve the end of the security and preservation of the state. And, moreover, one of Machiavelli's most prominent and recurrent examples of this argument is Moses. Thus, in Book 3, Chapter 30 of the *Discourses*, Machiavelli argues that "He who reads the Bible intelligently sees that if Moses was to put his laws and regulations into effect, he was forced to kill countless men who … were opposed to his plans."[8] Spinoza doubtless would have been aware of this argument, and he would also have been perfectly conscious of how the emphasis on the utility of the law in Chapter 4 of the *Theological-Political Treatise* would have aligned his own position with the Florentine's—despite the fact that neither Machiavelli is named in the book, nor is Moses' violence ever explicitly discussed.[9]

The eschewal of a direct link between utility and violence, as well as Spinoza's immediate distinction between two senses of the utility, one for human and one for divine law, may give the appearance that he is evading the problem. But if we pause to consider the connection with Machiavelli, we are able to see Spinoza's gesture in a different light. The crucial point for Machiavelli is that the violence provided through instrumental reason is justified on condition that it leads to forms of legitimacy. Violence is justified only on account of state-building and state-preserving. Spinoza wants to retain this instrumental reason, and in fact, he generalizes it to such an extent that in Propositions 65 and 66 of Part IV of the *Ethics*, as well as in Chapter 16 of the *Theological-Political Treatise*, calculating one's advantage becomes the ontological principle describing the human's being in the world and being with others. But at the same time, Spinoza severs the direct link between justification and legitimacy provided by Machiavelli. Within the overall argument of the *Treatise*, divine law performs the function of staging the complex and unresolvable relation between justification and legitimacy. I will return to this point shortly.

If the utility of human law is the preservation and security of the state, then what is the utility of divine law? As soon as he has redefined law in terms of utility, Spinoza turns to address the problematic of the utility of the divine law. He introduces this topic by saying that "by divine law I mean that which is concerned only with the supreme good, that is, the true knowledge and love of God" (*TTP* 49). In other words, he moves away from the definition of the divine as absolute necessity—that is, the definition with which he draws the distinction between divine and human law in the opening of the chapter. Instead, now he approaches divine law through its *particularity*, that is, by examining its effects on humans. The question that he needs to answer is to what extent divine law can be understood in instrumental terms.

Spinoza first approaches this topic through natural knowledge. He uses here two arguments that are familiar to Spinoza readers. Specifically, and in brief, the more natural knowledge we have, the closer we are to God, since God is the same as nature. And the more we understand the nature of causality, the closer we come to understanding the immanent causality of the divine. In addition, he argues that love of God, as the love of the most perfect thing, also brings the supreme good to the human. For a reader of the *Ethics*, Spinoza is going here through well-trodden ground.

After this, Spinoza states:

> This, then, is the sum of our supreme good and blessedness, to wit, the knowledge and love of God. So the means required to achieve this end of all human action [*Media igitur, quae hic finis omnium humanarum actionum*]—that is, God insofar as his idea exists in us—may be termed God's commands, for they are ordained for us by God himself, as it were, insofar as he exists in our minds. So the rules for living a life [*ratio vivendi*] that have regard to this end can fitly be called the divine law [*lex divina*]. (*TTP* 50/60)

Spinoza reproduces here the instrumental understanding of the law, not only conceptually, but also using similar vocabulary to the passage in which he first defined human law as utility a page earlier. For instance, the rules of life, the logic of living, is denoted here with exactly the same phrase he used to describe the instrumentality of human law, to wit, "ratio vivendi." And this *ratio vivendi* is described in unambiguously instrumental terms. The means (*media*) required to achieve the end (*finis*) of human action can be called the commands of God, or divine law.

Note that divine law is not defined here in terms of its essential properties, such as eternity and necessity. Instead, divine law is defined in terms of its particularity. In other words, we can understand divine law in instrumental terms when we inquire into how divine law contributes to our supreme good—which also means, into how divine law contributes to our well-being or blessedness. Such an inquiry, Spinoza indicates, belongs properly speaking to a treatise on ethics (*TTP* 50), that is, the very treatise whose writing Spinoza postponed to compose the *Theological Political Treatise*. This means that the divine law has an intrinsic utility. The divine law is not essentially instrumental. Rather, the divine law is instrumental for us, in the here and now. We can use the divine law to achieve happiness. The divine law is instrumental so long as it pertains to the means that motivate human action. In other words, divine law is ethically instrumental.

At this point, then, Spinoza has made a distinction between *two instrumentalities*. They are both about the *ratio vivendi*. But the instrumentality of the human law is prescriptive, whereas the instrumentality of the divine law is ethical. Or, differently put, the instrumentality of the human law follows Machiavelli in showing the link between justification and legitimacy, whereas the instrumentality of the divine law indicates that this link is not a matter of absolute necessity. Justification is always present but—as we will learn in a moment—God cannot be conceived as a lawgiver, and hence he is unconcerned with a project of legitimation. God, Spinoza reminds Machiavelli, is not Moses.

And yet, this only further displaces the problem, namely, to the prophets like Moses, who are the paradigmatic figures of authority in the *Theological-Political Treatise*, and who, as figures of authority, have a genuinely political function. How are the prophets to be understood politically through this disjunction between justification and legitimacy? The answer is that the figure of the prophet—as the paradigmatic figure of authority—is used by Spinoza to account for the *genesis* of the human law. The concept of human law brings justification and legitimacy into contact, and it is to authority, as the concept that produces human law, that Spinoza turns to explain the relation between justification and legitimacy. More specifically, Spinoza does not turn to all prophets, not even to Moses who is otherwise the protagonist in the *Treatise*. Instead, Spinoza turns to Adam, who, as the figure of the first prophet, is pertinent to address the genesis of human law.

Before I proceed with my reading of the use of Adam in Chapter 4 of the *Theological-Political Treatise*, I should make one point clear: I am indebted to Gilles Deleuze's interpretation of Spinoza's discussion of Adam, even though it seems to me that by concentrating on the correspondence with Blyenbergh, Deleuze privileges precisely Blyenbergh's questions about this passage on the Fall, which have to do with the existence of evil.[10] The effect of this is that the overtly political positioning of Adam as prophet and lawgiver is elided in Deleuze's interpretation.[11] This has had a profound influence in reading this passage from the *Theological-Political Treatise* in terms of Deleuze's distinction between ethics and morality.[12] And even though there are other interpretations which do not bear Deleuze's mark as heavily, still none of them aspires to an explicitly political reading of this passage. For instance, Hasana Sharp concentrates on the relation between Adam and Eve, while Nancy Levene reads this in the context of biblical interpretation, for instance, Maimonides' reading of the Fall.[13] But the connection to authority, legality and history is not addressed. It is this constellation that is of the utmost importance in the discussion of Adam in Chapter 4 of the *Theological-Political Treatise*. So let us turn to Spinoza's account of the Fall.

Now, as is well known—and Deleuze is particularly clear on this—Spinoza describes Adam's Fall as the result of a miscognition. God told Adam that it will essentially follow from his nature that were he to eat the forbidden fruit, then he will leave paradise. Adam, however, misunderstood this as a commandment, that is, as if God prohibited him from eating the fruit. God presented him with a divine law that is a matter of absolute necessity, whereas Adam understood it as a law whose necessity will be enforced only if the breaking of the law is discovered. Or, differently put, God told him what was the case, and Adam misunderstood this information as an order which needed to be obeyed. But what does this account of the miscognition tell us about the relation between the utility of divine and human laws? Or, what amounts to the same question, what does it tells us about how the relation between justification and legitimation is thereby construed? To answer this question, we need a slower and more patient reading of Spinoza's account of the Fall.

Immediately after distinguishing between the two laws, divine and human, in terms of their utility, Spinoza lists and briefly comments upon the main characteristics of divine law. Divine law is (1) universal in the sense that it is "common to all mankind" (*TTP* 51); (2) it "does not demand belief in historical narratives" regardless of the fact that such a historical narrative may apply "to Adam as to any other man" (*TTP* 51); (3) its "goodness" does not derive from "authority and tradition" because these "cannot perfect our intellect" (*TTP* 52); and, (4) it is linked to a project of freedom. To paraphrase, divine law binds all humans together because it does not rely on contingent knowledge, which is produced through *auctoritas*, and in that sense develops our intellect and contributes to our freedom. Or, more succinctly, the political import of the divine law consists in the harmony between law and cognition. To put this in terms of utility, divine law tells us what is our true advantage in order to achieve our political end, namely, freedom.

It is only after having established this that Spinoza asks the question as to whether "by the natural light of reason we can conceive God as a law giver or ruler, ordaining laws for men" (*TTP* 52). Differently put, can we conceive of God as a kind of *auctoritas*? Are the above characteristics of God possible to translate as "marks" of sovereignty? Spinoza turns to the Adamic narrative to answer this question.

Spinoza outright rejects the idea that God is a lawgiver and hence analogous to a sovereign. He says that this is obvious from what has been said thus far, but he also formulates it in the following manner: "God's will and God's intellect in themselves are in reality one and the same thing; they are distinct only in relation to the thoughts we form when we think of God's intellect" (*TTP* 52).[14] If the divine law showed the harmony between the legal and the cognitive, the nature of God shows in turn the harmony between action and cognition. Conversely, it will be this lack of harmony between law, action and cognition that will characterize human law. From this perspective, the production of *auctoritas*, as a human figure, needs to exhibit this discord between law, will and comprehension. Adam's miscomprehension does precisely that.

Spinoza's account starts with a logical contradiction: "So if, for example, God said to Adam that he willed that Adam should not eat of the tree of knowledge of good and evil, it would have been a contradiction in terms [*contradictionem implicaret*] for Adam to be able to eat of that tree. And so it would have been impossible [*impossibile*] for Adam to eat of it, because that divine decree must have involved eternal necessity and truth [*aeternam necessitatem et veritatem debuisset involvere*]" (*TTP* 53/63). In Spinoza's account, the fact that the will and the intellect of God are one and the same, and God's omnipotence, as well as the fact that divine law is eternal and necessary express exactly the same point from different perspectives. If this point is correct, then there is indeed a profound contradiction in saying that God "willed" that Adam does not eat from the tree of knowledge, because that would make God's will violable.

How can we side-step such a flagrant contradiction? The text continues: "However, since Scripture tells us that God did so instruct [*praecepisse*] Adam, and that Adam did nevertheless eat of the tree, it must be accepted that God revealed to Adam only the bad consequences he must necessarily incur [*malum tantum revelavisse, quod eum necessario sequeretur*] if he should eat of that tree;, while the necessary entailment of these bad consequences [*at non necessitatem consecutionis illius mali*] was not revealed" (*TTP* 53/63). The first thing to note here is that Adam is treated as a prophet since God "revealed" something to him. God revealed to Adam only what was going to happen if he ate the fruit, namely, the expulsion from the Garden of Eden. But he did not reveal to Adam this was a necessary consequence. This consequence is, as the account of Chapter 2 had explained, the acquisition of knowledge, not natural knowledge, but rather the kind of knowledge that is divorced from divine law. Adam, as a prophet, did not comprehend divine omniscience—he did not understand the inviolability of the divine law. The necessary entailment of Adam's actions qua prophesy and *auctoritas*, then, is the creation of the dissymmetry between cognition and the law's necessity. In other words, Adam's act did not create evil (as Augustine argued, and as Blyenbergh emphasized in his correspondence with Spinoza), but rather created the idea of human law. It defined what acts can be punished within certain contingent contexts.

The discrepancy between the necessity of natural knowledge and the human knowledge of punishment is described as an act of miscomprehension. "Consequently, Adam perceived this revelation not as an eternal and necessary truth but as a law [*revelationem non ut aeternam et necessariam veritatem perceperit, sed ut legem*], that is to say, an enactment from which good or ill consequence would ensue not from the necessity and nature of the deed [*non ex necessitate et natura actionis*] performed but from the sole will and absolute sovereignty of some ruler [*ex solo libitu et absolute imperio alicujus Principis*]" (*TTP* 53/63). Adam failed to understand that he was confronted with a divine—that is, an eternal and necessary—law. He thus broke the link between the act and the application of the law. His miscomprehension led to the rupture of the symmetry between will and intellect, and hence failed to conform to the ethical. Instead, it conformed to the structure of sovereignty, whereby the one who controls the law is also the one who controls the punishments that are delivered when one is caught breaking the law.

The full significance of both the determination of all the prophets as misunderstanding God's omniscience or the essence of divine law, and the designation of Adam as a prophet come to the fore at this point. There are three important consequences that follow from Spinoza's recount of the Fall.

First, essentially, Spinoza describes here a parable for the creation of contingency, and hence for the creation of history. Adam's disobeying of the law is the first act of history if history is understood as that which is not absolutely necessary—as that which is contingent. This in itself is not uncommon, as Augustine, who was the one who provided the determinative account of the Fall in the Christian tradition, also described it as the starting point of history. But instead of the moral tragedy narrated by Augustine, for whom the Fall is the expulsion from paradise, Spinoza presents a comedy of errors.[15] There is a failure of communication between God and Adam, resembling the failures of communication that lead to all sorts of comical happenings in theater. God as the creator of the free will: how hilarious, says Spinoza. If God represents the symmetry between will and intellect, then the first human misunderstanding and the first moment of history represent a cognitive dissonance that breaks that symmetry. The narrative of the Fall is about this miscognition of divine law, which in turn creates the idea of both a lawgiver and human law. Differently put, God is not a lawgiver because he cannot be either obeyed or disobeyed. The moment there is disobedience, at that very moment contingency is created—a creation that brings with it authority, lawgiving, legitimacy as well as the opening up of historical time.

Second, the political stakes of this transformation of the narrative of the Fall into a comedy of errors are profound. What the misunderstanding creates is the figure of authority or the prophet. Adam is a prophet because God communicated something to him *and* because Adam misunderstood it by failing to comprehend its absolute necessity—or God's omnipotence. And as a prophet Adam can perform the function of the lawgiver whose authority is beyond dispute and in that sense—according to the second Annotation to Chapter 1 of the *Treatise* —he can resemble the status of the modern monarch in the "now" when there are no longer any prophets. Differently put, the structural similarity between prophets and monarchs outlined by Spinoza suggests that the comedy of errors is not an isolated episode confined to the obscure starting point of history, but rather the necessary condition for the creation of *auctoritas* which continues to be repeated today through the figure of the sovereign. Thus, the monarchs, whose authority allows them to be lawgivers, thereby occupying a structurally similar position to lawgivers in general, appear as representatives of God—that is, they appear, in Hobbes' expression, as "mortal gods"—but only because their representations of the divine are false. *Auctoritas* is beyond disputation not because her judgments are inviolable but rather because her judgments are erroneous, relying—as Spinoza has described in the earlier chapters of the *Theological-Political Treatise*—on the contingent or historical circumstances of their enunciation.

Third, *auctoritas* is further eroded if we ponder what authority produces. Specifically, authority creates laws which can only function because of obedience, according to Spinoza. The key feature of human law is obedience, and that's why human law requires for its operation a system of both rewards and, more importantly, punishments for the law-breakers. But—we can ask at this point— what is it that creates this structure, or even what is it that creates this obedience?

What is it that conceptually makes obedience possible, in Spinoza's narrative of the Fall? Well, it is nothing other than disobedience! Adam is presented with an absolute necessity—he is presented with a divine law. And what his actions produce is not obedience, but rather the idea that the law can be broken. This misunderstanding of the nature of divine law—which cannot be broken because it is absolute—creates the idea of the human law, which is contingently necessary and hence breakable. The miscognition of the divine law is an act of disobedience—not to the divine law, as this is by definition impossible—but to the human law, which in Adam's case did not exist before and which, thus, is created by this act of miscognition–cum–disobedience. Or, more succinctly, disobedience is the condition of the possibility of obedience.

What do these three points about the narrative of the Fall amount to? They point to the creation of historical time as contemporaneous with the creation of *auctoritas*, to the creation of human law, and to the dependence of *auctoritas* and of human law on disobedience. This is not a complex way of saying something that is perhaps obvious in Chapter 4 of the *Treatise*, namely, that the divine law has precedence over the human law. This would have amounted to considering the two laws only from the perspective of necessity. Instead, as Spinoza insists, they should be considered from the perspective of utility. And from this perspective of instrumental rationality, the narrative of the Fall suggests that justification is the cause of legitimacy. The utility of divine law does not require a "lawgiver" as it is common to all humankind and it does not require any institutions to fulfill its function. And yet, we live in a "fallen world," which in this context means that we can never realize the utility of the divine law alone as our contingent being and historical time are caused by disobedience. This act of disobedience is the act that creates legitimation—in the widest and most complex and diverse ways possible. Disobedience is that which inserts the possibility of legitimacy—through figures such as *auctoritas* and the institution of human law—within the utility of divine law. But in this sense legitimacy is an aftereffect of justification.

The primacy of justification over legitimacy has also important repercussions in how we understand the *genesis* of human law. You will recall that I summarized the production of authority as consisting in obedience producing authority, which in turns produces legality and legitimacy. In Chapter 4 of the *Theological-Political Treatise*, Spinoza reverses this structure. His chain of reasoning can be schematically presented as follows: (1) Law is understood as utility, that is, through the *particularity* of how it is expressed in and through human actions. (2) God is not a lawgiver because he can be neither obeyed nor disobeyed—that is, he is not a figure of authority. (3) The creation of authority springs from an act of disobedience, which thus also becomes the source of the law. From this chain of reasoning, it follows that the genetic moment of the law is dependent on the particularity of its articulation. And this entails that the genesis of the law is not pushed to a remote past. Rather, the genetic moment can—and must—be staged every time anew. Spinoza's subversion of the "primal sin" consists in the thesis that, so long as there is authority, there is disobedience. Without this disobedience, there is no human law. We are all little Adams, and this is not a sin from which we need to be purified, but rather the reality of living in historical time, while our relation to other human beings is expressed through legal means.

We can say, then, that we are all Adams in the sense that we disobey and this disobedience stages the singular expression and the universal dimension of the law. Human law, as I put it earlier, is contingently necessary. Jacques Derrida also underscores the interplay of singularity and universality as constitutive of legality.[16] But while Derrida emphasizes that this is an aporetic relation that can never be resolved, Spinoza emphasizes the fact that it needs to be restaged every time anew. We, little Adams, need to perform our acts of miscognition. And this is not only to align history with a comedic narrative. It will also give Spinoza the means—as I will suggest in the last section—to develop a theory of judgment.

Where does that leave Spinoza's concept of authority as it is connected to the law? Paradoxically, the law's justification is more primary than its legitimation. Before the various forms of state formation implied in the propagation of the institution of human law, which requires legitimacy, come the various ways in which utility is to be assessed and comprehended. The calculation of one's advantage is not antithetical to the law, but rather restages the first miscognition that created human law. But even if justification is more primary, the creation of human law through an act of miscognition entails that the relation between justification and legitimacy can never be satisfactorily resolved. Any form of legitimacy must be justified, but its inherent basis on disobedience means that it also ought to be dejustified. This is, then, a sense of the law influenced by an authority that holds the processes of justification and legitimation apart. The distance between the two is fundamental for Spinoza.

Judgment: On justification and legitimacy

This above construal of the law may appear to face the difficulty of accounting for political change. Usually, political change is understood as the change of the law. This can be the change of particular laws—for instance, to protect the rights of specific groups. Or it can be the wholesale change of the entire legal framework supporting a state—which is the result of a revolution. But—one might ask—how is either option possible when the divine law is understood as having no outside? What does political change, then, consist in?

As we saw above, Spinoza's account of divine and human law results in the irresolvable relation between justification and legitimacy, even as justification is posited as more primary. This entails that Spinoza does not need to reduce political change to the transformation of legitimacy, and hence does not equate political change with the change of the law—as is usually the case. All he has to do for an account of political change is to point out the way in which justification collapses the inviolability of any established form of legitimation. In effect, this suggests a theory of judgment, even though Spinoza himself never explicitly thematizes such a theory. Let me provide an example from Chapter 19, the penultimate chapter of the *Theological-Political Treatise*.

Chapter 19 is structured as an affirmation of the Erastian principle that there should be a single authority in charge of both civil and religious law. Spinoza bases this principle on "catholica religio" (*TTP* 214/231), which here is synonymous with what he calls in Chapter 11 "true religion." The main characteristic of "true religion" is that it is subject to reason—it is not simply a matter of obeying through the mediation of prophetic authority. This also means that the Apostles now acquire didactic authority, or the "authority to teach [*authoritas ad docendum*]" (*TTP* 141/155), since knowledge that can be rationalized can also be transmitted and communicated. Having bestowed such a didactic authority, "God has no special kingdom over men [*nullum singulare regnum in homines habere*], save through those who hold the sovereignty [*imperium*]" (*TTP* 212/228). How are we then to account, asks Spinoza, for the fact that the successors of the Apostles, that is, precisely those endowed with *authoritas ad docendum*, are now insisting on safeguarding for themselves an ecclesiastical authority which is nothing but an attempt to hold political—which also means, sovereign—power?

To answer this question, Spinoza provides a quick historical account. He explains that "the first teachers [*primi docuerunt*] of the Christian religion [were] men of private station [*viri privati*]" (*TTP* 219/237) who not only lacked political authority, but whose teaching actually put them [in] on a collision course with political authorities. Later, when Christianity was instituted as the official religion of the empire, the Churchmen not only gained "recognition as its [i.e., religion's] teachers and interpreters [*doctores, et interpretes*]" but also as "virtually God's representatives [*Dei vicarii agnoscerentur*]" (*TTP* 220/237).

But this was not enough to guarantee the preservation of their power. They also needed the means to separate the basis of their legitimacy from that of the sovereigns'—that is, they needed a criterion to separate ecclesiastical from political legitimacy. Their strategy—which Spinoza calls seditious—consisted in the following:

> they multiplied religious dogmas to such an extent [*Religionis dogmata ad tam magnum numerum auxerant*] and confused them with so much philosophy [*cum Philosophia*] that the supreme interpreter of religion had to be a consummate philosopher and theologian [*summus ejus interpres summus Philosophus et Theologus*] and to have time for a host of useless speculations [*inutilibus speculationibus*]. This effectively ruled out all but men of private station with abundant leisure. (*TTP* 220/237)

Recall the moment that inaugurated human history: Adam misunderstood the utility of the command not to eat from the tree of knowledge. As Spinoza explains in Chapter 4, Adam thought that God's law was of the nature of human law, which can be disobeyed. But in fact it was a divine law, which is absolutely necessary. In this account of sedition as the separation of ecclesiastical from sovereign power, the speculations of those who have inherited didactic authority are useless (*inutilibus*) precisely because they willfully seek to perpetuate the Adamic mistake. Christian history, or history seen from the Christian perspective, is nothing but the ingrained misunderstanding about the necessity of God and the utility of divine law as it is perpetuated indefinitely by the Church. This perpetuation takes the guise of the proliferation of theology. Further, what theology shows is that the miscognition that opened up history is not simply a cognitive matter, but moreover the way in which authority seeks to reinscribe itself in history through legitimation.

Spinoza's strategy consists in identifying a form of power that claims legitimacy and to start questioning how this legitimacy is justified. Just as obedience presupposes disobedience in his account in Chapter 4, so justification presupposes dejustification. This gives Spinoza the means to form judgments about established forms of power.[17] Spinoza performs his critique of legitimate power by showing how the process of legitimation relies on the comedy of errors that characterized Adam's miscognition. In other words, Spinoza's account of authority and the law, which shows the privileging of justification over legitimacy, entails that any form of authority relying on a legitimate power is an authority that has either misunderstood or misrepresented the utility of divine law. As such, any form of legitimation is—to use Derrida's expression—

autoimmune. It is inherently possible to expose its misunderstandings and misrepresentations. The production of authority contains within itself the seeds of its own deconstruction. In Chapter 20 of the *Theological-Political Treatise*, Spinoza expresses this idea—which is at the core of his thinking of democracy—by invoking authority anew. But this is a strange kind of authority, an *authoritas abrogandi* (*TTP* 228/245), an authority to abrogate, or an authority that stages the disobedience that makes possible and unstable any form of legitimacy.

In Spinoza's account of authority and the law, legitimation is based on the foundations of disobedience and dejustification. Thus, Spinoza's historical narrative focuses on the forms of misrecognition that seek to make us believe in the inviolable legitimacy of power. From this perspective, the concept of the divine law not only fails to lend support to forms of political power, but rather becomes the means for radical change. Paradoxically, this is because divine law is coupled with authority, but in such a way as to avoid leading to authoritarian politics and paving the way to a critique of any form of legitimacy.

Notes

1 Spinoza, *Theological-Political Treatise*, trans. by Samuel Shirley (Indianapolis: Hackett, 2001). Hereafter abbreviated as *TTP* and cited parenthetically followed by page number. I have on occasion altered the translation. For the Latin, I have used *Opera*, ed. by Carl Gebhardt (Heidelberg: Carl Windters Universitätsbuchhandlung, 1924). The *Tractatus Theologico-Politicus* is contained in Volume 3. All references to this edition follow after the English edition.

2 The Latin term for authority Spinoza uses is "auctoritas." Spinoza also uses two variant spellings, "authoritas" and "autoritas." There is no evidence to suggest that these are anything but different ways of rendering the same concept. See Spinoza, *Opera*, Volume 3, 370. In fact, in his edition of Spinoza's works, Bruder normalizes the spelling throughout the *Tractatus Theologico-Politicus* to *auctoritas*. See *Opera quae supersunt omnia*, ed. by Carolus Hermannus Bruder (Leipzig: Bernhardi Tauchnitz, 1843–1846), Volume 3. Consequently, I will treat these three different spellings as interchangeable.

3 Cicero famously makes this point by distinguishing between potestas, which belongs to the people, and auctoritas, which pertains to the senate. He says in *De legibus*: "supreme power [*potestas*] is granted to the people and actual authority [*auctoritas*] to the Senate." Cicero, *De Legibus*, trans. by Clinton W. Keyes (Cambridge, Mass.: Harvard University Press, 1928), 492. For the most important philosophical work on authority, see Hannah Arendt, "Authority", *Between Past and Future: Six Exercises*

in Political Thought (New York: Viking, 1961), 91–141. The notion of authority runs through Arendt's entire work, with particularly important ramifications in books such as *On Revolution* (1962) and *On Violence* (1970). I will have to defer an analysis of Arendt's use of *auctoritas* for a different occasion.

4 Spinoza added some annotations to the *Theological-Political Treatise* after its first publication. These annotations were included in the edition of his collected works that his friends prepared immediately after his death.

5 I should note here that the only exception provided by Spinoza is the figure of Christ. This exception will prove important later, in Chapter 11 of the *Theological-Political Treatise*, while discussing "true religion" and the "authority to teach" vested upon the Apostles. I cannot take up the various issues that arise as a result of this exception, other than to note their effect on the concept of authority, which now transformed into *authoritas ad docendum* is no longer immune from disputation. A full account of the transformation from the *sola autoritas* of the prophet to this new sense of authority will have to wait for a different occasion.

6 See Hasana Sharp, *Spinoza and the Politics of Renaturalization* (Chicago: University of Chicago Press, 2011).

7 See Graham Hammill, *The Mosaic Constitution: Political Theology and Imagination from Machiavelli to Milton* (Chicago: University of Chicago Press, 2012); and, Eric Nelson, *The Hebrew Republic: Jewish Sources of the Transformation of European Political Thought* (Cambridge, Mass.: Harvard University Press, 2010).

8 Niccolò Machiavelli, *Discourses on the First Decade of Titus Livius*, trans. by Allan Gilbert, in *Machiavelli: The Chief Works and Others*, volume 1 (Durham: Duke University Press, 1989), 496.

9 The violence alluded to by Machiavelli here is the ordering of the massacre of those who venerated to golden calf while Moses was on Sinai for the first time to receive the divine law (*Exodus* 32: 26–28). This passage is important for Spinoza, especially in Chapter 18, and yet Spinoza never explicitly addresses Moses' violence there. Indeed, one of the most intriguing aspects of the *Theological-Political Treatise* is that the issue of violence is never foregrounded.

10 There are good reasons that the narrative of the Fall and the question of evil are connected. Historically, Augustine used the story of the Fall to solve one of the most intractable problems faced by early Christianity, namely, how it is possible to account for the existence of evil given that God is omnipotent. However, this problematic is not primarily what is at stake in Chapter 4 of the *Theological-Political Treatise*.

11 See Gilles Deleuze, *Expressionism in Philosophy: Spinoza*, trans. by Martin Joughin (New York: Zone Books, 1992), 247–48. See also Deleuze, *Spinoza: Practical Philosophy*, trans. by Robert Hurley (San Francisco: City Lights, 1988), 2 and 30–43. An exception to this is Kiarina Kordela's reading of this Fall as extrapolated in Chapter 4 of the *Theological-Political Treatise* both by criticizing Deleuze and by

highlighting political implications. See Kordela, $urplus: Spinoza, Lacan (New York: SUNY, 2007), 7–10.

12 For the influence of Deleuze's interpretation, see, for instance, Gabriel Albiac, "The Empty Synagogue", in ed. by Warren Montag and Ted Stolze, *The New Spinoza* (Minneapolis: University of Minnesota Press, 1997), 108–43.

13 Sharp, *Politics of Renaturalization*, 208–9; and, Nancy Levene, *Spinoza's Revelation: Religion, Democracy and Reason* (New York: Cambridge University Press, 2004), 38 ff.

14 This is a direct reference to *E* II, P49, which is the last and longest Proposition in Part II of the *Ethics*. The most obvious correlation is to its Corollary: "The will and the intellect are one and the same" (*E* II, P49C). But the similarities run much deeper. I will not take this up now, I will only note how concerned he is in the Proposition of the *Ethics* to link error to the conception of the free will, and how he lapses into a kind of humor himself to prove this point with reference to Buridan's ass—who in fact is the Cartesian subject.

15 For the narration of the Fall as a tragedy that attributes melancholia to humankind, see the analysis of St Hildegard in Raymond Klibansky, Erwin Panofsky, and Fritz Saxl, *Saturn and Melancholy: Studies in the History of Natural Philosophy, Religion and Art* (Nendeln/Liechtenstein: KRAUS Reprint, 1979), 78–80.

16 Jacques Derrida, "Before the Law", in *Acts of Literature*, ed. by Derek Attridge and trans. by Avital Ronell and Christine Roulston (New York: Routledge, 1992), 181–220.

17 For an account of dejustification as a kind of judgment, see Vardoulakis, *Sovereignty and its Other: Toward the Dejustification of Violence* (New York: Fordham University Press, 2013).

Bibliography

Albiac, Gabriel. "The Empty Synagogue," in ed. by Warren Montag and Ted Stolze, *The New Spinoza*. Minneapolis: University of Minnesota Press, 1997, 108–43.

Arendt, Hannah. "Authority," *Between Past and Future: Six Exercises in Political Thought*. New York: Viking, 1961, 91–141.

Cicero, *De Legibus*, trans. by Clinton W. Keyes. Cambridge, MA: Harvard University Press, 1928.

Deleuze, Gilles. *Expressionism in Philosophy: Spinoza*, trans. by Martin Joughin. New York: Zone Books, 1992.

Deleuze, Gilles. *Spinoza: Practical Philosophy*, trans. by Robert Hurley. San Francisco: City Lights, 1988, 2 and 30–43.

Derrida, Jacques. "Before the Law," in ed. by Derek Attridge and trans. Avital Ronell and Christine Roulston *Acts of Literature*. New York: Routledge, 1992, 181–220.

Hammill, Graham. *The Mosaic Constitution: Political Theology and Imagination from Machiavelli to Milton*. Chicago: University of Chicago Press, 2012.

Klibansky, Raymond, Erwin Panofsky, and Fritz Saxl. *Saturn and Melancholy: Studies in the History of Natural Philosophy, Religion and Art*. Nendeln/Liechtenstein: KRAUS Reprint, 1979.

Kordela, Kiarina A. *$urplus: Spinoza, Lacan*. New York: SUNY, 2007.

Levene, Nancy. *Spinoza's Revelation: Religion, Democracy and Reason*. New York: Cambridge University Press, 2004.

Machiavelli, Niccolò. *Discourses on the First Decade of Titus Livius*, trans. by Allan Gilbert, in *Machiavelli: The Chief Works and Others*, volume 1. Durham: Duke University Press, 1989.

Nelson, Eric. *The Hebrew Republic: Jewish Sources of the Transformation of European Political Thought*. Cambridge, MA: Harvard University Press, 2010.

Sharp, Hasana. *Spinoza and the Politics of Renaturalization*. Chicago: University of Chicago Press, 2011.

Spinoza, Baruch. *Opera*, ed. by Carl Gebhardt. Heidelberg: Carl Windters Universitätsbuchhandlung, 1924.

Spinoza, Baruch. *Theological-Political Treatise*, trans. by Samuel Shirley. Indianapolis: Hackett, 2001.

Spinoza, Baruch. *Opera quae supersunt omnia*, ed. by Carolus Hermannus Bruder. Leipzig: Bernhardi Tauchnitz, 1843–6.

Vardoulakis, Dimitris. *Sovereignty and Its Other: Toward the Dejustification of Violence*. New York: Fordham University Press, 2013.

4

Hobbes and Spinoza on Scriptural Interpretation, the Hebrew Republic and the Deconstruction of Sovereignty

James R. Martel

Introduction

In thinking about Spinoza as a radical thinker, someone who understands the contingent nature of law and authority, we tend to grant him these credentials as a matter of course. In this chapter, I will be challenging that assertion just a bit by making what might seem at first to be a highly unlikely claim; that, when it comes to exploring the contingent nature of the bases of legal and political authority, Spinoza is at times exceeded by that most unlikely of his contemporaries: Thomas Hobbes. More accurately, both of these thinkers are radical but, as I will show, the challenges they pose to orthodoxy come in different forms and with different emphases; Hobbes, as I will try to show, is more radical when it comes to epistemology and Spinoza is more radical when it comes to an appreciation of how that epistemology can be applied to the historical record. Any claim that puts Hobbes and Spinoza on a par when it comes to radicalism may seem surprising at the outset; while Hobbes is renowned as an authoritarian and a conservative thinker, Spinoza is seen as being either far more moderate or radical (depending on how one reads him). Yet, I will claim that Hobbes and Spinoza share the same basic understanding of the origin and nature of politics and that, of the two of them, Hobbes is often more willing to countenance the extreme forms of that argument. In this way, I am not seeking to detract from Spinoza's own radical bona fides but rather to add a consideration of and appreciation for Hobbes— at least in this way of reading him—as being equally (and sometimes more) subversive to the liberal tradition that lays claim to him. In the process, I hope to shed light on the nature of both thinkers when it comes to the intersection between theology and politics, the way contingency is not merely a fact of politics but a condition to be embraced (for Hobbes even more than for Spinoza) as constituting perhaps the critical feature of political authority.

When we read Hobbes and Spinoza side by side in their consideration of the genesis and nature of political authority, we see a curious phenomenon. Both of these thinkers offer fairly stern, centralized (especially in Hobbes' case) understandings of the bases of sovereign power and authority. Hobbes is famous (perhaps infamous) for his arguments about a sovereign prerogative that comes directly at the expense of popular authority and individual liberty. Spinoza, for his part, writes in the *Theological-Political Treatise* that private individuals must obey the sovereign in all things, even in those cases where the sovereign is clearly acting against "the natural light of reason."[1] Both of these authors, it would seem, seek to limit the forms of public and individual interpretation—and the political authority that comes from it—that might serve as rivals to or alternatives for a more unitary form of political decision making and judgment, at least insofar as such alternative interpretations manifest themselves as an actual challenge to sovereign power.

Yet, at the same time, both of these thinkers offer extremely decentralized— and indeed contingent—notions of interpretation when it comes to reading Scripture. For all of his stated desire to give the sovereign the "last word" on all matters of state and politics, Hobbes' method of interpretation suggests that interpretation cannot and should not be the monopoly of one reader and that meaning comes out of complicated and highly diffused social and linguistic processes. Spinoza for his part similarly sees interpretation as a decentralized and individualistic process. Although both thinkers supply clear rules and methodologies of interpretation that suggest that there is a "right way" to read Scripture, both of them pull back from asserting that the Bible can mean one thing only. They both insist on interpretation as a process rather than a simple act of decoding. They also insist on myriad private readings even as they acknowledge that such readings lead to the very dissent and difference of opinion that they perceive as a threat to sovereignty.

The questions that I will pose in this essay engage with why these generally centralizing political thinkers offer such a radical (taking the term in its contemporary, political sense as meaning subversive to centralizing narratives of authority and power) form of textual interpretation, with a corresponding implication about the politics that emerge from such interpretations. If such a form of reading seems to threaten the edifice of political order, why promote it as they do? How does this radical form of reading sit with their own professed political stances and how are we to reconcile these different approaches to readings of text and nation?[2]

I recognize that this argument runs against two scholarly traditions. First, the overwhelming majority of works on Hobbes read that thinker as being unabashedly conservative in word and effect.[3] Second, there is a smaller but very influential literature on Spinoza that reads him as being far more radical than he has traditionally been considered to be.[4] In making my claims, I am not asserting anything about the intentions of these authors. I am only saying that the implications of Hobbes' method of interpretation and exegesis—when extended to its logical conclusion—is itself more radical, more undermining of the sovereign power he seems to promote so ardently in his texts than the method of his younger and seemingly more easy going Dutch counterpart.[5] As I will argue further, Spinoza's own not insignificant radicalism is tempered somewhat by his fairly conservative understanding of reason but, when read in conjunction with Hobbes, the more subversive implications of his work stand out more clearly.

Both Hobbes and Spinoza are well known for the way they make interpretation of Scripture a basis for their broader agenda.[6] What has been less noted however is the way that this basis itself complicates their arguments, leading to tensions and paradoxes in their texts which have important implications for how we read them.

This essay also seeks to address another lacuna in the literature on Hobbes and Spinoza, namely, in terms of their respective treatments of the transition from the so-called "Kingdom of God"—the time when God was king of ancient Israel (what Spinoza calls "the Hebrew Republic")—to "ordinary" monarchies when humans are king.[7] Both thinkers formally describe the Hebrew theocracy as a model for modern forms of sovereignty—this can be argued to be one of two origin stores that Hobbes tells about the genesis of political authority, along with the more famous one he tells about the state of nature—but, as I will argue, this example similarly serves to undermine, rather than bolster, the formal political arguments these authors seek to make.

In terms of both the interpretive and historical/theological questions that I am treating with Hobbes and Spinoza, we see a similar phenomenon at play; whether it comes to asserting an authoritative (and sovereign) meaning in a text, or depicting a perfect (and divine) authority in ancient Israel, the author's formal desire for sovereign decision is undermined in both instances by the very popular vehicle that is otherwise seen as bearing and producing that authority, and for similar reasons. As I will argue further, for all of their deference to sovereign power, for both writers, the general population is seen as the source of the basic meaning of words. Likewise, in the case of the Hebrew Republic, the Hebrew people—as opposed to their leadership—are shown to be the true depository of interpretive authority (in a way that is not repeated in later iterations of sovereignty).

It might seem counterintuitive—and even problematical—to argue that under a theocracy, popular forms of interpretation are enhanced and decentralized, especially when discussing the works of Hobbes and Spinoza, two writers who turned to the interpretation of Scripture in the first place in order to avoid the onset of a theocracy in their respective countries. Yet, I will argue that in their respective treatments of the Hebrew Republic (and, by extension, in their concurrent treatment of the question of interpretation more broadly), we will see how God's rule over ancient Israel produces, in the view of these writers, less certainty, more plural readings and a general decentralization of interpretive and political authority. In this way, the Hebrew Republic is not like contemporary theocracies (whether in Hobbes and Spinoza's own time or our own), nor is it like any other kind of state that currently exists. Most critically, in the Hebrew Republic, God—and hence the sovereign of the nation—is not represented but only interpreted, as we will see further. Here, the myriad complexities of interpretation become central to the politics of the Hebrew Republic and, in this way, both Hobbes and Spinoza's more subversive interpretive methods become clearly and markedly political.

While in general, I will argue that Spinoza's interpretive methods are more centralizing and less related to collective and multiple (as opposed to sovereign and singular) acts and judgments than what we find with Hobbes, in looking at their mutual understanding of the Hebrew Republic/Kingdom of God, I will argue that there are many moments of convergence between these thinkers.[8] In his (admittedly only partial) appreciation for this arrangement, Spinoza's radical potential becomes more clearly legible, somewhat aligning him with the radical implications of Hobbes' own methodology and tying into a larger literature of reading Spinoza as a radical—including in this volume.

Reading, interpretation and sovereign authority

Hobbes' method of reading

To begin this inquiry, let me examine Hobbes and Spinoza's respective methodologies for reading and, in particular, their methods for reading Scripture. For both authors, as for virtually everyone who wrote or perhaps even lived in the seventeenth century in Western Europe, the question of interpretation was principally a question of Scriptural interpretation. The Bible enjoyed a status as *the* source of spiritual as well as political authority and both thinkers lived through periods of great tumult (Hobbes with the English civil war and Spinoza with the struggles between Arminianism and Calvinism in the Netherlands, among other events) that were principally inspired by and related to the question of Scriptural exegesis.

For Hobbes, misreading of Scripture was responsible for what he called a "kingdome of darknesse." This "kingdom" was produced "by abusing and putting out the light of the Scriptures" (*L* 4.44, 418).[9] It superimposes "Idols, or Phantasms of the braine" on the text, "mixing with the Scripture divers reliques of the [Pagan] Religion, and much of the vain and erroneous Philosophy of the Greeks, especially of Aristotle" (*L* 4.44, 418). This systematic style of misreading leads to the "Seducing of men by abuse of Scripture" and was, in Hobbes' view, a widespread peril that threatened England to its very core (*L* 4.44, 419).

Hobbes' response to this practice of misreading was to revisit Scripture and painstakingly eliminate these "Idols" of the text. In Part III of *Leviathan*, he sets out his overall method of reading, telling us:

> It is not the bare Words, but the Scope of the writer that giveth the true light, by which any writing is to bee interpreted; and they that insist upon single Texts, without considering the main Designe, can derive no thing from them cleerly; but rather by casting atomes of Scripture, as dust before mens eyes, make everything more obscure than it is; an ordinary artifice of those that seek not the truth, but their own advantage. (*L* 3.43, 415)

By referring to the "Designe" of the text and the "Scope" of the writer, Hobbes is drawing upon his own roots as a renaissance humanist. While, paradoxically, as we have already seen, he sets his ire against Greek philosophy, nonetheless his style of reading is informed by the classical traditions of Greece and Rome.[10] He thus treats Scripture like any text and subjects it to a form of structural analysis whereby any one part must be read in the context of the whole. In reading Scripture, he tells us that he avoids: "such texts as are of obscure, or controverted Interpretations; and to alledge none, but in such sense as is most plain, and agreeable to the harmony and scope of the whole Bible" (*L* 3.43, 414–15). In this regard, Hobbes, much as Spinoza will do after him, subjects the books of Scripture to a philological scrutiny that seeks to demystify them.[11] He shows us for example (again, as Spinoza will do after him) that the five books of Moses could not have been compiled by Moses himself (since Moses is shown to have died in them). Without denying their status as sacred texts (he concedes that the Pentateuch contains "all that which [Moses] is said to have written"), he subjects the Bible to a written, human history and thus highlights its nature as a physical, tangible text (*L* 3.33, 262). In this way, Scripture must conform to human-derived meanings, logics and senses that can then guide our interpretation.

At the same time as Hobbes focuses on the overall scope of the text, he pays a great deal of attention to the way we read individual words and phrases. True to his rhetorical sensibilities, Hobbes insists that we do not take metaphors too literally. To do so is to engage in what he calls "Daemonology" (*L* 4, 44, 418). This practice gives false life to rhetorical figures in Scripture (among other texts). Here, the text becomes read through an idolatrous lens, leading to the "kingdome of darknesse." In several of his works, he speaks of the error of *Separated Essences*, the act of ascribing body and reality to purely figurative terms (*L* 4.46, 466). In *Leviathan*, he tells us:

> seeing [the daemonologists] will have these Forms [i.e the terms and figures in question] to be reall, they are obliged to assign them *some place*. ... And in particular, of the Essence of a Man, which (they say) is his Soule, they affirm it to be All of it in his little Finger, and All of it in every other Part (how small soever) of his Body; and yet no more Soule in the Whole Body, than in any of those Parts. Can any man think that God is served with such absurdities? And yet all this is necessary to believe, to those that will believe the Existence of an Incorporeall Soule, Separated from the Body. (*L* 4.46, 466)

Here we see how the figure of the soul—originally a mere stand in for a person—takes on a daemonological life of its own, becoming an "Idol ... of the braine." The soul is made immortal and superior to the body which it figuratively represents. In *Behemoth*, Hobbes tells us that related separated essences (largely thanks to Aristotle) have led us to believe in falsities like free will and transubstantiation.[12]

In fighting such errors, particularly in *De Cive* and the second half of *Leviathan*, Hobbes engages directly with Scripture in order to highlight the fact that metaphors used to describe God are just that. In both of those texts he tells us not to read terms like "the Spirit" or the "Word" of God literally (and Spinoza says exactly the same thing) but rather as metaphors for wind or faith (among other concepts). In this way, Hobbes returns words to the human realm that they originate from, showing us how these words are created by human beings in order to speak of things that we cannot otherwise understand.

Accordingly, Hobbes can be said to democratize the meaning of Scripture, to show how anyone can learn to read it because the words and meaning of the Bible are produced and understood by ordinary individuals (by extension any one of us can also learn how to resist the superimpositions of idols by would-be "daemonologists"). Similarly, and by implication, Hobbes allows for an appreciation for the contingent nature of authority, the way it is built not on absolute truths but on commonly determined (and argued over) notions that are derived from human interaction and discourse on the most ordinary of levels. This is a sentiment that Hobbes explicitly suggests in his Introduction to *Leviathan* when he famously tells us that his reader should *"Read thy self."* He writes:

> that for the similitude of the thoughts, and Passions of one man, to the thoughts, and Passions of another, whosoever looketh into himself, and considereth what he doth, when he does *think, opine, reason, hope, feare,* &c; and upon what grounds; he shall thereby read and know what are the thoughts and Passions of all other men, upon the like occasions. (*L* Introduction, 10)

Here, through the common focus on reading, we see a connection whereby reading becomes neither an exclusive activity for elites nor an activity for purely isolated individuals. Rather, reading serves as a general engagement with language, a basic metaphor for politics itself. Although it seems that Hobbes' method boils down meaning to its most basic level (so that if we all read by his method we would all come to roughly similar conclusions), nonetheless it seems vital for Hobbes that we all actually engage in this activity in all of our plurality. Language, and the beliefs we produce out of it, are, for Hobbes, a process (and one that never concludes). Thus interpretation must occur on a widespread basis to reflect the way that the process forming meaning is itself collective and decentralized. We should recall that for Hobbes the cause of the English civil war is not widespread and multiple readings of Scripture but *bad* and idolatrous readings (for which a book like *Leviathan* serves as a corrective). Good and widespread readings, it would seem, are not only harmless but even necessary for the promulgation of understanding, for the very basis of meaning itself (whether Scriptural or otherwise).

Individual vs. sovereign readings

There is however a great tension throughout Hobbes' work (and not just in *Leviathan*) wherein the widespread reading that he requires comes up against the reading of the sovereign. If these readings do not converge, whose reading then shall serve as the definitive interpretation of meaning? Whose reading will be law? For Hobbes, the answer seems very clear; we see in the Introduction of

Leviathan that right after Hobbes tells us that each reader must "*Read thy self*" he trumps such private readings by a turn toward the sovereign's own reading:

> But let one man read another by his actions never so perfectly, it serves him onely with his acquaintance, which are but few. He that is to govern a whole nation, must read in himself, not this, or that particular man; but Man-kind. (*L* Introduction, 11)

In the shift from the individual reader reading "all other men" to "his acquaintance, which are but few," we see private reading become depoliticized, no longer a rival to the sovereign's reading of "Man-kind."[13]

Here we see that the more democratic and decentralized form of reading Hobbes was referring to earlier is overwritten but it is not erased. Throughout his texts, there remains an ongoing tension between Hobbes' calls for widespread (and nonidolatrous) readings and the reading of the sovereign. Permitting or requiring the former always offers a rival and a threat to the latter. Insofar as reading is by its nature multiple, interpretive and individual, by making reading a, or the, key metaphor for politics, we see that in Hobbes' system the sovereign's absolute authority over reading is never fully secure, never independent of the reading public that it sits athwart.

In *Behemoth*, which he wrote later in his life, Hobbes directly addresses the tension between individual and sovereign readings. At one point in the text, B., the pupil, asks A., the master, about the widespread availability of Scripture and the effect this has on the political climate of England. B. says:

> if men be to learn their duty from the sentence which other men shall give concerning the meaning of the Scriptures, and not from their own interpretation, I understand not to what end they were translated into English, and every man not only permitted, but also exhorted to read them. For what could that produce, but diversity of opinion, and consequently (as man's nature is) disputation, breach of charity, disobedience, and at last rebellion?[14]

Interestingly, one of the forms of rebellion that B. mentions is that of the Apostles rebelling against Roman rule and the Jewish high priests, suggesting a case where a rebellion against the state and church was in fact justified. If that is the case, could other rebellions be justified by Scripture as well? B. goes on to ask if it is (therefore) wise to have Scripture available in English. Noting that the ancient Jews had access to their own Scripture "in the Jewish language" he goes on to say that "it was nothing to the duty of Jews, whether [Scripture was] understood or not, seeing nothing is punishable but the transgression of some law."[15] Here, B. is implicitly asking why people should have access to Scripture if it only causes trouble and when all that really matters is that they obey the laws that Scripture conveys to them.

A.'s answer to this series of questions is telling. On the one hand, he reaffirms, as always, the supremacy of sovereign readings. He suggests (exactly as Spinoza does) that when the apostles' interpretation of Christ's message trumped the rule of their king, it was permitted because they "did know he was God, and consequently ... their disobedience ... was just."[16] Here the presumption seems to be that if you are not dealing with Jesus himself, if there is any doubt as to the Godlike nature of a theologically based challenge to state authority, the benefit should be given to the sovereign. As for questions of interpretation in modern times A. says: "Where the King is head of the Church and by consequence (to omit that the Scripture itself was not received but by the authority of Kings and States) chief judge of the rectitude of all interpretations of Scripture, to obey the King's law and public edicts, is not to disobey, but to obey God."[17]

For all of this, despite all of the threat that access to Scripture clearly produces in the population, A. insists that Scripture be widely available in English. He further tells B.:

> There are so many places of Scripture easy to be understood, that teach both true faith and good morality ... of which no seducer is able to dispossess the mind (of any ordinary readers), that the reading of them is so profitable as not to be forbidden without great damage to them and the commonwealth.[18]

Hobbes (in his guise as "A.") seems here to hope that there is a convergence between individual readings and the sovereign one (if reading is done, once again, in an appropriate, nonidolatrous fashion). And yet this "solution" papers over several difficulties. What if these readings do not converge? What if the sovereign is a bad reader, actually worse than the citizenry taken both as a collective and as a set of individuals?

Despite Hobbes' desire to give the sovereign the last word in interpretation, he cannot and will not avoid the fact, stated plainly in *Behemoth*, that "the power of the mighty hath no foundation but in the opinion and belief of the people."[19] Popular interpretation is indispensible for Hobbes, an idea he reinforces in *Leviathan* when he notes (speaking of the time of the early Christian Church) that:

> When a difficulty arose, the Apostles and Elders of the Church assembled themselves together, and determined what should bee preached, and taught, and how they should interpret the Scriptures to the People; but took not from the People the liberty to read, and interpret them to themselves. The Apostles sent divers Letters to the Churches, and other Writings for their instruction; which had been in vain, if they had not allowed them to Interpret, that is, to

consider the meaning of them. And as it was in the Apostles time, so it must be till such time as there should be Pastors, that could authorize an Interpreter, whose Interpretation should generally be stood to: But that could not be till Kings were Pastors, or Pastors Kings. (*L* 3.42, 355–56)

Here we see that in the absence of a unity of pastors and kings (i.e., the state of his—and our—current polity), public interpretation cannot be written out of the picture. Indeed for Hobbes, the bases of meaning are not found in any given or received sets of knowledge but come instead from the kind of ordinary discourses of language that create the fabric of our collective reality. In his radical nominalism, Hobbes holds that words only mean what we collectively decide them to mean; even in the face of a "great decider" like the sovereign, there is a yet deeper power of determination that comes from the community as a whole. It is this recognition of the power of communities informing and shaping their own beliefs that holds Hobbes back from insisting that Scripture be treated like a guarded secret for kings and bishops to interpret as they see fit.

Even as he claims that sovereign pronouncements should trump and override all others, we see that for Hobbes the underlying authority lies not with the sovereign but with the people who "author" it. Despite the tensions this produces in his texts, there remains at the heart of Hobbes' method and approach to reading a kind of radically democratic possibility that the authors of meaning (i.e., the speaking, reading public) might be able to lay claim to. For all his political conservatism, Hobbes does not turn his back on this possibility even when he reflects on the horrors of civil war that were unleashed by allowing for multiple and unauthorized readings to occur. Insofar as a sovereign is just as capable of a bad idolatrous reading as a member of the public (maybe even more so since they don't have the check on their sense of individual interpretation that ordinary citizens have with each other), the question of interpretation does not turn on rank but rather on method in reading.

Spinoza's method of reading

As already mentioned, there are an enormous number of congruencies between Hobbes and Spinoza's respective interpretive methods. For Spinoza, "the knowledge of Scripture must be sought from itself alone" (*TTP* 108), which is somewhat akin to Hobbes' comments about reading Scripture (or any text) according to its "Scope" and "Designe." Like Hobbes, Spinoza insists on treating Scripture as a physical, humanly derived document wherein meaning must be demonstrated in the text rather than inferred to it.

Also as with Hobbes, Spinoza understands that meaning itself has an anchor in popular usage, even in the face of the kind of superior, rational readers that Spinoza generally looks to. He writes:

> [T]he masses and the learned alike preserve language, but it is only the learned who preserve the meaning of particular sentences and books; thus, we may easily imagine that the learned having a very rare book in their power, might change or corrupt the meaning of a sentence in it, but they could not alter the signification of the words; moreover, if anyone wanted to change the meaning of a common word he would not be able to keep up the change among posterity, or in common parlance or writing. (*TTP* 107)

Spinoza rejects (what he characterizes as) overly philosophical forms of interpretation. He is only interested in those parts of the Bible that are, in his view, extremely clear and straightforward. In rejecting much of the Talmudic tradition, he argues that any part of Scripture that requires lengthy exegesis is potentially distorting, substituting a learned opinion for what is "evident" on the page. Of this, he further writes:

> The precepts of true piety are expressed in very ordinary language, and are equally simple and easily understood. Further, as true salvation and blessedness consist in a true assent of the soul—and we truly assent only to what we clearly understand—it is most plain that we can follow with certainty the intention of Scripture in matters relating to salvation and necessary to blessedness; therefore we need not be much troubled about what remains. (*TTP* 113)

In this way, the popular meaning of words is a foundation for Spinoza's interpretive methods, and here again he is in good company with Hobbes.

Finally for Spinoza, as with Hobbes, the interest in myriad public readers sits in tension with the idea that the state should act as a "public interpreter" of Scripture.[20] With Hobbes, as we have already seen, the sovereign's reading serves to trump (at least formally) that of the general public. The sovereign also guards against myriad and dangerous interpretations of Scripture by the clergy (whose disagreements destroyed the English state and religion). In Spinoza's case too, the sovereign serves to protect the polity from religious rivals to its authority. As J. Samuel Preus tells us, Spinoza understood the question of Scriptural interpretation in distinctly political terms.[21] He writes: "as with Hobbes [for Spinoza] the secular rulers have the right to act as the 'interpreters' of public religion, because in the realm of public law, sovereignty must be undivided."[22] Yet it is precisely this unity of meaning that remains in question for both authors.

Reason in Spinoza (and Hobbes)

Where Hobbes and Spinoza do begin to differ—with important consequences for how we think about them politically—comes in terms of how they think meaning is engaged with and responded to by various readers. While for Hobbes, as we have seen, meaning is an ever shifting construct, a product of myriad collective decisions that have no constant or set value, for Spinoza meaning seems to be somehow suspended between common usage and what he calls "the natural light of reason." Hobbes, of course, believes in reason, but his approach to it is far more materialistic (and skeptical) than Spinoza's. In Part I of *Leviathan*, Hobbes introduces the idea of reason relatively late; starting with the senses and then memory and imagination, Hobbes takes us through a process that leads on to speech and then reason. For Hobbes, reason is not separate from speech and may be an artifact of it.[23] He tells us that:

> When a man *Reasoneth*, hee does nothing else but conceive a summe totall, from *Addition* of parcels; or conceive a Remainder, from *Subtraction* of one summe from another: which (if it be done by Words,) is conceiving of the consequence from the names of all the parts, to the name of the whole, or from the names of the whole and one part, to the name of the other part. (*L* 1.5, 31–32)

For Hobbes then, reason is a response to the physical and mechanical aspects of thought as language, a kind of quasi-mathematical calculation.[24]

For Spinoza, on the other hand, reason produces a parallel set of beliefs to divine law. While he strenuously argues that reason and faith are separate registers and that to subsume the one to the other (as Maimonides attempts to do) is to be "utterly in the wrong," for Spinoza reason nonetheless is not unconnected to God's truth (*TTP* 190). He calls the mind that reasons "the true handwriting of God's Word" and the text that reason discerns "the reflection and image of God's Word" (*TTP* 192). Spinoza says repeatedly that God's revealed religion accords exactly with what reason would figure out on its own (given that it is a God given ability to understand the world that God created). He says, for example, that a good man "whether he be taught by reason only or by the Scripture only, has been in very truth taught by God, and is altogether blessed" (*TTP* 80). At the same time, Spinoza makes it clear that reason does not actually reveal eternal truths and cannot replace Scripture. He tells us for example that "we cannot perceive by the natural light of reason that simple obedience is the path of salvation." This, he tells us, is taught by "revelation only," hence the ongoing need for Scripture (*TTP* 198).[25]

This understanding stands in contrast to Hobbes who is much sterner in his insistence that we can know nothing whatsoever about God as when he writes:

> [T]he nature of God is incomprehensible; that is to say, we understand nothing of *what he is,* but only *that he is*; and therefore the Attributes we give him, are not to tell one another, *what he is,* nor to signifie our opinion of his Nature, but our desire to honor him with such names as we conceive most honorable amongst ourselves. (*L* 3.34, 271)

Both thinkers insist on placing a curtain between human endeavors toward knowing divine truth (i.e., the process of reason) and that truth itself but Hobbes' policing of that barrier is more strident (which makes sense, given his worries about idolatry). The differences between Hobbes and Spinoza on this question are to some extent more a matter of degree than kind; Hobbes too sees reason as a "talent which [God] hath put into our hands to negotiate till the coming again of our blessed Saviour" (*L* 3.32, 255). But this is a talent that operates in complete opacity. For Hobbes, reason can discern natural law, but natural law in this case is concerned with forbidding "that which is destructive of [a person's life], or taketh away the means of preserving the same" (*L* 1, 14, 91). While natural law may in some ways correspond to God's law, such a convergence can only be inferred. For Hobbes, God and God's will can only be honored, as we see above by "what we conceive most honorable [or in the case of natural law, prudent,] amongst ourselves." He tells us that we cannot presume (as we can with the case of Spinoza) to duplicate God's laws, rather we can only gesture at it.

The thinkers also are differentiated (again not in kind but in degree) by their respective understandings of how well people reason and with what consequence.[26] Spinoza tells us that whereas "the intellect alone lays down laws for the wise," for the unwise masses a different sort of persuasion is needed (*TTP* 66). Spinoza distinguishes reason from "experience" as when he writes:

> if anyone wishes to persuade his fellows for or against anything which is not self-evident, he must ... convince them either by experience or by ratiocination; either by appealing to facts of natural experience, or to self-evident intellectual axioms. (*TTP* 77)

The narratives that predominate in the Bible offer examples of tangible experiences for the unlearned reader. Although he concedes "Experience can give no clear knowledge of [doctrine] ... it can nevertheless teach and enlighten men sufficiently to impress obedience and devotion on their minds" (*TTP* 78).

For his part, Hobbes makes a somewhat similar distinction between science and prudence. He tells us that though we all "have the use of Reasoning" yet it "serves … to little use in common life." Similar to Spinoza, for Hobbes experience leads to prudence which can actually be better than science if the latter engages in "mis-reasoning" (*L* 1.6, 36). Yet, for Hobbes "mis-reasoning" comes less from a lack of reason per se than from the presence of idolatry. What Spinoza would consider unreasoning, Hobbes would consider a mind distorted by the "Idols, and Phantasms of the braine."

One could argue that Hobbes is simply more pessimistic about human beings and doesn't place as much store in ratiocination as Spinoza does. For Spinoza, as we have seen, great minds can independently discern God's laws (at least as far as humans are able to) and live happily and well. For Hobbes, it seems, there is no one who can read the world (or even Hobbes' own texts) that well (very much including the sovereign "reader"). Or, perhaps more accurately, he hopes for such a reader but is not sure he will get one. In *Leviathan,* at the end of Part II, after lamenting that he finds his work potentially "as uselesse, as the Commonwealth of *Plato,*" Hobbes famously tells us:

> I recover some hope, that one time or other, this writing of mine, may fall into the hands of a Soveraign, who will consider it himselfe (for it is short, and I think clear,) without the help of any interested, or envious Interpreter; and by the exercise of entire Soveraignty, in protecting the Publique teaching of it [that is to say of *Leviathan*] convert this Truth of Speculation, into the Utility of Practice. (*L* 2.31, 254)

Spinoza is more confident than this (in that he has far more than "some hope"). Because he is guided not only by the materiality of language (i.e., by a Hobbes style nominalism) but also by "the natural light of reason," he comes closer to arguing for a convergence (as we have already seen) between God's law and our own. Even if he refrains from calling such laws "divine truths," for Spinoza the divide between the human and the divine is far more porous than it is for Hobbes.

In Spinoza's rendering then, reason is less a simple quasi-mathematical response to the material presence of sensory data and more a source of knowledge in and of itself. This difference has consequences for the notion of reading that each author subscribes to; while we have seen that Hobbes *hopes* that various readings will converge more or less (especially if they read according to Hobbes' own philological and rhetorical methods), we see that Spinoza seems to *expect* that they will. The problem for Spinoza is that people often replace their reason with various desires and thus do not reason at all when they are interpreting, whereas for Hobbes, desire is the font of everything, including reason itself.

Reading and democracy

The political upshot of this difference is that while Spinoza is far more democratic than Hobbes in terms of his political prescriptions and formally far more tolerant of (even insistent on) free speech, his method of interpretation, I would argue, is in fact less democratic than Hobbes, less based in popular and collective conceptions and meanings.

As is well known, Spinoza argues (contra Hobbes) that democracy is the most "natural" form of government (*TTP* 207). Although he also argues that a society that is used to monarchy or aristocracy is probably best kept that way, he tells us that a society that has a history of being democratic (such as the Netherlands) offers the best and most harmonious form of government possible. But Spinoza's democratic tendencies, I would argue, are dampened by his own understanding of reading, interpretation and meaning and their relationship to reason, the way that the collective conversations that form interpretation are, for him—and in a way that is very much unlike Hobbes—beholden to and entangled with a higher, and divine, authority.

For Spinoza, it is true, democracy is highly harmonious with reason.[27] He tells us that:

> In a democracy, irrational commands are still less to be feared: for it is almost impossible that the majority of a people, especially if it be a large one, should agree in an irrational design: and, moreover, the basis and aim in a democracy is to avoid the desires as irrational, and to bring men as far as possible under the control of reason, so that they may live in peace and harmony: if this basis be removed the whole fabric falls to ruin. (*TTP* 206)

And yet, the style of reason itself inflects a peculiarly authoritarian aspect into Spinoza's account of democracy. Such is Spinoza's faith in this kind of reason that he harshly advocates for an absolute power by the sovereign authority. Sounding not unlike Hobbes himself, Spinoza tells us that just as an individual who lives in the state of nature is "bound to live according to his own laws, not according to anyone else's, and to recognize no man as a judge, or as a superior in religion":

> Such, in my opinion, is the position of a sovereign, for he may take advice from his fellow-men, but he is not bound to recognize any as a judge, nor anyone besides himself as an arbitrator on any question of right, unless it be a prophet sent expressly by God and attesting his mission by indisputable signs. Even then he does not recognize a man, but God Himself as His judge. (*TTP* 211)

In fact, as we will see, even in the case of prophecy itself, Spinoza is reluctant (more reluctant than Hobbes) to cede too much authority from the sovereign. More generally, and very much like Hobbes, Spinoza argues that the sovereign "retain[s its] natural rights, and may do whatever they like" (*TTP* 210).[28] Even when the sovereign *is* unreasonable, when it "commands anything contrary to religion," Spinoza tells us that:

> If a sovereign refuses to obey God as revealed in His law, he does so at his own risk and loss, but without violating any civil or natural right. For the civil right is dependent on his own decree; and natural right is dependent on the laws of nature, which latter are not adapted to religion, whose sole aim is the good of humanity, but to the order of nature—that is, to God's eternal decree unknown to us. (*TTP* 210)

In other words, we should follow the sovereign virtually no matter what when we do not have a clear divine mandate (in other words, when it comes to just about everything we try to interpret). Like Hobbes, Spinoza sees the rebellion fomented by Christ as a major exception to the duty to obey sovereign leaders. Short of a messianic event of the stature of Christ's life on earth, we must obey the sovereign in all that it says and demands of us.[29]

One might still say, well but the sovereign in Spinoza's case, at least in some cases, is all of us and it is not so odious to follow a sovereign when it is ourselves. And this is exactly what Spinoza does say. But the constitution of "ourselves" is somewhat unclear. In what way do we wear a sovereign "hat" for Spinoza as opposed to being a mere subject of that rule? Spinoza seems to suggest a majority rule type of democracy (as when he says that in a democracy subjects "only hand [their natural rights] over to the majority of a society, whereof [they are] a unit," *TTP* 207). Yet, the idea of reason as inhering not in the common pool of experience and language but in some autonomous font of knowledge (which, as we have seen, Spinoza sets distinctly apart from experience) suggests a less than democratic form of decision making, one that threatens to become yet another "Idol ... of the braine" in Hobbes' terminology, a basis for determining who does and who does not have the right to interpret.

The specter of an unchecked majority succumbing to widespread, and idolatrous phantasms in the name of its own reason may seem slightly ahead of (and behind) its time, as when, some two hundred years later, we come to Tocqueville's analysis of the democratic majority in America. And yet, we might be able to discern, by Hobbes' methodology, how such an outcome is possible in Spinoza's telling. Because Spinoza does not share Hobbes rigorous struggle against all "Idols ... of the braine," or "Separated Essences," he may be more vulnerable to precisely the kinds of misreadings that he and his own methodology are directed to root out.

Spinoza's ongoing insistence on discerning good from bad (or at least non- or less reasonable) readers helps point to the potentially troubling nature of his political theory as well. For Spinoza, Scripture not only serves to disseminate valuable stories (as Hobbes argues as well) but allows the nonreasoning (or less reasoning) masses a way to understand the messages of reason without the direct presence of reason itself. If the masses form the basis for the basic understanding of words and meaning, it seems as if reason is superimposed on to this base in the same way that Hobbes' sovereign is meant to sit atop an edifice of language to serve as "the great decider." Yet there are some key differences between Hobbes and Spinoza in terms of their respective approaches to this question. In Hobbes' case, the tension is ongoing and unresolved, indeed unresolvable. There is always going to be a need for collective and individual forms of reason, even if it threatens the sovereign monopoly on interpretation. For Spinoza on the other hand, reason's trumping or overwriting of experience and the settling of meaning seems to be a genuine "resolution"; it offers a solution to the problem of interpretation which in fact masks the way a (potentially idolatrous) conformity overwrites the agonic and multiple layers of interpretation that serve as the heart of democratic practices.

Another key difference is that unlike Spinoza, Hobbes keeps the sovereign distinctly separate from the people. In this way, he preserves a space for multiple and discordant readings. Spinoza, by making the sovereign and the people the same thing, superimposes the expectation for a single reading on everyone, lessening the radical potential of his notion of interpretation in the process. Although both of them trump individual readings with sovereign ones, Hobbes' superimposition is more tentative (recall that Hobbes hopes that various readings will concur while Spinoza expects them to). This is why I argue that Spinoza's method of interpretation is less democratic than his formal espousal of democratic politics would lead us to expect (and why for Hobbes it is the other way around).

The Hebrew Republic

Having made this argument, I want to turn the focus of this essay away from reason and interpretation per se and toward one area where I think Spinoza demonstrates a more radical and subversive tendency. This comes in his discussion of the time when God was the king of Ancient Israel. Here, once again, Spinoza shares an interest with Hobbes who devoted an entire chapter of *De Cive* and large parts of the latter half of *Leviathan* to a consideration of this unique political form. While Hobbes and Spinoza diverge in their understanding of reading and interpretation more generally, I would argue that in his own evocation of the "Kingdom of God," Spinoza approaches Hobbes' own more subversive possibilities in the latter's consideration of that kingdom.

Hobbes and Spinoza's interest in the period is not unique to these thinkers. In his book, *The Hebrew Republic*, Eric Nelson describes the fascination many seventeenth century scholars had with ancient Israel. Nelson argues that rather than moving toward a greater secularism (as is generally held), seventeenth century thought moved toward a greater involvement with religion. While the renaissance was a time of increasing secularism, the seventeenth century put Scripture and its interpretation at the center of political thought.[30] The Reformation brought with it an appetite to return to the Old Testament, to the Hebrew language and to the Judaic rabbinical tradition as a way to do an end run around Catholic orthodoxies. This had serious consequences for the way that politics were thought about. Nelson writes:

> Readers began to see in the five books of Moses not just political wisdom but a political constitution. No longer regarding the Hebrew Bible as the Old Law—a shadowy intimation of truth, which had been rendered null and void by the New Dispensation—they increasingly came to see it as a set of political laws that God himself had given to the Israelites as their civil sovereign. Moses was now to be understood as a *lawgiver*, as the founder of a *politeia* in the Greek sense.[31]

The idea that God set up a "perfect constitution" offered European scholars an idea of the political that was in fact openly theological even as it set the standard for the practice of secular politics. Thinkers ranging from Bodin and Grotius to Cunaeus wrote about the political system of ancient Israel with strong implications for their own contemporary practices.[32]

In terms of Hobbes and Spinoza themselves, Nelson traces a genealogy of interest from John Selden who wrote numerous texts on ancient Israel to Hobbes and thence to Spinoza. Nelson writes that even as Hobbes was greatly influenced by Selden, "Hobbes's approach to this paradigmatic constitution would, in turn, deeply influence what is perhaps the most famous seventeenth-century text on the *respublica Hebraeorum* ... Baruch Spinoza's *Tractatus theologico-politicus*."[33]

In the case of both Hobbes and Spinoza, a discussion of the Kingdom of God ostensibly serves as a model for contemporary sovereignty as well; after all,

God's kingdom would seem to constitute an ideal model for how any kingdom (or any political order at all) ought to be run. Yet, it is precisely through the sublimity of the concept of a nation ruled by God that we see a subversive element to this discussion; God's sovereignty, in contrast to the sovereignty of terrestrial kingdoms that follow, is not arbitrary. God's authority is perfect and uncompromised by various human faults and errors. By definition, it is not bedeviled by the idolatry that Hobbes at least sees as being endemic to human society.

And yet, although perfect, God's authority is still subject to interpretation, to human judgment. Indeed, the question of interpretation—and the subversive possibilities it suggests—becomes most pointed when it comes to God's regency. When God is king, there is a radical aporia in the heart of the political structure. With no terrestrial sovereign to dominate and control interpretation, we have a form of authority that has no single, central voice. The more decentralized and democratic forms of interpretation and authority both Hobbes and Spinoza describe emerge from the shadows of sovereign decisionism (even if it is the intention of both writers to trump them with sovereignty in the end). For both thinkers, therefore, the connection between the Kingdom of God and contemporary sovereigns unsettles as much as it anchors (then) current forms of rule.

One of Hobbes' most strident complaints about contemporary church practices was the idea that the Kingdom of God was still extant: "The greatest, and main abuse of Scripture, and to which almost all the rest are either consequent, or subservient, is the wresting of it, to prove that the Kingdom of God, mentioned so often in the Scripture, is the present Church" (*L* 4.44, 419). Such an error sanctifies a set of contemporary church practices as if God were directly manifest in them. It allows the Pope and various other clergy to claim to be speaking for God and creates an artificial (for Hobbes) distinction between "*Civill* and the *Canon* Laws" (*L* 4.44., 421).

In fact, for Hobbes, to use the human word "kingdom" to speak of God requires an actual, terrestrial kingdom. For him, this kingdom existed only once, in ancient Israel (he tells us that it will be restored when Christ comes back to reign on earth). Hobbes tells us that the "Kingdome of God was first instituted by the Ministery of Moses, over the Jews onely" (*L* 4.44, 419). This kingdom lasted throughout the period of Hebrew Judges and ended (except for a temporary afterlife following the Jews' return from the Babylonian captivity) "in the election of Saul, when [the Hebrews] refused to be governed by God any more, and demanded a King after the manner of the nations" (*L* 4.44, 419)—although, as I'll show even under the first few kings, some version of this kingdom continued, at least insofar as the question of public interpretation was concerned.

For Spinoza too, God's kingdom literally (and only) existed in ancient Israel. He calls this moment the "Hebrew theocracy" as well as the "Hebrew Republic." He writes that "God alone, therefore, held dominion over the Hebrews, whose state was in virtue of the covenant called God's kingdom, and God was said to be their king" (*TTP* 219).

For both writers, one of the key aspects of the kingdom of God was that God's rule was mediated, first by Moses and then by a subsequent series of high priests, judges and prophets (although Spinoza has a more ambivalent relationship to this later group, as I will show).[34] Despite this division of authority, for Spinoza (and Hobbes echoes this notion) "in the Hebrew state the civil and religious authority, each consisting solely of obedience to God, were one and the same" (*TTP* 219). Even if there was a functional division of labor in the Kingdom of God between clerics and military (and political) leaders, all the laws had one source: God.

A fractured sovereignty

For both thinkers, the upshot of this kingdom was a fractured and decentralized form of rule. Insofar as no human authority had ultimate power, the various nodes of authority led to a more diffuse form of sovereignty than we currently practice (either in these author's lifetimes or our own). Perhaps most importantly, under the conditions of the Kingdom of God, interpretation as such was much more obviously the basic political practice than it would be in later expressions of sovereignty in that at the heart of the state lies an entity (God) that had to be spoken for, whose words did not directly result in rule but was always mediated by some set of political and social actors.

In practice, this led to a highly exceptional and undetermined form of politics during the time of the Hebrew Republic/Kingdom of God. In *De Cive*, Hobbes writes that in this kingdom, the role of prophets tended to disrupt the ordinary interpretive role of the Levite high priests:

> [t]he supreme civil power was therefore *rightly* due by God's own institution to the high-priest; but *actually* that power was in the prophets to whom (being raised by God in an extraordinary manner) the Israelites, a people greedy of prophets, submitted themselves to be protected and judged, by reason of the great esteem they had of prophecies.[35]

Hobbes tells us further that the executive aspects of government too were diffuse and decentralized in this kingdom:

> though penalties were set and judges appointed in the institution of god's priestly kingdom; yet, the right of inflicting punishment depended wholly on private judgment; and it belonged to a dissolute multitude and each single person to punish or not to punish, according as their private zeal should stir them up. And therefore Moses by his own command punished no man with death; but when any man was to be put to death, one or many stirred up the multitude against him or them, by divine authority, and saying, *Thus saith the Lord*. Now this was conformable to the nature of God's peculiar kingdom. For there God reigns indeed, where his laws are obeyed not for fear of men, but for fear of himself.[36]

Here we see the de facto fracturing of authority that marks the kingdom of God. When the sovereign only "speaks" via those who interpret God's will, sovereignty shares in the decentered and displaced nature of larger interpretive practices. In this way, the contradiction that we normally see in both Hobbes and Spinoza between sovereign power and popular interpretation is resolved, if only under these circumstances.[37]

Perhaps more to the point, for Hobbes, the authority of the prophets comes, not directly from God but from the people's decision of whether they are actually hearing God speak through the prophets or not:

> others did judge of the prophets, whether they were to be held for true or not. For to what end did God give signs and tokens to all the people, whereby the true prophets might be discerned from the false; namely the, the event of predictions, and the conformity with the religion established by Moses; if they might not use those marks?[38]

In other words, God set a series of marks and signs in the world and these remain available for the people "to read" in order to interpret the words of the prophets (who are in turn interpreting the word of God). By evacuating the center of political and interpretive authority (by having God be king), popular interpretation is not just useful but actually critical. Ultimately, it is people who "read" God's will and serve as the font of its authority over and above the priestly authority that is formally set above them. In this depiction, then, we see the tensions that are inherent in all of Hobbes' depictions of political community come down firmly on the side of the people. With the removal of a rival, human sovereign, interpretative authority returns to the people from whom it is originally derived.

Spinoza too sees the "Hebrew Republic" as a fractured and decentered place. He tells us that Moses left no successor to combine his dual function of combining canonical and civil authority, leaving the former job to a high priesthood (the Levite tribe). The executive power, such as it was, was left to a set of twelve tribal "captains," each responsible for his own tribe. Of this arrangement, Spinoza writes:

> From these directions, left by Moses to his successors, we plainly see that he chose administrators, rather than despots, to come after him; for he invested no one with the power of consulting God, where he liked and alone, consequently, no one had the power possessed by himself of ordaining and abrogating laws, of deciding on war or peace, of choosing men to fill offices both religious and secular: all these are the prerogatives of a sovereign. (*TTP* 223)

For Spinoza, the conditions produced by such a fractured form of government meant that "In respect to their God and their religion [the Hebrews] were fellow-citizens; but in respect to the rights which one possessed with regard to another, they were only confederated" (*TTP* 224). God's kingship was the only thing that these subcommunities had in common.

In practice, Spinoza tells us this arrangement worked quite well; ancient Israel suffered little factionalism and virtually no civil war prior to the advent of human kings. Spinoza tells us that "the power of evil-doing was greatly curtailed" insofar as the executive captains were beholden to the Levites for interpretation of God and the Levites for their part "had no share in the government, and depended for all their support and consideration on a correct interpretation of the laws entrusted to them" (*TTP* 226). In addition, Spinoza writes: "the whole people were commanded to come together at a certain place every several years and be instructed in the law by the high-priest; further, each individual was bidden to read the book of the law through and through with scrupulous care" (*TTP* 226). For Spinoza, the upshot of this arrangement is less the subservience of the people to the priestly caste and more their own empowerment as a community. Even as tribal captains were independent of all central power structures (except the command of God), there is an even more fundamental power that resides in the very same people who form a consensus over the meaning of words. In this way, the connection between a general discussion of interpretation and the polity of the Hebrew Republic is made clearer.

Spinoza offers several instances in the Bible where popular and decentralized decisions are determinant. For example, he writes:

> When Joshua was dead, the children of Israel (not a fresh general-in-chief) consulted God; it being decided that the tribe in question contracted a single

alliance with the tribe of Simeon, for uniting their forces and attacking their common enemy. (*TTP* 224–25)

In this way, decisions are made literally by the people themselves over and above any formal forms of representation. Here again we see some evidence that, as with Hobbes, Spinoza sees that people's interpretive power is both required and powerful in the Kingdom (or in his case "republic") of God. He tells us that even the power of the captains was checked by popular opinion, since to defy God's law would mean to bring on "the virulence of theological hatred" (*TTP* 227). Spinoza also writes:

> If this independence of citizen soldiers can restrain the princes of ordinary states [he spoke of Alexander's soldiers and their resistance to imperial decrees] … it must have been still more effectual against the Hebrew captains, whose soldiers were fighting, not for the glory of a prince, but for the glory of God, and who did not go forth to battle till the Divine assent had been given. (*TTP* 227)

Here, Spinoza reminds us that the individual Hebrews (the males at least; the female Hebrews seem to be generally left out of both his and Hobbes' overall analysis) formed a powerful and self-aware body of "readers" keen on preserving God's law and fomenting trouble and resistance against various forms of its implementation. As with Hobbes, we see that for Spinoza, the people's interpretive authority—the same power that they wield over language more generally—has far less risk of being overwritten and trumped than it does in future political iterations.

Such a state of affairs points to a different model of sovereignty and authority than that which Spinoza seems to offer in his comments about contemporary sovereignty. For Spinoza, in an "ordinary" state (i.e., a state where God is not king) the sovereign is an expression of the people in their collectivity, represented by their government and united by a common conception of reason. In the Hebrew Republic, however, the collective judgment of the people is, in a sense, set against, or at least in tension with, the government; as opposed to the interpretive authority of the Levites, which offers one kind of "reason" in the state, the people seem to have another form that, by definition, will not come to the same conclusion(s). Furthermore, violating even this delicate equilibrium, are the disruptions from prophecy (more on this soon). It seems then that in the case of the Hebrew Republic, reason itself, which for Spinoza normally serves as a great uniter of people, becomes in this case just as fractured as the authoritative structures it was supposed to bolster. It seems that when the source of interpretation is actually God, Spinoza's tendencies to overwrite popular discourse with central tenets of reason give way. Compared to God's perfect truth, the people's interpretations—however reasoned they may be—are necessarily more plural and decentralized and, in this case, Spinoza seems to accept—and even appreciate—that state of affairs.

Clearly for Spinoza there is a great value in depicting the Hebrew Republic as a democracy. He explicitly links that polity to his own when he writes that the citizens of ancient Israel were confederated and free and "in much the same position (if we except the Temple common to all) as the United States of the Netherlands" (*TTP* 224). Yet in fact this model may not so much illuminate or bolster the Dutch Republic as show up many of the problems with contemporary forms of democratic rule that the comparison produces.

The end of the republic

For both Hobbes and Spinoza, the Kingdom of God was a unique form of government. But, of course, this kingdom did not last. Eventually, the Hebrews decided to have a human king instead of a divine one, effectively ending the Kingdom of God. In the view of both writers, the transition to terrestrial kingdoms ushered in the kinds of government that we have to this day. The key question to ask is what does the earlier existence of God's kingdom, the Hebrew Republic, mean for contemporary forms of authority? In what ways do the diffuse and myriad forms of authority inform, or call into question the kinds of unitary notions of sovereignty that both Hobbes and Spinoza formally subscribe to?

For Hobbes, the end of God's kingdom was due to the corruption that periodically visited the Hebrews and which, finally, brought down God's government:

> Again when the sons of *Samuel*, being constituted by their father Judges in *Bersabee*, received bribes, and judged unjustly, the people of Israel refused any more to have God to be their King, in other manner than he was King of other people; and therefore cryed out to *Samuel*, to choose them a King after the manner of the Nations. So that Justice fayling, Faith also fayled: Insomuch as they deposed their God, from reigning over them. (*L* 1.12, 85)

As Hobbes makes clear, it is not that God abandoned the Hebrews but that they abandoned God ("Justice fayling, Faith also fayled").

For Hobbes, the transition from God as king to human kings ushered in a new form of sovereign authority. He tells us that "there was no authority left to the Priests, but such as the King was pleased to allow them" (*L* 3.40, 329).

Even so, he concedes that along with the Hebrew kings, prophets continued to arise whose teachings sometimes contradicted or went against the kings. In this way the authority of the kings was not as complete as it would be in later, post-Hebraic iterations of terrestrial sovereignty. In *De Cive* Hobbes writes of this period that "the civil power therefore, and the power of discerning God's word from the words of men, and of interpreting God's word even in the days of the kings, was wholly belonging to [prophets, among others]."[39] Hobbes argues that kings did not always need to follow the prophet's teachings, but this rival source of interpretation serves as an ongoing remnant of the diffused version of sovereignty that reigned during the kingdom of God itself.

In both *De Cive* and *Leviathan*, the two principle texts in which he discusses the Kingdom of God, Hobbes insists that the sovereign authority God bestowed on Moses descends through the kingdom of God and down to the future kings, including the kings of his own time. Yet, his own depiction of the uniqueness of God's kingdom serves as a counterweight to such arguments. Although he is careful to show that even in the time of Moses and the judges that followed, there was always one voice that spoke for God, we see that human sources of political authority are consistently undermined by God (via the prophets), a state of being that survives God's kingdom itself for some time. Such divine or alternative sources and forms of authority and interpretation mean that there is not one simple and clear form of sovereign authority that can be passed down to future kings, regardless of what Hobbes insists. When God is king of Israel, the center of authority is literally evacuated. To leave God as an aporia (as Hobbes always insists) means that God's authority comes to the world in diffuse and highly mediated forms, a state of affairs, as we have as seen, that can persist even when there are earthly kings. To argue that the Kingdom of God serves as a kind of model for the highly centralized and unilateral sovereign forms that we find with terrestrial kings is to ignore the deep contrast that Hobbes sets up by highlighting the uniqueness of the Kingdom of God in the first place. It further suggests that Hobbes' various discussions of interpretation are not merely a matter of individual vs. sovereign forms of reading (in which case the sovereign simply trumps and supersedes the popular) but offer an alternative form of politics as well, one that potentially persists even to Hobbes' (and our) own day.

In Spinoza's view, the Hebrew Republic "might have lasted forever" (*TTP* 237). However, he goes on to write "it would be impossible to imitate it at the present day, nor would it be advisable to do so" (*TTP* 237). Such a sentiment perfectly expresses the ambivalence with which Spinoza views the Kingdom of God as it relates to our own time. As with Hobbes, Spinoza sees that the end of the republic stemmed from the disobedience of God's subjects. He argues that when God appointed the Levites as the priestly tribe, he did so as a punishment to the other tribes, because only the Levites refrained from worshipping the Golden Calf (*TTP* 233). In doing so, God set into motion a source of resentment that would eat away at the republic. Spinoza writes: "If the state had been formed according to the original intention, the rights and honour of all the tribes would have been equal and everything would have rested on a firm basis. Who is there that would willingly violate the religious rights of his kindred?" (*TTP* 234).[40] Even as he earlier praised the separation of the Levites as being a major factor in suppressing private ambition and corruption in the Hebrew Republic, Spinoza comes to argue that it would have been better to have priests drawn from every tribe rather than making one tribe apart from the others. He writes that "the obligation to keep in idleness men hateful to them, and connected by no ties of blood" led to discord (*TTP* 233). Instead of a harmonious and everlasting form of government, resentment against the Levites led to greater resentment and distortion until "at last the people, after being frequently conquered, came to an open rupture with the Divine right, and wished for a mortal king, so that the seat of government might be the Court, instead of the Temple" (*TTP* 235).

For Spinoza, the move toward more ordinary forms of government was catastrophic for the Hebrews; the election of kings provided a "vast material for new seditions." With the rise of kings, jealousy of alternative forms of power arose. While the first kings respected the authority of the high-priests (more or less), over time they "began gradually to introduce changes, so as to get all the sovereign rights into their own hands" (*TTP* 235). These struggles produced almost constant strife and civil war.

As with Hobbes, for Spinoza, the reign of the Hebrew kings is a kind of hybrid between contemporary unitary forms of sovereign authority and the kind of diffuse sovereignty that we find in the Kingdom of God itself (*TTP* 235). The interpretive authority of the kings was challenged by the people's tenacious belief in their religion, the ongoing political authority of God and the challenges posed by the high priests and by the prophets. In such an atmosphere, Spinoza labels the rule of the Hebrew kings as a "precarious sovereignty" (*TTP* 235).

While Hobbes is somewhat accepting of the ongoing role of prophecy in the reign of the Hebrew kings (recall that he says that the kings were not obliged to always obey them even when they were correct), Spinoza is quite set against their rival sources of authority. He argues that the prophets "rather irritated than reformed mankind by their freedom of warning, rebuke and censure" (*TTP* 239). He also tells us that the prophets were "often intolerable even to pious kings, on account of the authority they assumed for judging whether an action was right or wrong" (*TTP* 239). It may seem peculiar that Spinoza, who, once again is generally seen as far more tolerant of diversity of opinion, would be more intolerant of rivals to sovereign authority than Hobbes is himself.

One explanation for this is offered by Steven B. Smith who argues that the *Theological-Political Treatise* was written in opposition to an attempt to theologize the Dutch Republic as "a new Israel." The Dutch clergy, he tells us further, "saw their own position as akin to ancient prophets."[41] In this way, Spinoza may have been denigrating prophecy to avoid theological challenges to the Dutch state (although, as we have seen, he himself seeks to relate the Dutch and the Hebrew Republics).

But there may be other reasons for the distaste he displays toward the political challenge of prophecy as well. I would argue that here once again, we may also be seeing the effects of Spinoza's allegiance to reason as he conceives of it—especially in a context in which God is no longer king. Insofar as the transition to ordinary and contemporary forms of government suggests the coming reign of the "natural light of reason," Spinoza turns against prophecy as a direct challenge to such an authority (in a parallel to his concern that the Dutch Republic not be overcome by its clergy). For Spinoza reason and sovereignty are linked in a way that they are not for Hobbes (the sovereign for Hobbes is once again not necessarily more reasonable than anyone else). Thus, in the period when prophecy exists side by side with terrestrial monarchy, Spinoza strongly turns against the former for the sake of the unity and authority of the latter.

In this way, once again, we see the more conservative (at least in the sense of being more centralizing and authoritarian) aspects of Spinoza's political philosophy in contrast to the more radical implications of Hobbes' work. Yet at the same time, it is Spinoza who spends far more time than Hobbes on showing exactly how fractured, how diffuse authority is during the period of the Kingdom of God. His very use of term "the Hebrew Republic" suggests this fracturing. Spinoza describes the decentralization of the tribes, the roles of the captains and the autonomy and authority of the average citizen-soldiers in ways that Hobbes does not. If Spinoza turns against the forms of authority found in the Hebrew Republic as soon as it becomes a direct rival to the kinds of sovereignty that he finds in his own time, it remains true that he leads our attention directly to the radical implications of that republic in the first place. In Spinoza's writing, we see the way such a republic serves as a true alternative to contemporary sovereignty even as he then overwrites such an authority with the authority produced by the "natural light of reason."

In this way, I am arguing against the claims of a scholar like J. Samuel Preus, who sees in Spinoza an attempt to undermine theology in the guise of "interpreting" it. Preus tells us "the *Theologico-Political Treatise* belabors the connection between theology and politics in order once and for all to end the influence of theology on politics."[42] Preus claims that for Spinoza, theology itself is an impediment to political freedom and anathema to a republic like Holland. I am arguing, on the other hand, that even if Spinoza's intention is to dismiss theology (that is, even if Preus is correct about this, which I suspect he is) his return to theology does not undermine itself so much as undermine the nascent construction of his secularism as well as the political order that comes along with it.

Conclusion

In this way, we see that both Hobbes and Spinoza can be read as subversive; Hobbes by dint of his more radical method of reading and interpretation (one that is not tempered by an idea of reason as an independent source of real knowledge) and Spinoza by dint of the careful way he extrapolates the fracturing and diffusion of sovereign authority in the Hebrew Republic/Kingdom of God. It is particularly when we look at that kingdom that we see how the question of interpretation takes on its most explicit political connotations. Without the rivalry of contemporary forms of sovereignty we see the underlying fonts of collective interpretive authority that such sovereignty usually overwrites. While the authority of God is spoken for by priests and prophets in the Kingdom of God, such an authority remains diffused across the many readers who interpreted and responded to God's law as laid down to the Hebrew people. It is also diffused by the active participation of the Hebrews both in their religion and in their state.

Rather than offering a kind of continuity of sovereignty from that time to our own, I argue that the contrast between the forms of authority we find in the Kingdom of God/Hebrew Republic and our own serves to highlight the interpretive tensions we find in both Hobbes and Spinoza's method of reading Scripture, with important consequences for how we read these authors politically as well.

If Spinoza emerges as being radical but somewhat more constrained than Hobbes, this should illuminate our discussions of Spinoza's contributions—in ways both positive and negative—to considerations of the genesis and nature of political authority. We can see that in terms of the implications for resistance,

Spinoza offers insight into the ways that sovereign authority—even as he formally countenances and accepts it—is never as certain, never as absolute and unified as it seeks to appear. If Spinoza has his reasons for seeking to paper this over, his analysis nonetheless shares with Hobbes the characteristic of making such a realization possible, thus undermining, in a sense, the very kind of political power he seemingly seeks to promote.

Notes

This essay expands upon an earlier essay that appeared as a chapter in *Divine Violence: Walter Benjamin and the Eschatology of Sovereignty* (New York: Routledge, 2011). My thanks to Dimitris Vardoulakis and Kiarina Kordela for their help with this later version of the essay and to Victoria Kahn, David Bates and other members of the Berkeley early modern sodality for help with the earlier version.

1   Benedict (Baruch) de Spinoza, *A Theologico-Political Treatise* (New York: Dover Press, 1951), 211. For more *on* Spinoza, sovereignty and interpretation see Eugene Garver, "Spinoza on Constitutional Interpretation," *Law, Culture and the Humanities* 6.2 (2010), 274–95. For the "natural light of reason," see *TTP*, 100 (among many examples).

2   In treating these authors in tandem, it is worth noting that Hobbes and Spinoza were roughly contemporary and did in fact read one another's work. Obviously the much younger Spinoza was more likely to be influenced by Hobbes than the other way around. William Sacksteder tells us that Spinoza had a copy of *De Cive* in his library, writing "[Spinoza] borrowed and adapted freely from that book in the sole major work he published during his lifetime, the *Tractatus Theologico-Politicus*." William Sacksteder, "How Much of Hobbes Might Spinoza Have Read?" in ed. by Genevieve Lloyd, *Spinoza: Critical Assessments of Leading Philosophers* (New York: Routledge, 2001), 222. He goes on to speculate that Spinoza may well have read other works of Hobbes' as well, almost certainly including his response to Descartes in the latter's *Meditations*. He speculates that Spinoza possibly even read *Leviathan* (at least the Latin edition which was published in Amsterdam in 1668), along with *De Corpore, De Homine* and *De Cive*. Ibid., 231. Sacksteder also tells us that Hobbes read the *Theological-Political Treatise*; citing Aubrey, he tells us that Hobbes said of himself upon reading the Treatise that he "durst not speak so boldly." Ibid., 227. See also Edwin Curley, "I Durst Not Write So Boldly," *Hobbes and Spinoza, Scienza e Politica Atti del Convegno Internazionale Urbino,* Ottobre 14–17, 1989. This connection between these writers (Sacksteder calls Hobbes Spinoza's "teacher") may help to explain the resemblance between their works but in fact there are significant differences between

them as well. While Spinoza, in his call for free speech and religious tolerance appears far more "progressive" than Hobbes, I would argue that in fact the upshot of Hobbes' interpretive method is more radical than Spinoza (although, as I will argue there is a radical potential in Spinoza's work as well). Accordingly, the disjuncture between Hobbes' interpretive and political models may be greater—and more subversive—than the seemingly more "left-leaning" works of Spinoza.

3   Thus, for example, Hobbes scholars ranging from Richard Tuck to Gregory S. Kavka, while disagreeing on much else, agree on this basic reading of Hobbes. See Richard Tuck, *Hobbes* (Oxford: Oxford University Press, 1989); Gregory S. Kavka, *Hobbesian Moral and Political Theory* (Princeton: Princeton University, 1986).

4   For those who read Spinoza as a radical, see, for example Antonio Negri, *Savage Anomaly: The Power of Spinoza's Metaphysics and Politics* (Minneapolis: University of Minnesota Press, 1999); Etienne Balibar, *Spinoza and Politics* (New York: Verso Press, 2008). Negri's interpretation is perhaps the most foundational for rethinking Spinoza. Although Negri acknowledges the way that Spinoza participates in a kind of proto liberal discourse, his claim is that Spinoza's form of liberalism is self destructive, leading to a far more radical outcome, a near total materialism and the deep and utter subversion of the liberal or bourgeois metaphysics that his work appears to espouse.

5   I make a much fuller analysis of Hobbes' (inadvertent?) radicalism in my book, *Subverting the Leviathan: Reading Thomas Hobbes as Radical Democrat* (New York: Columbia University Press, 2007).

6   For example, for Hobbes, see A. P. Martinich, *The Two Gods of Leviathan: Thomas Hobbes on Religion and Politics* (New York: Cambridge University Press, 1992); Patricia Springborg, "*Leviathan* and the Problem of Ecclesiastical Authority," *Political Theory* 3 (1975), 289–303; J. G. A. Pocock, *Politics, Language and Time: Essays on Political Thought in History* (New York: Atheneum, 1971); Tracy Strong, "How to Write Scripture: Words, Authority, and Politics in Thomas Hobbes," *Critical Inquiry* 20 (1993), 128–59. For Spinoza, see J. Samuel Preus, *Spinoza and the Irrelevance of Biblical Authority* (New York: Cambridge University Press, 2001); Steven B. Smith, *Spinoza, Liberalism and the Question of Jewish Identity* (New Haven: Yale University Press, 1997); Theo Verbeek, *Spinoza's Theologico-Political Treatise: Exploring "the Will of God"* (London: Ashgate, 2003); Nancy Levene, *Spinoza's Revelation: Religion, Democracy and Reason* (New York: Cambridge University Press, 2004).

7   The Latin term "Hebraorum Republica" used by Spinoza is similar to "De Republica Hebraorum" ("Of the Hebrew Republic") the title of a then widely known book by the Dutch Hebraist, Petrus Cunaeus. See *The Hebrew Republic* (Jerusalem: Shalem Press, 2007).

8   Because the interpretive methods for receiving God's commands in the Hebrew Republic are, as we will see further, fractured and de-centered (produced by a rivalry between the priests and the prophets), we find a much greater role for popular

interpretation in ancient Israel than in future "ordinary" societies where a unitary sovereign trumps popular forms of interpretation.
9 Thomas Hobbes, *Leviathan*, ed. by Richard Tuck (New York: Cambridge University Press, 2005). Hereafter cited parenthetically as *L*, part number followed by chapter, and then page number.
10 For discussions of Hobbes' humanist background and its relationship to his modernism see Quentin Skinner, *Reason and Rhetoric in the Philosophy of Hobbes* (New York: Cambridge University Press, 1996); Victoria Kahn, *Machiavellian Rhetoric: From the Counter-Reformation to Milton* (Princeton: Princeton University Press, 1994); David Johnston, *The Rhetoric of Leviathan: Thomas Hobbes and the Politics of Cultural Transformation* (Princeton: Princeton University Press, 1986).
11 Preus tells us that while Hobbes sought to submit Scripture to interpretation, Spinoza went a step further and sought an explanation. Preus, *Spinoza and the Irrelevance of Biblical Authority*, 208.
12 Thomas Hobbes, *Behemoth or the Long Parliament* (Chicago: University of Chicago Press, 1990), 42, 43.
13 There is yet another way that Hobbes undermines the sovereign's reading. He also offers his own reading as a private individual as being perhaps superior to that of the sovereign (as when, at the end of the Introduction in *Leviathan*, he tells us of the sovereign's reading: "[Y]et, when I shall have set down my own reading orderly, and perspicuously, the pains left another [i.e., the sovereign], will be only to consider, if he also find not the same in himself" (*L* Introduction, 11).
14 Hobbes, *Behemoth*, 52.
15 Hobbes, *Behemoth*, 52.
16 Hobbes, *Behemoth*, 53.
17 Hobbes, *Behemoth*, 53.
18 Hobbes, *Behemoth*, 53.
19 Hobbes, *Behemoth*, 16.
20 Preus, *Spinoza and the Irrelevance of Biblical Authority*, 2.
21 Preus, *Spinoza and the Irrelevance of Biblical Authority*, 2.
22 Preus, *Spinoza and the Irrelevance of Biblical Authority*, fn 48, 15. He goes on, citing Spinoza himself, to show that "in their function as 'interpreters' however, it is *not* the task of the state to establish true religion or to root out idolatry, but the 'welfare of the people, to which all laws both human and divine, must be made to conform.'"
23 When Hobbes writes: "the Greeks have but one word Logos, for both *Speech* and *Reason*; not that they thought there was no Speech without Reason; but no Reasoning without Speech," he seems to endorse this position as his own. (*L* 1.4, 29).
24 He also tells us that the "Latines calle Accounts of money *Rationes*, and accounting, *Ratiocinatio* … they extended the word *Ratio*, to the faculty of Reckoning in all other things" (*L*. 1.4, 29).

25 Although for Spinoza reason cannot know divine law it can help us to "grasp with moral certainty what is revealed" (*TTP* 195). Reason, he tells us, enables us to live with and prosper under God's Law. Citing the wisdom of Solomon (as found in Scripture) he offers that "wisdom and knowledge flow from God's mouth, and that God bestows on us this gift … our understanding and our knowledge depend on, spring from, and are perfected by the idea or knowledge of God, and nothing else" (*TTP* 67).

26 Preus contends with the claim that Spinoza "took the Bible 'out of the hands of the people' and turned it over to the professoriate" by arguing that the superiority of interpretation granted to scholars does not extend to "readers seeking *religious guidance.*" Preus, *Spinoza and the Irrelevance of Biblical Authority*, fn 44, 14. Yet this answer begs the question of what is the *political* (as opposed to religious) upshot of understanding reading in this fashion. Interestingly, Preus writes that Spinoza "echoes Hobbes, who wrote that 'whatsoever is necessary for these [i.e. ordinary readers] to know [for salvation] is so easy as to not need interpretation; whatsoever is more does them no good'" (ibid.).

27 Nancy Levene writes that Spinoza "reveals … that rationality (reason, truth) and religion (morality, piety) depend upon democracy (independence, freedom)—that each depends upon the others, without which "the peace of the commonwealth," as Spinoza puts it, cannot be secure." Levene, *Spinoza's Revelation*, 1.

28 He goes on to write that the sovereign "may take advice from his fellow-men, but he is not bound to recognize any as a judge, nor anyone besides himself as an arbitrator on any question of right, unless it be a prophet sent expressly by God and attesting his mission by indisputable signs" (*TTP* 211).

29 Nancy Levene argues that there is no basic contradiction between following the sovereign and following God's law, even when the two laws appear to diverge. She writes: "The divine law is rational, universal, and true, and is the foundation of enlightenment in all senses. Yet religion also refers to human laws, to those laws that are enacted in particular times and places as interpretations of the divine law, or as manipulations of it. This second notion of religion is at once rooted in political life and also a dire threat to it. For those laws that claim divine authority will be most effective at galvanizing the majority, for good and for ill, and they will also, inevitably, attempt to set themselves up as an autonomous power, a 'dominion within an dominion' … in competition with legitimate sovereign political power. That the divine law taken in itself is rational does not prevent its turbulent involvement in human conflicts." Levene, *Spinoza's Revelation*, 1. Thus, the practice of interpreting divine law will be imperfect but its source remains part of a larger fabric of a rational order.

30 Eric Nelson, *The Hebrew Republic: Jewish Sources and the Transformation of European Political Thought* (Cambridge, MA: Harvard University Press, 2010), 2.

31 Nelson, *The Hebrew Republic*, 16.

32 Nelson cites Bodin's *Methodus ad facilem historiarum cognitionem* for one. See also, for example, Petrus Cunaeus, *The Hebrew Republic* (Jerusalem: Shalem Press, 2007).
33 Nelson, *The Hebrew Republic*, p. 22.
34 For Hobbes, this kingdom was not instituted directly by God's word but rather via the mediation of Moses. Citing the Scriptural passage whereby the Hebrews say to Moses "*speak thou with us, and we will hear, but let not God speak with us lest we die*," Hobbes tells us "Here was their promise of obedience, and by this it was they obliged themselves to obey whatsoever he should deliver unto them for the Commandment of God" (*L* 3.40, 324, 325).
35 Thomas Hobbes, *De Cive* in *Man and Citizen* (Indianapolis, IN: Hackett Publishing, 1991), 323.
36 Hobbes, *De Cive*, 323.
37 Here we see evidence for my initial claim that in the Hebrew Republic (as these writers viewed it) the sovereign is not represented but only interpreted.
38 Hobbes, *De Cive*, 325.
39 Hobbes, *De Cive*, 326.
40 Levene argues that the problem here for Spinoza is the separation between church and state that it implies. Levene, *Spinoza's Revelation*, 211.
41 Smith, *Spinoza, Liberalism and the Question of Jewish Identity*, 146.
42 Preus, *Spinoza and the Irrelevance of Biblical Authority*, 5. Levene takes a slightly more nuanced approach. She speaks of Spinoza's "reluctance to dismiss theology outright" and an "equal reluctance to define what it is." Levene, *Spinoza's Revelation*, 99.

Bibliography

Balibar, Etienne. *Spinoza and Politics*. New York; Verso Press, 2008.

Cunaeus, Petrus. *The Hebrew Republic*. Jerusalem: Shalem Press, 2007.

Curley, Edwin. "I Durst Not Write So Boldly," *Hobbes and Spinoza, Scienza e Politica Atti del Convegno Internazionale Urbino*, Ottobre 14–17, 1989.

Garver, Eugene. "Spinoza on Constitutional Interpretation," *Law, Culture and the Humanities* 6.2 (2010), 274–95.

Hobbes, Thomas. *Behemoth or the Long Parliament*. Chicago: University of Chicago Press, 1990.

Hobbes, Thomas. *Leviathan*, ed. by Richard Tuck. New York: Cambridge University Press, 2005.

Johnston, David. *The Rhetoric of Leviathan: Thomas Hobbes and the Politics of Cultural Transformation*. Princeton: Princeton University Press, 1986.

Kahn, Victoria. *Machiavellian Rhetoric: From the Counter-Reformation to Milton*. Princeton: Princeton University Press, 1994.

Kavka, Gregory S. *Hobbesian Moral and Political Theory*. Princeton: Princeton University, 1986.

Levene, Nancy. *Spinoza's Revelation: Religion, Democracy and Reason*. New York: Cambridge University Press, 2004.

Martel, James. *Subverting the Leviathan: Reading Thomas Hobbes as Radical Democrat*. New York: Columbia University Press, 2007.

Martinich, A.P. *The Two Gods of Leviathan: Thomas Hobbes on Religion and Politics*. New York: Cambridge University Press, 1992.

Negri, Antonio. *Savage Anomaly: The Power of Spinoza's Metaphysics and Politics*. Minneapolis: University of Minnesota Press, 1999.

Nelson, Eric. *The Hebrew Republic: Jewish Sources and the Transformation of European Political Thought*. Cambridge, MA: Harvard University Press, 2010.

Pocock, J. G. A. *Politics, Language and Time: Essays on Political Thought in History*. New York: Atheneum, 1971.

Preus, J. Samuel. *Spinoza and the Irrelevance of Biblical Authority*. New York: Cambridge University Press, 2001.

Sacksteder, William. "How Much of Hobbes Might Spinoza Have Read?" in ed. by Genevieve Lloyd, *Spinoza: Critical Assessments of Leading Philosophers*. New York: Routledge, 2001, 222–35.

Skinner, Quentin. *Reason and Rhetoric in the Philosophy of Hobbes*. New York: Cambridge University Press, 1996.

Smith, Steven B. *Spinoza, Liberalism and the Question of Jewish Identity* (New Haven: Yale University Press, 1997).

Spinoza, Benedict de (Baruch) *A Theologico-Political Treatise*. New York: Dover Press, 1951.

Springborg, Patricia. "*Leviathan* and the Problem of Ecclesiastical Authority," *Political Theory* 3 (1975), 289–303.

Strong, Tracy. "How to Write Scripture: Words, Authority, and Politics in Thomas Hobbes," *Critical Inquiry* 20 (1993), 128–59.

Tuck, Richard. *Hobbes*. Oxford: Oxford University Press, 1989.

Verbeek, Theo. *Spinoza's Theologico-Political Treatise: Exploring "the Will of God."* London: Ashgate, 2003.

5

Spinoza's Politics of Error

Siarhei Biareishyk

> *It is a guilty reading, but not one that absolves its crime on confessing it. On the contrary, it takes the responsibility for its crime as a "justified crime" and defends it by proving its necessity.*
>
> Louis Althusser, Reading Capital

> *when an error makes its appearance a repression lies behind it*
> Sigmund Freud, Psychopathology of Everyday Life

"I know that I am human and may have erred" reads the penultimate sentence of Spinoza's *Theological-Political Treatise* (*TTP* 259).[1] Georges Canguilhem points to the difficulty of accounting for this uncharacteristic "I" in view of Spinoza's thought and its political intervention: "this philosophy that refutes and rejects ... the *cogito*, the affirmation of freedom in God and people—this philosophy without subject ... gave its author the strength of mind or spirit [*ressort*] required to rebel against *le fait accompli*"—all that under the auspices of a possible error?[2] If in Spinoza's ontology, because thought and extension are two attributes of God or nature, all bodies participate in thinking, then what is the function of error? and what or who errs? In the face of the eternal and infinite substance, what is the epistemo-ontological status of error? "[L]ife," Michel Foucault says, commenting on the thought of Canguilhem, "is what is capable of error."[3] In saying this, Foucault suggests that life generates errors beyond the subject-object relation. Insofar as "error is the root of what produces human thought and its

---

For their support in publishing my work, insightful comments and numerous productive discussions, I thank the co-editors of this volume, A. Kiarina Kordela and Dimitris Vardoulakis. This text emerged in part as a response to the seminar of Étienne Balibar, to whom I am also indebted for critical suggestions as well as relevant references. My gratitude extends to Charles Gelman, Ilya Kliger, Jacques Lezra, Warren Montag, Ross Shields and Sonia Werner for their direct input, support, and inspiring conversations at different stages of this project.

history," this history is considered in terms of and through its interruptions and discontinuities.[4] In a similar vein, the Spinozan theory of error, entailing also the process of error becoming truth, enables one to think the dynamics underlying epistemological ruptures as well as shifts in political regimes—which in Spinozan philosophy prove to be two sides of the same epistemo-ontological process.

In what follows, I unfold three kinds of error in Spinoza that correspond to his three kinds of knowledge, thereby also demonstrating the political modality of error. While every kind of error participates in truth, only the third kind, functioning according to the logic of immanent causality, can constitute a political or epistemological event—the event of error becoming truth. Elucidating Spinoza's strategy of interpretation in the context of his ontology, I will consider the processes underlying error-becoming-truth in light of the following conditions: first, error is neither a matter of a decision nor subjectivity; second, error manifests itself not as an exception, but as a mode of political or epistemological existence; third, the epistemological value of error as truth or falsity is not determined by representation, but by the production of its own effects—of knowledge, of political regimes. Reading Spinozan theory of error in conjunction with Louis Althusser's conception of epistemological rupture as symptomatic reading and the Freudian/Lacanian status of the unconscious enables a conceptualization of the process of error becoming truth through a theory of the encounter—between interpretation and the third kind of error. Finally, I propose to approach Spinoza's *Theological-Political Treatise* itself as a production of the theory of the democratic republic through an encounter with a persistent erring inherent in the first commonwealth of the Hebrew state.

The first and second kinds of error

The concept of error must be understood in its relation to imagination, which, while not reducible to error, constitutes its condition of possibility. Spinoza defines imagination in the following way: "the affections of the human body whose ideas set forth external bodies as if they were present to us we shall call images (*imagines*) ... And when the mind regards bodies in this way, we shall say that it 'imagines' (*imaginari*)" (*E* II, P17S). This definition of imagination is congruent with what Spinoza claims in *Theological-Political Treatise* to be a fundamental law "which necessarily follows from human nature": "when a man recalls one thing he immediately remembers another which is similar or which he had seen along with the first thing" (*TTP* 57). While the production of images is a necessary process under the attribute of thought, the same necessity does not pertain to the emergence of errors—Spinoza insists: "the imaginations of the mind, looked at in themselves, contain no error; i.e. the mind does not err from the fact that it imagines" (*E* II, P17S). In order to distinguish an image from error, Spinoza gives the following example: "when we gaze at the sun, we see it as some two hundred feet distant from us. The error does not consist in simply seeing the sun in this way, but in the fact that while we do so we are not aware of the true distance and *the cause of our seeing it so*" (*E* II, P34S, my emphasis). That we perceive the sun in such a way means that our body is affected by the sun and therefore produces an image. This image of the sun, however, does not entail an adequate knowledge of the external body, but only an adequate knowledge of our own body (*E* II, P25). An adequate idea of this image would express the state of the body thus affected—or, in other words, the very principle of the production of images—because, even if we know the true distance of the sun, "we shall nevertheless continue to see it as close at hand" (*E* II, P34S). One commits an error in confusing an image of an external body with knowledge of that body (e.g., in drawing a conclusion that the sun is two hundred feet away). Error attributes the cause of the image (the affection of the body) to the determination of the sun.

Most generally, then, error stems from the misattribution of cause and effect. Although error takes root in the privation of knowledge or ignorance, "to be ignorant and to err are different things" (*E* II, P35Pr). The concept of error additionally entails an *excess of signification*: "[error] consists in the privation of knowledge which inadequate knowledge … involves" (*E* II, P35Pr). Error, therefore, is not merely privation of knowledge—its absence or lack—but consists rather in a certain modality of attributing to an image the status of an idea. Or, more precisely: *error is the formation of an idea from an image by a false attribution of causality*. This error pertains to Spinoza's conception of "the first kind of knowledge," wherein "from having heard or read certain words we call things to mind and we form certain ideas of them similar to those through which we imagine things" (*E* II, P40S2). Because the error that comprises ideas from a misattribution of cause in the necessary production of images belongs to the sphere of the first kind of knowledge, I propose to call this an "error of the first kind."

Another kind of error that figures in Spinoza involves the passage from the particular to the universal. Evald Ilyenkov succinctly explicates the logic of such error: "Error … begins only there, where the limited correct mode of action is given a universal meaning, there, where the relative is taken for the absolute."[5] This mode of error is apparent in Spinoza's critique of the so-called "transcendental terms" and "universal notions," such as "entity," "man," and "dog." The transcendental terms arise as a result of the mind producing an exceeding amount of images, whereupon the mind "is unable to imagine the unimportant differences of individuals ... and their exact number, and imagines distinctly only their common characteristic" (*E* II, P40S1). Yet, this "common characteristic" must not be confused with a "common notion"—an adequate idea of that which is "common to all things and [is] equally in the part as in the whole" (*E* II, P38). A "common characteristic" arises as the result of a particular disposition of a singular body, insofar as "the body was affected most repeatedly" by a given image, to which it consequently gives the status of a "universal notion" or "transcendental term" (*E* II, P40S2). This "common characteristic," however, is not constitutive of a given set of images (e.g., dog, man, entity), since "not all men form these notions in the same way"; rather, the formation of the "common characteristic" merely reflects the state of a singular body: "each will form universal images according to the conditioning of his body" (*E* II, P40S2). Consequently, this kind of error consists in the attributing of a universal meaning to the effect of a concrete and particular situation. In other words, this error arises as a function of a mode of interpretation that attributes to the essences of particular things or situations the status of "common notions." Insofar as the second kind of knowledge is based on "common notions," one can call this error—"the error of the second kind."

As misattributions of causes, these two kinds of error are variants of one another. The error of the first kind explicates the essence of a singular thing through the images it generates in the existing body, whereas the existence of the affected body does not pertain to the essence of a singular thing affecting it. The error of the second kind explicates "common notions" through the essences of things (or vice versa), whereas common notions do not "constitute the essence of any particular things" (*E* II, P40S2).

Demarcation and regimes of proximate causes

The explication of these two kinds of error illustrates Spinoza's own strategy of interpretation. If error takes root, to use Ilyenkov's formulation, in a "limited correct mode of action," Spinoza determines its truth in the demarcation of the field of effectivity of such action.[6] Ilyenkov argues that, for Spinoza, a thinking body and its mode of action are constituted "by virtue of a particular set of circumstances"—as a result of "the intersection and conjunction of a plurality of causal chains."[7] Error arises, Ilyenkov argues, when the thinking body "transfers this particular mode of action onto another thing"—onto a different singular conjuncture.[8] For instance, while the attribution of universal meaning to the edicts decreed by Moses in the formation of the Hebrew state would constitute an error of the second kind, the same edicts (as well as their proclamation as universal at the time) must be considered a correct mode of action limited to a particular historical situation; as Spinoza writes, "the Laws revealed by God to Moses were nothing but the decrees of the historical Hebrew state alone, and accordingly ... no one needed to adopt them but the Hebrews, and even they were only bound by them so long as their state survived" (*TTP* 9). And yet, the enunciation of these laws *as* eternal was politically necessary, comprising thus a correct mode of action for the constitution and the persistence of the historical Hebrew state. "Correct mode of action" thus means *correct within the inherent logic of a particular situation*, a singular conjuncture determined by its historical circumstances and political effectivity. In turn, if we take the example of our perception of the sun, an adequate idea of this image pertains to a demarcated field that only includes the affected body (and not the external object) and its production of images. Hence, *Spinoza demonstrates the "truth" of a given error by demarcating the field that determines it: an error of a given "truth" arises when interpretation reaches beyond this demarcated field.*

Significantly, Spinoza's strategy of interpretation as demarcation is able to consider one and the same thing as both false and true by shifting between different demarcated fields. The latter insight is manifested, for instance, in Spinoza's invocation of Paul: "if the circumcised break the law, their circumcision will become uncircumcision, and on the other hand if the uncircumcised obey the command of the law, their uncircumcision is regarded as circumcision" (*TTP* 52–53). From the logic of the Hebrew state, it would be erroneous to forego circumcision on grounds of piety, for circumcision is a decree that pertains to the essence of the particular political pact constituted by Moses. In the logic of Christianity, however, because "God is the God of the Jews and the gentiles," "the uncircumcision is regarded as circumcision" as an effect of being pious, for the act of circumcision no longer pertains to the effectivity of a political entity (*TTP* 52–53). This work of demarcation enables an interpretation to consider the same element within contradictory logics; one and the same element appears as either true or false if considered in different fields of historical effectivity.

The work of demarcation moves in ever expanding fields, from an individual affection, to the revelation of a particular prophet, to a people or a particular formation of a state. Each demarcated field contains an inherent logic that corresponds to its essence, as that "without which the thing [i.e., the demarcated field] can neither be nor be conceived" (*E* II, D2). In the interpretation of singularities in view of their political significance—for example, a particular state—the demarcated field with its inherent logic coincides with the limits of sovereignty constituted by a particular form of pact. The process of state-formation consists in the law of transfer, wherein if "someone surrenders to another a portion of the power they possess, they necessarily transfer the same amount of their own right to the other person"; in this way, a state as a singularity also inherits the notion of "natural right," that is, to "strive … to persist in its own state" where "the right of nature extends as far as its power extends" (*TTP* 199, 195). Consequently, the pact grounding a state is predicated solely on its effectivity: the pact persists only as long as it has the power to persist, that is to say, as long as it reproduces itself as its own effect. Spinoza's mode of interpretation aims at the demarcation of a singular state's field of effectivity: this demarcated field, comprising the inherent logic of a singularity in question, is the sole standard of truth and falsity.

If, as Étienne Balibar argues, "Spinozist history aims at historical singularity," one must insist that Spinoza's mode of reading such historical singularities cannot rely on reason, or the second kind of knowledge.[9] Because the second kind of knowledge is based on "common notions," which do not pertain to the essences of particular things, "the basic principles of reason [the second kind of knowledge] … do not explicate the essence of any particular thing" (*E* II, P40S2). Thus, while the natural light of reason understands things through their first causes, Spinoza stresses the necessity of a mode of interpretation that relies solely on proximate causes. Spinoza insists: "a general consideration of necessity and the connectedness of causes cannot help us at all in the formation and ordering of particular things"; hence, "we ought to define and explain things by their proximate causes" (*TTP* 58). Just as Spinoza reads the Bible on its own terms, in this injunction to read according to proximate causes, each pact and each historical state must be understood according to its own inherent logic. Each pact, consequently, constitutes a *regime of a particular ordering of proximate causes*, which determines the state's political significance, singularity, and effectivity. As Balibar argues: "a pact … *by itself* includes no guarantee … which amounts to saying that the [proximate] causes sought are not of the order of juridical representation but of political practice."[10] In turn, the function of sovereignty—and the effectivity of its political practice—lies in the *distribution* of proximate causes and in the *reproduction* of its regime.

The third kind of error

It is in the ascription and reproduction of proximate causes that the political function of error and interpretation is to be located. The work of demarcation, in considering one and the same thing as both error and truth, enables one to conceptualize a political error that pertains to the third kind of knowledge. In constituting a regime of proximate causes, a given social whole or sovereignty at the same time designates a realm of error as that which falls outside its constitutive logic. In reproducing itself, sovereignty must also reproduce the logic of proximate causes that constitutes it as a political singularity. For this reason, Spinoza insists that the "divine law depends solely upon the decree of the sovereign authorities, and hence also … they are its interpreters" (*TTP* 242). For instance, even if a true prophet produces a revelation that is outside the logic of a given regime of proximate causes, this prophet commits an error; the sovereign must rightfully punish the prophet and prohibit this revelation (*TTP* 222). Thus, for Spinoza, because the sovereign authorities retain a monopoly on interpretation, political practice entails a constitutive epistemological dimension: sovereignty is the name for the process of demarcation of "error" from a "correct mode of action." A political error, then, is everything that falls outside the perpetuation and reproduction of a given political singularity.

Political error is exemplified in Spinoza's analysis of treason, which is defined as an attempt "to seize the right of supreme power in some way or to transfer it to someone else" (*TTP* 204). The crime of treason is considered solely from within the regime of proximate causes of an established state, since it pertains only to "subjects or citizens who by a tacit or express agreement have transferred all their power to a state" (*TTP* 204). Although political error aims at injuring the sovereign right, it is not determined in a utilitarian calculation of loss and gain, since it makes no difference "whether the state as a whole would lose or gain even in the most obvious way from it" (*TTP* 204). This is because a political error, beneficial or not, necessarily stakes a claim on the interpretative monopoly of the sovereign authorities. Spinoza demonstrates this position in the limit-case of the free state, in which the "subversive opinions"—errors—

are "those views which, simply by being put forward, *dissolve the agreement* by which each person *surrenders their right to act according to one's own judgment*" (*TTP* 253–54, my emphasis). That is, in acting according to one's own judgment in such a way that does not comply with the sovereign's distribution of proximate causes, one dissolves the agreement that grants the sovereignty the sole authority of interpretation. Because Spinoza equates "right" with "power," the sovereign right of interpretation is not of the order of juridical legitimation, but pertains to the power with which a political singularity reproduces itself. Political error thus diminishes the sovereign power in the attempt to usurp its monopoly on interpretation.

A political error of this kind entails a specifically ontological dimension. Drawing attention to the definition of treason as an *attempt* to seize or modify sovereign right of supreme power, Spinoza elucidates it as follows: "I say 'has attempted,' for if it were the case that such persons could only be condemned after the deed was done, a state would generally be seeking to do this too late, after its right had been seized or transferred to someone else" (*TTP* 204). It is important to insist that treason is committed only if an attempt to undermine sovereignty *fails*. Indeed, a failed attempt is an attempt the result of which *cannot come into being* (within a given regime of proximate causes); if, on the other hand, the power of sovereignty is seized—if an error does come into being—in Spinoza's reading, it would be incorrect to interpret this act *within* the demarcated field of subverted sovereignty, whose interpretation deems it an error. In other words, to the extent that the attempt succeeds, it ceases to be an error, for it comes to constitute a different distribution of power and effectivity—a different logic of distribution of proximate causes. Spinoza's association of right with power, on the one hand, and power with interpretation on the other, implies that right is both an ontologically and epistemologically accomplished fact. Treason—a failed attempt to usurp this right—is by contrast a non-accomplished fact, an epistemological error and ontological non-entity. Political error thus underscores the necessity to situate the theory of error in both epistemological and ontological registers; indeed, as Spinoza says: "As regards the difference between a true and a false idea ... *the former is to the latter as being to non-being*" (*E* II, P43S; my emphasis).

A political error of this kind still remains within the general definition of error in Spinoza as misattribution of cause and effect, because it is the sole right of the sovereign authorities to administer the distribution of causes and effects within a given regime. Yet, a political error differs from the first two kinds of error in that it is an attempt at re-demarcating the domains of error and the correct mode of action—that is, an attempt to usurp interpretation is an attempt to restructure the regime of proximate causes established in a singular form of the state. Whereas treason is error and thus relegated to non-being—or, more precisely, it is repressed or even foreclosed—the very same act may have the status of an accomplished fact in a different singular political conjuncture. A political error, then, consists in calling into being that which is relegated to non-being in a given singular regime of proximate causes. Unlike the first and the second kind of error, a political error of this kind entails potential ontological realization—a process that also necessitates an epistemological reconstitution of the relation between error and correct mode of action.

Because a political error threatens to undermine sovereign's monopoly on interpretation, it aims at the very essence of singular sovereignty. As Spinoza argues, "by the annulling [of the essence of a thing] the thing is annulled" (*E* II, P10CS). Because the natural right of sovereignty extends only so far as its power extends, the essence of a singular sovereignty can be determined by way of political error: since the political error threatens to "annul" the power of a singular sovereignty, it points to the very essence of this sovereignty as "that without which the thing can neither be nor be conceived." The political error thus determines the limits of the sovereignty's interpretative power—the demarcation of what it can and cannot allow without thereby undermining its essence. Insofar as the third kind of knowledge seeks to explicate the essences of singular things under the species of eternity (*E* V, P22–29), this kind of political error can be termed "the third kind of error": on the one hand, it explicates the essence of a singular sovereignty, and, on the other hand, it calls into being that which can be regarded as "actual" only *sub specie aeternitatis* (wherein the status of virtual and actual coincide).

Political error of the third kind cannot be considered in terms of a subjective decision, but must be conceptualized as a necessary mode of political existence. Just as a state consists of its citizens, for Spinoza, every singularity is necessarily a composite singularity (*E* II, L3A2). The inherent logic of a singularity coincides with its conatus, which constitutes "the actual essence of the thing," amounting to the power "with which each thing endeavors to persist in its own being" (*E* II, P7). Sovereignty, whose right extends as far as its power (to reproduce its regime of proximate causes), consists of the singularities retaining a conatus that is not reducible to any greater unity to which they belong. Balibar aptly notes that an individual thing—for example, state, citizen, concept—must be conceived "as a determinate level of *integration*, incorporating other individuals ('lower' levels of integration) and itself incorporated in 'higher' levels or forms of integration."[11]

With respect to the political error this means that, considered on the level of the integration of the state as a composite singularity, treason is a swerving away by one of the component parts of the state from the logic of proximate causes that constitutes the essence/conatus of the greater body (the state).

According to Spinoza's strategy of interpretation by work of demarcation, the individual body can be said to commit a political error only when considered in the regime of proximate causes that includes the state. At the same time, the very same act of treason, considered on the level of the integration of the erring component part, is a manifestation of a conatus endeavoring to persist in its own being. Spinoza argues that individuals "proceed to reject the laws and act against the magistrate" not because they willingly choose to become criminals, but because they "*are so constituted*" to act in this manner if "the opinions they believe to be true should be outlawed" (*TTP* 255, my emphasis). In other words, if the outlawed doctrines pertain to the essence of a single body, this body commits an error simply by persisting in its own being—in this case this body, as Spinoza says, "*will be unable to obey*" (*TTP* 255, my emphasis). The erring of a conatus, then, is the manifestation of the necessity of a single eternal and infinite substance, insofar as it is an expression of a mode persisting in its own being. The status of such a conatus as error is, therefore, constituted only in a singular regime of proximate causes, and not *sub specie aeternitatis*. *The erring of a conatus does not pertain to its essence, but is one mode of its existence*: the same conatus can be or be conceived without constituting an error.

Neither is a political error an exceptional event, for error is a necessary part of a political existence inherent in any logic of sovereignty. Error as a political potentiality becomes possible due to the fact that no distribution of proximate causes can fully correspond to the order of nature; thus, something that is "real" in the realm of nature—a singular essence—is necessarily repressed in the determination of any logic of sovereignty. On the one hand, even in the limit-case of democracy, "if every person transfers all the power they possess to society, [then] society alone retains the supreme natural right over all things"; on the other hand, "[n]o one will ever be able to transfer his power and (consequently) his right to another person in such a way that he ceases to be a human being" (*TTP* 200, 208). While the sovereign authorities must necessarily proceed *as if* they retain full monopoly on interpretation in the complete transfer of power, every such transfer entails a remainder. Despite the "theoretical" conceptualization of sovereignty that entails "right of sovereign powers to all things," Spinoza points out that in practice "we must admit that each person retains many aspects of his right" (*TTP* 208–9). The distribution of proximate causes as the standard of truth and falsity in the formation of political singularity, thus, necessarily forecloses in its inscription some elements that nonetheless belong to this political singularity at different levels of integration. Just as a political error threatens to diminish the power of the sovereign authorities, it is equally true to say that error is the product of the determination of sovereignty itself.[12] In this respect, Foucault's analysis of error in the work of Canguilhem proves instructive; as Foucault says: "at the most basic level of life, the processes of coding and decoding give way to a chance occurrence that, before becoming a disease, a deficiency, or a monstrosity, is something like a disturbance in the informative system, something like a mistake."[13] In Spinozan terms, this means that error is neither a decision nor an exceptional event, but that *errors are perpetually generated on different levels of integration in the distribution of truth and falsity of a particular regime of proximate causes.*[14]

Unlike the first and second kind of error, the third kind of error becomes truth only retroactively, *in its effects*. The causality implied in the error of the third kind becoming truth differs radically from the causality inherent in the first and second kinds of error. This difference manifests itself in two different conceptions of knowledge: the "representational mode of knowledge," on the one hand, and knowledge as production, on the other. Pierre Macherey insists on Spinoza's radical departure from the Cartesian mode of knowledge, which, in seeking to return effects to their proper causes, "addresses its objects from the point of view of their representation in thought."[15] Contrary to this, Spinoza's central thesis reads as follows: "Nothing exists from whose nature an effect does not follow" (*E* I, P36), thus conceiving of knowledge "in a progression that goes from cause to effects."[16] Macherey elucidates the critical difference between these two conceptions of knowledge: "in Spinoza's statement the principle of causality literally inverts the terms of the traditional principle: from the well-known formula 'nothing is without cause' ... he substitutes 'no cause is without effect,'" thereby short-circuiting the conception of knowledge as a proper representation of an object by a subject. Insofar as an idea consists in the chain of effects it engenders, Macherey argues, Spinoza establishes "a necessary relationship between knowledge and the process of its production."[17] This insight is manifested in the third kind of error: while the error of the first or the second kind seeks to *represent* the cause of a certain effect (in misattributing the relation between the two), the error of the third kind seeks to *engender* a series of effects that open a possibility for the *production* of a new regime of proximate causes. In other words, the truth of the first two kinds of error is established in the proper demarcation of the respective regimes of proximate causes; establishing the truth of the third kind of error, on the other hand, demands a production of an entirely new regime of proximate causes. Hence, only the third kind of error functions according to Spinoza's logic of immanent causality: its truth or falsity is determined solely in its effects; that is, the truth of the third kind of error is produced as an effect of its own effects.

Symptomatic reading

It is now possible to pose the central question: what is the process underlying an error of the third kind becoming truth? If it is the interpretation by the work of demarcation that is able to consider one and the same element both as truth and as falsity on different levels, it must be asked: What is the function of interpretation with regard to the aforementioned process?

These questions outline the task of Althusser's project in *Reading Capital*, especially as regards to his conception of symptomatic reading as epistemological rupture. Althusser investigates the mode of reading that underlies the emergence of a new problematic (or, otherwise put, the "terrain" and "horizon" of a field), wherein the element that manifests itself as a "symptom" in the old problematic becomes a central concept in the coherence of the emergent problematic. Drawing on the shared conceptual constellation of the two projects in question, I propose to consider Althusser's analysis of symptomatic reading as epistemological rupture in conjunction with the Spinozan theory of error: this notion of the symptom—adapted by Althusser from Freudian/Lacanian psychoanalytic theory—is congruent with Spinoza's third kind of error underlying the shift in regimes of proximate causes. In turn, this conjunction enables one to consider the process of error becoming truth in terms of the theory of the *encounter*—encounter between a certain mode of interpretation and the third kind of error.

Spinoza's injunction to interpret according to proximate causes figures centrally in Althusser's adaptation of the psychoanalytic notion of the "symptom" in his analysis of epistemological rupture. Just as Spinoza argues that "[a]ll of our knowledge of the Bible ... must be derived only from the Bible itself" (*TTP* 99), Althusser insists that, rather than imposing an external standard of truth and falsity on the text in question, in the symptomatic reading "we never compare classical theory with anything *except itself*."[18] Akin to Althusser's approach to the text, as Warren Montag succinctly puts it, "[f]or Spinoza nature is a surface without depth; Scripture as part of nature conceals nothing, holds nothing in reserve."[19] It is precisely in this sense that the introduction of the psychoanalytic notion of the symptom proves productive: as Jacques Lacan points out, far from hiding a secret, "symptom acts as a language that enables repression to be expressed."[20] But if a symptom—whether a dream, a slip of the tongue, a joke or a lapse in memory—is an expression, it is so only through interruption, deviation, pulsation—a kind of swerving away from an established logic.

The axiom underlying Althusser's discussion of symptomatic reading as epistemological rupture is that every problematic, which determines the subject and the object as well as their relation in the production of knowledge, includes a blind spot as its structuring condition—a blind spot that manifests itself as symptom, contradiction, equivocation. In this sense, it is not the subject but the problematic itself that determines the questions that can be posed and the answers that can be given: "[science] can only pose problems on the terrain and within the horizon of a definite theoretical structure, its problematic, which constitutes its absolute and definite condition of possibility."[21] At the same time, the limits of a problematic entail a necessary exclusion of elements (objects, problems, questions) not by virtue of their existence outside these limits, but as the effect of the very problematic in question. In Spinozan terms, it is the regime of proximate causes itself that generates error; as Althusser says: "These new objects and problems are necessarily *invisible* in the field of the existing theory, because they are not objects of this theory, because they are *forbidden* by it."[22] Consequently, the possibility of posing the question about the conceptual being of the symptom-error—the very task of symptomatic reading—necessitates a shift in the theoretical problematic itself.

Althusser demonstrates that the symptomatic reading that inaugurates an epistemological rupture in Marx's analysis of classical political economy aims at such structuring omissions. For instance, Marx argues that, in seeking to determine the "value of labour," the classical political economy succumbed to "inextricable confusions and contradictions."[23] This is because labor, as Marx points out, "is … the immanent measure of value, but has itself no value."[24] Yet, in its attempt to determine the "value of labour," classical political economy unwittingly touched upon a question of the value of labor-power—a commodity that the laborer sells and that has to be reproduced, which is "as different from its function, labour, as a machine is from the operations it performs."[25] Yet this error does not merely consist in the misattribution of causes—the confusion of the cause of the value of labor-power for the value of labor—but, as Althusser argues, in the construction of an altogether new object (labor-power) that goes beyond the problematic at hand. As Althusser says, "*it is the correct answer to a question that has just one failing: it was never posed.*"[26] It is a correct answer that is correct only *within a different problematic*; thus, the posing of this question necessitates "a transformation of the *entire* terrain and its *entire* horizon."[27]

Consequently, it is neither Marx nor political economy alone that constitutes the advent of a new epistemological problematic. As Althusser notes: "it is not Marx who intervenes to impose from without on the classical text a discourse which reveals its silence—*it is the classical text itself which tells us that it is silent*: its silence is *its own words*."[28] Just as the process of the third kind of error becoming truth presupposes the *production* of a new regime of proximate causes, a shift in problematics must be grasped as the *production of knowledge*: "What made the *mistake* of political economy possible ... [is] ... the *transformation of the object* ... an object which it produced itself in its operation of knowledge and which did not pre-exist it."[29] Yet, the production of this new object is merely a symptom and must remain in the erring mode of existence until its encounter with the symptomatic reading that demarcates a new problematic in which it gains conceptual significance. Far from being any kind of guarantee, decision or exception, the symptom-error is merely an "unstable index of the possible production of a new theoretical *problematic*."[30] It is, then, only through Marx's intervention that this latent possibility realizes itself in an "epistemological rupture": an error-symptom, due to the new demarcation of the problematic, becomes a *concept*. Hence, such epistemological rupture arises neither as a result of symptomatic reading necessarily nor in the presence of the error-symptom alone, but in an *encounter between the third kind of error and a reading that unfolds its possible effects*.

If a symptom-error indeed gains its status as concept-truth only in an encounter with a particular mode of reading-production, what is the epistemo-ontological status of this symptom-error? In this respect, Lacan's characterization of the unconscious as "pre-ontological" proves decisive. Lacan says: "what truly belongs to the order to the unconscious, is that it is neither being, nor non-being, but the unrealized."[31] The symptom, then, as the expression of something that pertains to the order of the unconscious is witness neither to being nor to non-being; an encounter with interpretation, in turn, is the *realization* of the symptom as concept. This is the ontological presupposition that underlies the consequence that the encounter in an epistemological rupture is conceived in terms of the production of knowledge, which consists in, as Althusser puts it, "making manifest what is latent, but which really means transforming ... something which in a sense *already exists*"—that is to say, realizing it in production.[32]

A Spinozan theory of error further radicalizes this dynamic by collapsing ontology and epistemology: given that "the difference between a true and a false idea [is that] the former is to the latter as being to non-being," the epistemological value of a conatus—as truth or falsity—is of the same order as its ontological status. In other words, the truth of the third kind of error remains pre-ontological (unrealized) until an encounter that is the ontological realization of its effects. Hence, I propose to understand Spinoza's oft-cited dictum that "truth is the standard both of itself and falsity" quite literally: truth, as that which is ontologically realized, is the standard that determines itself (reproduction of itself as truth) and the false, as that which is ontologically unrealized or relegated to non-being as error. One can rephrase the same insight in political terms: the sovereign authorities—understood as the distribution of proximate causes in a singular regime—is the standard of itself (its own interpretation and self-perpetuation) and the error (prohibition of that which threatens to usurp its power). The ontological realization of power is at the same time the realization of its epistemological value as truth or falsity in its effects.

Spinoza's encounter

Althusser's posthumously published theory of the "materialism of the encounter" further clarifies the conditions of the ontological realization of the error-symptom as truth.[33] In the formation of a new problematic or the regime of proximate causes (what in his later writings Althusser calls an "established fact"), this encounter[34] "must be, not a 'brief encounter,' but a lasting encounter, which then becomes the basis for all reality, all necessity, all Meaning and all reason"—a Spinozan insight, for an interpretation according to demarcation of proximate causes considers each inherent logic of a singularity as the standard of distribution of truth and falsity.[35] And if error and its encounter with interpretation manifest themselves as contingency, such contingency is not "a modality of necessity, an exception to it"; instead, Althusser argues, "we must think necessity as the becoming-necessary of the encounter of contingencies"— and contingency as the process of becoming-necessary of the redistribution of proximate causes in a regime.[36] Because the truth of the third kind of error is determined solely in its effects, one must insist on the nonlinear temporality inherent in the production of error as truth: the error does not become truth in the immediacy of the erring conatus, nor does it remain truth forever. Spinoza expresses this insight with regard to the effectivity of Scripture: "Something intended to promote the practice of piety and religion is called sacred and divine and is sacred only *so long as people use it religiously*. ... If they devote that thing to impious purposes, the very object that before was sacred will be rendered unclean and profane" (*TTP* 165, my emphasis). The truth or sanctity of Scripture persists as long as the encounter between Scripture and its interpretation produces the effects of piety; once this encounter ceases, "both words and book will then likewise have neither use nor sanctity"—one and the same Scripture thus becomes a source of error (*TTP* 165). By the same token, an erring conatus may persist as error indefinitely if it fails to produce itself as truth in its effects, or, having fallen into error, it may manifest itself as truth once again in another, different, encounter. As Althusser notes, a lasting encounter "never guarantees that it will continue to last. ... Just as it might not have taken place, it may *no longer* take place."[37]

The theory of the encounter in the process of error becoming truth is exemplified in Spinoza's analysis of the transition from the monarchical form of government during the time of Moses to a lasting quasi-democratic theocracy of the first commonwealth. Although in the initial encounter with God in the formation of the Hebrew state the people commonly decided "to transfer their right to no mortal man but rather to God alone" (*TTP* 213), because the people were so terrified of the voice of God they "plainly abolished the first covenant"— that is, they committed an error with respect to the initial transfer of power— "and absolutely transferred their right to consult God and interpret his edicts to Moses" (*TTP* 214). Thus, the Hebrew state resembled a monarchy where Moses alone "held sovereign majesty" (*TTP* 214). The shift to the quasi-democratic theocracy, wherein Moses left no successor to hold absolute sovereign power after himself, took place in the form of treason. Spinoza locates this shift in a passage in which "two men are accused of having prophesied in the camp" without consulting Moses, thereby, in effect, "usurping the sovereign right" of his monopoly on interpretation (*TTP* 273). Joshua, in following the law, insists on the arrest and the persecution of the two men for this error. Yet, Moses acquits the two men, rebuking Joshua in the following manner: "Are you angry on my account? Would that the whole people of God were prophets" (*TTP* 273). Spinoza explicates this occurrence, in which Moses recognizes the truth of the attempted treason, in the following way: "That is, would that the right of consulting God would succeed in placing the government in the hands of the people themselves" (*TTP* 273). In other words, Moses' refusal to persecute the two men who committed treason is based on the ground of reverting to the initial (missed) encounter between Hebrews and God, wherein "as in a democracy ... [t]he right to consult God, receive laws, and interpret them remained equal for all, and all equally without exception retained the whole administration of the state" (*TTP* 214). The political error, thus, becomes an established practice. With regard to the accusation of treason and Moses' refusal to enforce it, Spinoza writes: "Joshua therefore was not ignorant of the law but of *the requirements of the time* and this is why he was reproached by Moses" (*TTP* 273, my emphasis). In other words, it is Joshua who commits an error (of the first kind), for his judgment of following the old law misses the correct demarcation of proximate causes, that is to say, the "requirements of the time." One must insist, then, that it was not Moses' sovereign decision that inaugurated the theocracy of the first commonwealth, but rather the "requirements of the time" that constituted what Althusser would call a "mutation of a theoretical problematic." Moses' interpretation by way of demarcating the new "requirements of the time" demonstrates that what Joshua—obsoletely—considers a political error is the truth of the new political conjuncture, that is to say, of a new distribution of proximate causes.

Yet, the very condition of the democratic distribution of proximate causes in the first commonwealth contained a potentiality of error threatening to collapse the Hebrew state into a monarchical regime. This condition is evident in the fact that the democratic potential of theocracy is predicated on positing an imaginary function of (an absent) God, since "all these things were more opinion than reality" (*TTP* 214). Likewise, after the death of Moses, both priests and administrative authorities "were seen to be substitutes for [Moses], administering the state *as if the king were absent rather than dead*" (*TTP* 244–45, my emphasis). Because "divine teachings ... acquire the force of a decree not directly from God, but from those who exercise the right of governing and issue edicts or by their mediation," this distribution of proximate causes perpetually retained a potential of usurpation of this interpretative relation to the absent God or king (*TTP* 241). Indeed, in the history of the first commonwealth, the function and authority of interpretation of God's revelations remained a point of continuing strife. In this respect, this history saw a proliferation of different manifestations of an erring conatus in the form of prophets, who "retained so much authority for themselves" and "had more success ... in antagonizing than reforming people by means of the liberty which they usurped to admonish, scold and rebuke" (*TTP* 232). And although "[t]he Hebrew state ... might have lasted for ever," this singular encounter of theocracy—singular, for "no one can now imitate it"—came undone on the very condition that gave it democratic potential: an error, wherein the Hebrews "openly violated the divine Law and demanded to have a man as their king"—that is, wherein they gave one man an absolute interpretative relation to God and to civil affairs (*TTP* 230, 228).

Can it be said that Spinoza's *Theological-Political Treatise* is not merely an analysis of the third kind of error in the theory of encounter, but that it is itself an interpretative encounter with the persistent error of the quasi-democratic theocracy of the first commonwealth? No doubt, Spinoza's text is an urgent intervention in a political conjuncture of his time: the Dutch State is ravaged by permanent turmoil on the basis of theological strife; Spinoza's intervention addresses, as Balibar succinctly puts it, "the collusion between the principle of monarchical authority and religious fundamentalism, which has mobilized the 'multitude' against the interests of the nation."[38] While a detailed inquiry into this point would reach beyond the scope of this paper, one cannot fail to recognize that this political crisis recapitulates the persistent erring in the first commonwealth, insofar as it was founded on the potentiality of the theological usurpation of political power. Indeed, Spinoza's text attempts to produce a theory of the democratic distribution of proximate causes that precludes the engendering of this particular error; namely, the central thesis of the *Theological-Political Treatise* states: "everyone should be allowed the liberty of their own judgment and authority to interpret the fundamentals of faith according to their own mind" (*TTP* 10). With this move, Spinoza seeks to neutralize the potential to usurp political power on theological basis. The relation to God and its interpretation, in Spinoza's view, should be available to everyone as an established practice: a continuous source of error in theocracy becomes truth in Spinoza's conceptualization of a democratic republic.

The penultimate sentence of the *Theological-Political Treatise* reads: "I know that I am human and I may have erred." Indeed, Spinoza's heresy is beyond doubt. Spinoza's reading strategy does not merely enable an analysis of the third kind of error, but also shows that to explicate this error is nothing short of *committing it,* that is, of participating in an encounter between error and interpretation, which means—submitting its potential truth to the judgment of its own effects.

Notes

1   All references to Baruch Spinoza, *Theological-Political Treatise*, ed. by Jonathan I. Israel. and trans. by Michael Silverthorne (Cambridge: Cambridge University Press, 2007).
2   Georges Canguilhem, "The Brain and Thought," trans. by Steven Corcoran and Peter Hallward, *Radical Philosophy* 148 (2008), 16, 17.
3   Michel Foucault, "Life: Experience and Science," trans. by Robert Hurley, in ed. by J. D. Faubion, *Aesthetics, Method, and Epistemology* (New York: New Press, 1998), 476.

4   Foucault, "Life," 476.
5   Evald Ilyenkov, *Dialekticheskaja logika. Ocherki istorii i teorii*, 2nd ed. (Moscow: Politizdat, 1984), 45. All translations of Ilyenkov are mine.
6   For Ilyenkov, the possibility of error in Spinoza is the specific capacity of a "thinking thing" or a thinking body in action. A thinking body is produced by the relations and forces in which it enters: "The intersection and conjunction of a plurality of causal chains may result in the emergence of a thinking body in one case, but in another case – a mere body, stone, tree, etc." (Ilyenkov, *Dialekticheskaja logika*, 43). Thus, a thinking body perpetually undergoes encounters with other bodies modifying and determining it: "a thinking body, when it is inactive, is no longer a thinking body" (Ilyenkov, *Dialekticheskaja logika*, 37). The specificity of the thinking body consists in the fact that it has no pre-determined structure, but has the ability to adapt and form itself in relation to the things it encounters: "not having a single ready-made schema of action in its interiority," the thinking body acts "according to the schema of arrangement and placement of all other bodies, also including its own body" (Ilyenkov, *Dialekticheskaja logika*, 41). For Ilyenkov, this relational determination of the thinking body is what makes error in Spinoza's system possible at all. When a body encounters a thing that is "in itself imperfect, i.e. contingent, then the mode of action adapted to it is also imperfect" (Ilyenkov, *Dialekticheskaja logika*, 45). That this particular mode of action is imperfect means that it is inapplicable and ineffective with regard to other singular things and encounters. The error thus consists in the adaptation of an imperfect mode of action to a thing different from the one that engendered and determined this action.
7   Ilyenkov, *Dialekticheskaja logika*, 43.
8   Ilyenkov, *Dialekticheskaja logika*, 45.
9   Étienne Balibar, "Jus-pactum-lex: On the Constitution of the Subject in the Theologico-Political Treatise," trans. by Ted Stolze, in ed. by Ted Stolze and Warren Montag, *The New Spinoza* (Minneapolis: University of Minnesota Press, 1997), 177.
10 Balibar, "Jus-pactum-lex," 180.
11 Étienne Balibar, *Spinoza: From Individuality to Transindividuality* (Delft: Eburon, 1997), 16.
12 See further the discussion of the importance of "necessary rebel" in Spinoza's notion of the political in Dimitris Vardoulakis, *Sovereignty and Its Other: Toward the Dejustification of Violence* (New York: Fordham University Press, 2013), 122–39.
13 Foucault, "Life," 476.
14 This insight is clearly evident in the mechanisms of biopower. Biopolitics, as a regime of proximate causes that aims at the sustenance of life, nevertheless necessarily precludes *certain forms of life* as errors. Foucault elucidates this dynamic in the function of biopolitical racism as means "to create caesuras within the biological continuum addressed by biopower," which, in turn, "is the precondition for exercising the right to kill"—a condition not only for "destroying the enemy

race," but also for eliminating internal errors, "as a way of regenerating one's own race" (Micheal Foucault, *"Society Must Be Defended": Lectures at the Collège de France*, 1975–6, trans. by David Macey (New York: Picador, 2003), 255–57). Kiarina Kordela further demonstrates that on the level of *sub species aeterninatis*, "the superfluity of life is the basis of the biopolitical normative situation" in which life is the objective (A. Kiarina Kordela, "Horror," *Political Concepts: A Critical Lexicon*, 2015, https://www.politicalconcepts.org/horror-kiarina-kordela/). In a biopolitical regime, therefore, a political error consists precisely in a persistence of a mode of life that such a regime excludes.

15 Pierre Macherey, *Hegel or Spinoza*, trans. by Susan M. Ruddick (Minneapolis: University of Minnesota Press, 2011), 54.

16 Macherey, *Hegel or Spinoza*, 55.

17 Macherey points out that this position comes close to Hegel's conception of knowledge, with a critical difference, however, that not only the Spinozan view remains radically anti-teleological, but also that, "in making thought an attribute of substance, [Spinoza] constitutes its movement as absolutely objective and delivers it from all reference to a subject, even if it be thought itself" (Macherey, *Hegel or Spinoza*, 59).

18 Louis Althusser (with Étienne Balibar), *Reading Capital*, trans. by Ben Brewster (London: Verso, 2009), 22.

19 Warren Montag, *Bodies, Masses, Power: Spinoza and His Contemporaries* (New York: Verso, 1999), 5. Cf. Chapter 1 "Scripture and nature: the materiality of the letter" in the aforecited book, as well as Montag's "Spinoza and Althusser against the Hermeneutics: Interpretation or Intervention?," in ed. by Ann Kaplan and Michael Sprinker, *The Althusserian Legacy* (London: Verso, 1993).

20 Jacques Lacan, *Book III: The Psychoses*, trans. by Russel Grigg, ed. Jacques-Alain Miller (New York: W.W. Norton, 1997), 60.

21 Althusser, *Reading Capital*, 22.

22 Althusser, *Reading Capital*, 27.

23 Karl Marx, *Capital: A Critique of Political Economy, Volume 1*, trans. by Ben Fowkes (London: Penguin Books, 1990), 679.

24 Marx, *Capital*, 677.

25 Marx, *Capital*, 678.

26 Althusser, *Reading Capital*, 22.

27 Althusser, *Reading Capital*, 25.

28 Althusser, *Reading Capital*, 23.

29 Althusser, *Reading Capital*, 25.

30 Althusser, *Reading Capital*, 25, 26.

31 Jacques Lacan, *Book XI: The Four Fundamental Concepts of Psycho-Analysis*, trans. Alan Sheridan, ed. by Jacques-Alain Miller (New York: Norton, 1998), 29, 30.

32 Althusser, *Reading Capital*, 36.

33 While positing a certain continuity between Spinoza's role in Althusser's work of the 1960s and his posthumously published writings, such as "The Underground Current of the Materialism of the Encounter" in *Philosophy of the Encounter: Later Writings, 1978–87*, trans. by G. M. Goshgarian, ed. by François Matheron and Olivier Corpet (London: Verso, 2006), is not without problems, Gregory Elliott and Vittorio Morfino show the pertinence of thinking these texts together. See Gregory Elliott, "Ghostlier Demarcations: On the posthumous edition of Althusser's writings," *Radical Philosophy* 90 (1998); Vittorio Morfino, "An Althusserian Lexicon," trans. by Jason Smith, *Borderlands* 4.2 (2005), http://www.borderlands.net.au/vol4no2_2005/morfino_lexicon.htm.

34 It is clear that this line of inquiry enables, and latently implies, the conceptualization of the third kind of error as an Epicurean-Lucretian *clinamen*. Without going into great detail, it is worth pointing out the consequences that a Spinozan theory of error would have for the theory of the *clinamen*. In his "Lucretius and the Simulacrum," Gilles Deleuze already observes that the *clinamen* "is a kind of conatus" (Gilles Deleuze, "Lucretius and the Simulacrum." *The Logic of Sense*, ed. by Constantin V. Boundas and trans. by Mark Lester and Charles Stivale (New York: Columbia University Press, 1990), 269). For Deleuze, this is justifiable because the *clinamen* is not a "secondary" but "the original determination of the direction of the movement of the atom" (Deleuze, "Lucretius and the Simulacrum," 269)—that is, the manifestation of atom's persistence in its being. In Alain Badiou's conception of the event, on the other hand, *clinamen* is considered a "vanishing term": "The clinamen is outside time, it does not appear in the chain of effects. All effects are subject to the law. The clinamen has neither past … nor future … nor present … It takes place only in order to disappear, *it is its very own disappearance*" (Alain Badiou, *Theory of the Subject*, trans. by Bruno Bosteels (London: Continuum, 2009), 62). In other words, for Badiou, *clinamen* is an exceptional event. Mladen Dolar succinctly summarizes two ways in which *clinamen* has been taken up in the materialist tradition: either as a "constitutive exception" or as "an omnipresent 'universal' principle" (Mladen Dolar, "Tyche, clinamen, den," *Continental Philosophy Review* 46.2 (2013), 232). Dolar, in my opinion correctly, locates Badiou in the first category and Deleuze (together with the young Marx) in the second. The present rendition of the *clinamen* as erring conatus departs from both of these conceptions. On the one hand, the *clinamen* is not an exceptional event that through its swerve constitutes the world while vanishing thereafter: as the third kind of error, the *clinamen* is inherent in and produced by every law. On the other hand, the "swerve" or the error of the *clinamen* cannot be said to be a kind of "universal" principle of substance: this is because the erring of a conatus does not pertain to its essence, but is a mode of its politico-epistemological existence.

35 Althusser, "Materialism of the Encounter," 169.

36 Althusser, "Materialism of the Encounter," 193, 194.
37 Althusser, "Materialism of the Encounter," 174.
38 Étienne Balibar, *Spinoza and Politics*, trans. by Peter Snowdon (London: Verso, 1998), 23.

Bibliography

Althusser, Louis (with Étienne Balibar). *Reading Capital*, trans. by Ben Brewster. London: Verso, 2009.

Althusser, Louis. "The Underground Current of the Materialism of the Encounter," ed. by François Matheron and Olivier Corpet and by G. M. Goshgarian, *Philosophy of the Encounter: Later Writings, 1978–87*. London: Verso, 2006.

Badiou, Alain. *Theory of the Subject*, trans. by Bruno Bosteels. London: Continuum, 2009.

Balibar, Étienne. "Jus-pactum-lex: On the Constitution of the Subject in the Theologico-Political Treatise," ed. by Ted Stolze and Warren Montag, trans. by Ted Stolze, *The New Spinoza*. Minneapolis: University of Minnesota Press, 1997, 171–204.

Balibar, Étienne. *Spinoza: From Individuality to Transindividuality*. Delft: Eburon, 1997.

Balibar, Étienne. *Spinoza and Politics*, trans. by Peter Snowdon. London: Verso, 1998.

Canguilhem, Georges. "The Brain and Thought," trans. by Steven Corcoran and Peter Hallward. *Radical Philosophy* 148 (2008), 7–18.

Deleuze, Gilles. "Lucretius and the Simulacrum," ed. by Constantin V. Boundas, trans. by Mark Lester and Charles Stivale, *The Logic of Sense*. New York: Columbia University Press, 1990, 266–79.

Dolar, Mladen. "Tyche, clinamen, den," *Continental Philosophy Review* 46.2 (2013), 223–39.

Elliott, Gregory. "Ghostlier Demarcations: On the posthumous edition of Althusser's writings," *Radical Philosophy* 90 (1998), 20–32.

Foucault, Michel. "Life: Experience and Science," ed. by J. D. Faubion and trans. by Robert Hurley, *Aesthetics, Method, and Epistemology*. New York: New Press, 1998, 465–78.

Foucault, Michel. "*Society Must Be Defended*": Lectures at the Collège de France, 1975–6, trans. by David Macey. New York: Picador, 2003.

Freud, Sigmund. *The Psychopathology of Everyday Life*, trans. by James Strachey. New York: Norton, 1966.

Ilyenkov, Evald. *Dialekticheskaja logika. Ocherki istorii i teorii*, 2nd ed. Moscow: Politizdat, 1984.

Kiarina Kordela, A. "Horror," *Political Concepts: A Critical Lexicon*, 2015, https://www.politicalconcepts.org/horror-kiarina-kordela/

Lacan, Jacques. *Book III: The Psychoses 1955–1956*, ed. by Jacques-Alain Miller and trans. by Russel Grigg. New York: W.W. Norton, 1997.

Lacan, Jacques. *Book XI: The Four Fundamental Concepts of Psycho-Analysis*, ed. by Jacques-Alain Miller and trans. by Alan Sheridan. New York: W.W. Norton, 1998.

Macherey, Pierre. *Hegel or Spinoza*, trans. by Susan M. Ruddick. Minneapolis: University of Minnesota Press, 2011.

Marx, Karl. *Capital: A Critique of Political Economy, Volume 1*, trans. by Ben Fowkes. London: Penguin Books, 1990.

Montag, Warren. "Spinoza and Althusser against the Hermeneutics: Interpretation or Intervention?" ed. by Ann Kaplan and Michael Sprinker, *The Althusserian Legacy* London: Verso, 1993, 51–81.

Montag, Warren. *Bodies, Masses, Power: Spinoza and His Contemporaries*. New York: Verso, 1999.

Morfino, Vittorio. "An Althusserian Lexicon," trans. by Jason Smith. *Borderlands* 4.2, 2005, http://www.borderlands.net.au/vol4no2_2005/morfino_lexicon.htm

Spinoza, Baruch. *Theological-Political Treatise*, ed. by Jonathan I. Israel, trans. by Michael Silverthorne. Cambridge: Cambridge University Press, 2007.

Spinoza, Baruch. *Ethics: With the Treatise on the Emendation of the Intellect and Selected Letters*, ed. by Seymour Feldman, trans. by Samuel Shirley. Indianapolis: Hackett, 1992.

Vardoulakis, Dimitris. *Sovereignty and Its Other: Toward the Dejustification of Violence*. New York: Fordham University Press, 2013.

6

Spinoza's Immanent Sovereignty: Fantasy and the Decision of Interpretation

A. Kiarina Kordela and Joseph Bermas-Dawes

From absolute immanentism to atheist immanence

Essential to Spinoza's argumentation in the *Theologico-Political Treatise* is the link among power, truth and obedience. Spinoza analyzes these terms not by contrasting religion and politics but rather by analyzing the two spheres side by side. Obedience—to either God or political authority—can be produced out of ignorance and superstition when a subject's passions are manipulated, for example, through "fear of punishment, or from love of any other object" (*TTP* 60). This obedience, however, only "passes into love" when the decrees of authority—God or the state—are seen not as "human law" which is "laid down by man for himself … with a certain object," but as "divine command" which always "involve[s] necessity or truth" (*TTP* 277, n. 28; 59; 58; 63). Obedience that results out of love rather than fear and that perceives laws not as decrees of some potentate but as eternal truths, similar to scientific truths, coincides with freedom. For "man is free, in so far as he is led by reason," and so obeying laws based on their veracity, and not out of fear of punishment, is "to love [authority] out of free choice" (*TTP* 277, n. 27; 62). In this ideal or scientific religion and political state, true faith and obedience to political authority and its laws would become indistinguishable from reason, that is, indistinguishable

---

The query about the status of sovereignty within Spinoza's political philosophy, which motivated us to write the present essay, was first raised in conversations within a student-faculty collaborative research project on Spinoza in the summer of 2015. During that project, in addition to reading Spinoza's own work we edited and discussed the essays contained in the first volume of this collection, some of which have found their way into the present essay.

from observing eternal truths. This overlap of obedience and reason is the ideal of biopower or of what Jacques Lacan calls the university discourse where the new master is knowledge, specified as "not knowledge of everything ... but all-knowing [non pas *savoir-de-tout* ... mais *tout-savoir*]," that is, "nothing other than knowledge," not mastery or power, but *pure* knowledge, which, as such, is said to be "objective knowledge" or "science" or what "in ordinary language is called the bureaucracy."[1] In short, biopower bases itself on the illusion that that the function of knowledge is to reveal objective or eternal truths rather than to sustain authority. Biopower, therefore, appears to be the realization of Spinoza's own ideal State where "decrees" would be "perceived ... not as a law"—that is, not as "an ordinance followed by gain or loss" (i.e., reward or punishment), "depending ... on the will and absolute power of some potentate," and which one obeys only out of fear—"but as an eternal truth," not unlike the truth "that God ... has from eternity decreed that three angles of a triangle are equal to two right angles" (*TTP* 63). In this ideal State, revelation, as the incubator of faith, would be as obsolete as ideology is (purported to be) in biopower's most ideal dreams.[2]

However, Lacan's point about the presumably "objective knowledge" of the discourse of the university is that this knowledge hides the fact that in truth it is enunciated from, and sustains, a position of power. In other words, the hidden underside of this knowledge is the master's command, just as the underside of the discourse of the university is the discourse of the Master—that is, a discourse in which authority unabashedly and proudly presents itself as mastery. While the master in the master's discourse gives a clear order—"he gives a sign (master signifier), and everybody starts running," as Alenka Zupančič puts it[3]—the new master of the university discourse denies any relation to power and hides in the form of objective knowledge. Crucially, as Spinoza knows, the difference lies not in the effect—which in both cases is obedience—but in the subject's respective perspective and motive. In the discourse of the university, the motive of obedience is reason, insofar as the decrees of the law appear to the subject as eternal truths; in the discourse of the master, the motive is "love, or fear or (as is more frequently the case) ... hope and fear together"—but, "in any motive whatever," which includes both cases as well as any other conceivable case, the fact is that one obeys and acts "in submission to the sovereign, and not in virtue of his own authority" (*TTP* 215). And since "it is the fact of obedience, and not the motive for obedience, which makes a man a subject," the fact of obedience posits an absolute limit to freedom, which Spinoza defines by stating "a man is free, in so far as he is led by reason" (*TTP* 276, n. 26). Whether led by reason or love or fear or any motive whatever, whenever one "performs in accordance with the commands of the sovereign," one "is in submission to the sovereign." Hence, when it comes to obedience, the university discourse's reason is just as good as the master discourse's fear, love, or hope. What differs, however, and in fact decreases, in the passage from fear to love, and from there to reason, is the desire for resistance. For "he is most under the dominion of another who with his whole heart determines to obey another's commands," that is he who loves the one who has dominion (*TTP* 215). But loving the one who has dominion is precisely the state of not obeying commands but of observing "eternal truths" out of reason, that is, out of the "true knowledge" of the causes of the laws, that is, of these truths. In Spinoza's words, "[d]ivine rights appear to us … [as] commands, only as long as we are ignorant of their cause; as soon as their cause is known … obedience passes into love of God," hence, "[r]eason … leads us to love God, but cannot lead us to obey Him" (*TTP* 277, n. 28). In our relation to authority, there is no difference between love and reason—in both cases we do not experience ourselves as obeying—and where there is no obedience, there is no question of resistance either.

Several Spinozist thinkers take Spinoza's ideal state with its equation of political power with eternal truth at face value, thus developing politico-philosophical models of absolutely immanent and objective unfoldings of power relations. The epistemological corollary of this interpretation of Spinoza's political power as absolutely immanent finds one of its best formulations in Deleuze's concept of "expression," which rejects "impression" and the "sign" (representation) as a purely imaginary distortion of truth that occurs mostly through anthropomorphic projections. For Deleuze, philosophy and truth lie unambiguously on the side of expression, and revelation and faith equally unambiguously on the side of the sign. In Deleuze's words, a "revelatory" or "imperative sign is not an expression but a confused impression which leads us to believe that the true expressions of God, the laws of nature, are so many commandments."[4] And further, underscoring the imaginary mirror-like character of revelation:

> Revelation is not an expression, but a cultivation of the inexpressible, a confused and relative knowledge through which we lend God determinations analogous to our own (Understanding, Will), only to rescue God's superiority through his eminence in all genera (the supereminent One, etc.).[5]

In the political genus, this supereminent One whom the imaginary tends to render transcendent is the sovereign who, expectedly, becomes the target of critique among the absolute immanentist Spinozists. For instance, in Antonio Negri's words from his essay included in this collection, whether "it is by working on the concept of accumulation of powers," and however we want to understand this, the point is to "get rid of all the political theologies accompanying—as in the case of Schmitt and Agamben, on the right as well as on the left—the post-modern restoration of the concept of sovereignty."[6] Carl Schmitt sums up this tenet of absolute immanentism in the statement "[t]he machine now runs by itself," perfectly predicting Hardt and Negri's conception of a "sovereignty machine."[7] This enmity toward the concept of sovereignty can, according to Schmitt's thesis of a "systematic analogy" between "[t]he metaphysical image that a definite epoch forges of the world" and its "political organization," be read as representative of the political reflection of our era's metaphysical assumptions.[8] Just as the "conception of God [as transcendent] in the seventeenth and eighteenth centuries" matches "the notion of the transcendence of the sovereign vis-à-vis the state," so too does the dominance of the thinking characteristic of "natural science"—which "is based on the rejection of all 'arbitrariness,' and attempts to banish from the realm of the human mind every exception"—match a political structure which does away with the structural exception, that is, the sovereign decision. However, the elimination of this structural excess is impossible because, to invoke Schmitt's justification, the "legal prescription, and the norm of decision, only designates how decisions should be made, not who should decide"; that is, "the law does not designate to whom it gives authority," or, yet again, the "ascription" of the decision to a point "is not achieved with the aid of a norm; it happens the other way around. A point of ascription first determines what a norm is and what normative rightness is."[9] No order is based on itself alone; it always needs an exception on which to ground itself—even as, as we shall see, this excess or exception to structure is not of Schmitt's decisionistic type.

Like Negri, we do not want to restore sovereignty, whether in a contractual or other sense, but we also do not want to sustain Deleuze's thesis that the "opposition of expressions and signs is one of the fundamental principles of Spinozism."[10] For if one rejects "impression" or the "sign" as merely a confused knowledge, one ultimately reverts, in spite of all anti-emanetist intentions, to transcendentalist dualism insofar as such a rejection upholds the sanctity of the attributes against the corruption of the modes. This passage will help us clarify:

Expression itself no longer emanates, no longer resembles anything. And such a result can be obtained only within a perspective of univocity. ... Things in general are modes of divine being, that is, they implicate the same attributes that constitute the nature of this being. ... The things that are produced are not imitations any more than their ideas are models. There is nothing exemplary even in the idea of God, since this is itself, in its formal being, also produced.[11]

From a truly monist perspective, what follows from Deleuze's passage is that signs (modes) implicate the same attributes that constitute the nature of the divine being. Therefore, if modes involve a confused knowledge through which they endeavor to rescue God's superiority, this is due to the fact that the divine attributes *are themselves fallen* from their (transcendentalist) divine status and are craving to be restored in their superiority. To put it in Walter Benjamin's idiom, the "fallenness" of signs expresses that being (or the absolute) itself is fallen, that is, that it, too, is "enfolded into a material history strewn with ... transient ideas."[12] This is the sole coherent meaning of Deleuze's statement that there is nothing exemplary even in the idea of God, since this is itself also produced. It follows that one of the fundamental principles of Spinozism is that expressions and signs stand not in opposition but in an immanent relation with each other, as the true and the false ways in which substance makes itself known.

Accordingly, we want to propose a properly secular (non-transcendentalist or dualist) conception of immanence, on the basis of which we shall unfold the equally and similarly immanent relation between philosophy or truth and revelation or faith. For, above all, in Spinoza's scheme, where "*truth* is the standard both of itself and of the false," revelatory faith (false) must be as indispensable in the constitution of *truth* as the philosophical truth (*E* I, P43S; emphasis added). Implied in our position is also the thesis that the relation between, on the one hand, the *Ethics* and, on the other hand, the *Theologico-Political* and the *Political Treatises* is also one of immanence and continuity.

We maintain that a properly secular, non-transcendentalist—or, as Lacan would say, atheist—system of thought (and of being, i.e., a secular ontology) consists not in the elimination of transcendence but in enfolding it within the plane of immanence. This becomes clear by examining any transcendent concept within an atheist philosophical system, for instance, infinity within Jean-Paul Sartre's phenomenology. If infinity were creeping into our phenomenological immanence from some out-worldly heaven, then it would be fairly easy for secular thought to get rid of it, and absolute immanence could be achieved. However, infinity is wedded to the phenomenological experience as such because: (a) appearance presupposes a perceiving subject, and hence a theoretically infinite multiplicity of 'points of view' from one of which any given subject may perceive the appearing object; and (b) this infinity of points of view remains also within phenomenology a *transcendent* category, that is, a category that is never given empirically—there can never be empirically an infinite number of people perceiving an object. Therefore the transcendence in phenomenological immanence does not emanate from some extra-empirical beyond but is rather the effect of empirical experience itself.[13] This is Lacan's point when he states that "the true formula of atheism is not *God is dead*" but rather "*God is unconscious*"—that is, God is that aspect of conscious thought that is both transcendent to it (inaccessible by it) and enfolded in it, as both its precondition and its effect.[14] Transcendence does not die. Either it reigns from high above (as it does in transcendentalism), or it sinks deep below (as in proper immanentism)—though, as we shall see, its operations, mechanisms and structure in each case are neither the same nor symmetrical nor one another's inversion, but strictly distinct.

Interpretation as immanent sovereignty

We now turn to Spinoza's political writings to address first a question that directly concerns the theme of this collection: what is the relation between the resistance of the mob (*vulgus*, as presented in the *Theologico-Political Treatise*) or the multitude (*multitudo*, as extrapolated in the *Political Treatise*) and political authority (*imperium*)? Given that both authority and resistance are forms of political power, within Spinoza's philosophical edifice they cannot but relate to this power as the two attributes relate to substance. Note that this is the same logical relation of immanence that links truth, at the level of substance, and the true and false of which the prior, higher truth is the standard—according to Spinoza's principle, to repeat, that "truth is the standard both of itself and of the false" (*E* I, P43S). As we know from the *Ethics*, there is only "one substance" which is the immanent, not the transitive, cause of all things," and since "substance cannot be produced by anything else ... it will be the cause of itself" (*E* I, P14C, P18 and P6), which is to say, substance is the potentiality or power of actualizing itself. In the context of ontology, substance is the power of being to actualize itself in the form of modes of its two main attributes, thought and extension. In the political context, substance is the (political) power to actualize itself (as a concrete political formation) in the form, as it were, of its two main attributes:

authority and resistance. Cesare Casarino argues for the same relation between authority and multitude or resistance in his article "Grammars of Conatus; or, On the Primacy of Resistance in Spinoza, Foucault, and Deleuze," where he asserts that, for Spinoza, "resistance is the standard of itself and of power."[15] Warren Montag's analysis of the terms *multitudo* and *imperium* in the *Political Treatise* seems also to point to the same conclusion. Central to Montag's study is TP 3.2, where Spinoza claims that

> the right of the commonwealth, or ... the right of the supreme authorities is nothing else than simple natural right, limited, indeed, by the power, not of every individual, but of the multitude, which is guided, as it were, by one mind—that is, as each individual in the state of nature, so the body and mind of a dominion have as much right as they have power. (*TP* 3.1. and 3.2)

Other than the fact that, as Montag points out, this passage "displaces the individual from the center of political analysis," it is important to note Spinoza's equation of the relationship between mind and body to that of authority and multitude.[16] This becomes more explicit in the next paragraph, where Spinoza states:

> If the commonwealth grant to any man the right, and therewith the authority ... to live after his own mind, by that very act it abandons its own right, and transfers the same to him, to whom it has given such authority. But if it has given this ... authority to live each after his own mind ... to every citizen, it has thereby destroyed itself. (*TP* 3.3)

If authority corresponds to the mind or thought, and the multitude to the body or extension, then this passage reconfirms our thesis that, according to Spinoza's fundamental ontological scheme, authority and the multitude are not two oppositional or hierarchical terms but two expressions of power—not unlike the two attributes in which substance expresses itself.[17]

Now, Spinoza is explicit about three aspects of authority that clearly contradict the absolutely immanentist approach and, initially, might even appear to concur with decisionistic approaches. All three aspects are expressed in the following crucial passage, which in its attempt to define the conditions of resistance and revolution in effect defines authority:

> Contracts or laws, whereby the multitude transfers its right to one council or man, should without doubt be broken, when it is expedient for the general welfare to do so. But to decide this point, whether, that is, it be expedient for the general welfare to break them or not, is within the right of no private person, but of him only who holds dominion; therefore of these laws he who holds dominion remains sole interpreter. (*TP* 4.6)

First aspect: he who holds dominion (i.e., authority) is he who interprets; second aspect: interpretation is decision; and third aspect—as a supplement to the other two—the decision/interpretation of the one who holds dominion concerns ultimately not any laws but specifically sustaining or breaking the very foundational laws through which the multitude transfers its right to one council or man. Spinoza's equation of authority with interpretation *qua* decision seems to lie far from a purely procedural, structural, or mechanistic understanding of power, which is supposedly characteristic of the "modern master" who is reduced to the presumably objective "globalizing logic of the market and procedures," and whose "structure is [supposed to be] horizontal."[18] Michael Hardt and Antonio Negri's conception of "the model of imperial authority" as a kind of "governance without government" is representative of this procedural conception of power which is supposed to follow a "structural logic, at times imperceptible but always and increasingly effective, that sweeps all actors within the order of the whole."[19] Rather, here Spinoza seems to lie closer to Carl Schmitt's thesis that the "[s]overeign is he who decides on the exception," that is, he decides whether the situation of "the suspension of the entire existing order" is to occur.[20] Nevertheless, Spinoza's decision lies also far from Schmitt's corresponding concept, due to the former's intertwining of natural rights, power and civil rights. This is another way of saying that their difference owes to the fact that Spinoza does not begin with humans in a state of nature to which are then added rights and obligations; rather, nature is already strewn with rights and obligations.

It is due to this intertwining between nature and power, as we shall presently see, that the privilege of political interpretation or decision does not belong only to those who possess authority but also to the multitude. This is indicated in Chapter 4 of the *Political Treatise,* where Spinoza describes in what ways authority is bound by law. On the one hand, "if by 'law' we mean civil law … [then] we can not at all say that a commonwealth is bound by laws or can do wrong" because authority has the power "to lay down and interpret the laws, but also abolish the same" and therefore is not restricted by any decree. Hence, in terms of the civil law, authority is unlimited and always in the right. On the other hand, however, if we consider the word "law" as referring to "the general rules which concern all natural things," rather than laws of civil jurisprudence, then authority is bound by the natural law and "a commonwealth does wrong, when it acts against the dictate of reason," that is, "when it does, or suffers to be done, things which may be the cause of its own ruin." For, just as "in the state of nature a man is bound to take heed, that he preserve his independence and be not his own enemy, lest he should destroy himself," dominion is also bound by the natural law—that it not destroy itself through its own actions. "So far, then as" a commonwealth "acts against reason, it fails itself, or does wrong" (*TP* 4.4–5). It is exactly here that we can differentiate Spinoza from Schmitt. While for Schmitt sovereignty is a "principally unlimited authority," Spinoza sets a limit on authority's power—natural law.[21] And it is this limit of the natural law on political authority that interlaces the latter in an immanent relation with the multitude and, hence, with resistance. For this limit inheres in the multitude itself insofar as, as Spinoza states, "authority must be limited not only by the power of the agent, but by the capacity of the object"—that is, the very multitude that authority attempts to render obedient. Spinoza follows this with an analogy to help explain: while I might "say that I can rightfully do what I will with this table, I do not certainly mean, that I have the right to make it eat grass." Equally so, authority does not have "the right to make men wish for this or that, or (what is just as impossible) regard with honour things which excite ridicule or disgust" (*TP* 4.4). If authority, as the agent of power, demands from the multitude, its object, more than it can do, authority breaks its natural right and thereby destroys itself.

The consequence of authority breaking its own natural laws is the transformation of the multitude's fear into indignation. Spinoza states that for authority "to slay and rob subjects, ravish maidens and the like, turns fear into indignation and the civil state into a state of enmity." This occurs when authority does not observe reason and its "maxims and motives of fear and reverence"—that is, when it imposes laws that "cannot be broken, without at the same time weakening the commonwealth's strength, that is, without at the same time changing to indignation the common fear of most of the citizens." In such a case, "the commonwealth is dissolved" by its own actions and the "contract [between multitude and authority] is vindicated not by the civil law, but by the law of war" (*TP* 4.4–6). In other words, the indignation or revolt of the multitude coincides with authority's self-destruction. Since, as we have seen, authority and the resistance of the multitude correspond to the two attributes of substance—mind and body—and since, as we know from Spinoza, one attribute cannot limit another, the limitation of any attribute can come only from itself. Therefore, the revolt of the multitude is the manifestation (on the attribute of the body) of the authority's self-limitation or self-destruction (on the attribute of the mind). Put differently, the moment of revolt and the dissolution of authority is one in which two acts of interpretation coincide: the authority's decision to transgress the maxims of reason (its own natural law), and the multitude's decision that authority has indeed transgressed the maxims of reason by expecting its object (the multitude itself) to do or comply with things that oppose its own nature. To be sure, as will increasingly become clear below, the concept of "decision" is not in the least to be associated with any notion of "free will." It should also be noted that the authority's transgression of its own natural laws, or, what amounts to the same, the multitude's resistance, does not necessarily entail the triumph of resistance; sometimes, it can simply reinforce authority, that is, it can make it more authoritarian. In this regard too, Spinoza's scheme is not teleological.

As we have seen, far from being purely procedural, in Spinoza, power involves the sovereignty of decision, which is always made in the act of interpretation. Here we also understand that this decision is determined by the limitations on authority posed by its own natural law, which is at the same time the law that determines the limitations of the object (multitude). In other words, the ultimate arbitrator regarding the sovereign decision (and concomitantly the possibility of resistance on the part of the multitude) is the natural law that determines the limits of both authority and its object (multitude). It is because of this common determination of the limitations of the object (multitude) and the limitations of authority by these same natural laws that authority and the multitude's resistance stand in an immanent relation. This immanent relation between authority and the multitude is presupposed for modern power, which as Michel Foucault has put it, "is exercised only over free subjects, and only insofar as they are free," with the result that "there is no face-to-face confrontation of power and freedom."[22]

This immanent relation between authority and multitude entails that, in Spinoza's political theory, the function of interpretative decision far exceeds both the realm of jurisprudence and the realm of the decision regarding the state of exception or that regarding the moment of the revolution. In fact, the interpretative decision permeates every single aspect of the multitude's life. The point is not simply that he who "holds dominion [is he] to whom are entrusted by common consent affairs of state—such as the laying down, interpretation, and abrogation of laws," that is, the design, interpretation and suspension of the laws (*TP* 2.17). Rather, the point is that Spinoza's dominion extends beyond the interpretation of legal and political doctrine to "spiritual rights," of which sovereigns "ought to be the interpreters and the champions" (*TTP* 245). For "[t]he firmest dominion belongs to the sovereign who has most influence over the minds [*animos*] of his subjects," and "[w]e all know what weight spiritual right and authority carries in the popular mind [*animos*]. ... We may even say that those who wield such authority have the most complete sway over the popular mind" (*TTP* 215, 252).[23] For only by influencing spiritual matters does authority have the maximum influence on the minds of the multitude, which carry the interpretative task of deciding whether authority has infringed its own and the multitude's natural laws. In other words, what belongs within the limits of what the multitude's nature can suffer is not written in stone but is itself a matter of the multitude's interpretation, and, hence, malleable. It is for this reason that Spinoza adamantly opposes the separation between political authority and the church: "I do not pause to consider the arguments of those who wish to separate secular rights from spiritual rights, placing the former under the controls of the sovereign, and the latter under the control of the universal Church" (*TTP* 251). It is "the function of the sovereign only to decide the limits of our duty toward our neighbor—in other words, to determine how we should obey God," that is, how we should "rightly practice piety or obedience to God," which is the same as "obey[ing] the sovereign power's commands in all things" (*TTP* 249–50). In all respects—"[w]hether we look to the abstract truth, or the security of states, or the increase of piety"—"we are compelled to maintain that the Divine right, or the right of control of spiritual matters, depends absolutely on the decree of the sovereign, who is its legitimate interpreter and champion" (*TTP* 254). Thus, the business of this sovereign interpreter is not only the interpretation of law within the context of the legal order or, at least partly, the decision regarding the exception, but also to distinguish between piety and sacrilege in the minds of the multitude. *A fortiori*, in this Divine right—"the right of control of spiritual matters"—resides the very essence of sovereignty. For: "What is left for the sovereign power to decide on, if this right be denied him?" To which Spinoza responds: "Certainly nothing concerning either war or peace," for "if he has to ask another man's opinion" as to what is "pious or impious," everything "would depend on the verdict" of this other person who would have "the right of deciding ... what was pious or impious," and who, by this token would "gradually acquire ... complete control over the kings, till at last he himself [would] mount ... to the summits of dominion," as was the case with "the Pope of Rome" (*TTP* 253). Spinoza's sovereign interpretation, therefore, differs from Schmitt's in being immanent in the multitude and diffused in the everyday, insofar as it is determined by the limitations of the object (multitude) and permeates the process of subjectivation, that is, the constitution of subjects within the multitude at every moment and in every aspect of their existence.

Parenthetically, note that this granting of "spiritual rights" to the sovereign aligns with Spinoza's distinction between "the outward observances of piety" and the "inward worship of God." As he states, when it comes to the sovereign's right over spiritual matters, "I speak only of the outward observances of piety and the external rites of religion, not of ... the inward worship of God ... and piety," which "are within the sphere of everyone's private rights" (*TTP* 245-46). This privileging of outward piety over internal worship concurs with Robert Pfaller's analysis of the importance of a negative space between the subject and interpellation in Louis Althusser, especially in the context of Christian ideology. Pfaller claims that "[b]y metaphysically devaluing the materiality of Christian ideology"—the "enormous positivity materialized in a powerful apparatus at work in perfectly visible rituals"—"negation fulfills the function of 'internalizing' this ideology." In other words, "the theoretical misrecognition of the importance of rituals" is a "crucial feature of ideology" because it creates a negative space where the subject can distance himself from said ideology, and yet, continue to stay within it. In fact, this distance or "this 'gesture of calling into question the identity conferred on me by way of interpellation' is a necessary part of interpellation."[24] For Spinoza, this space is the sphere of private worship, which allows for "an imaginary transgression of imaginary subjectivity," that is, it allows us to assume that we are more than whatever identity has interpellated us.[25] Private worship is thus an imaginary space which is nevertheless necessary for the creation of obedient subjects.

From imagination to fantasy

Deleuze claims that "knowledge through signs is never expressive, and remains of the first kind [of knowledge]," that is, imaginary knowledge.[26] This means that revelation and faith pertain to the first kind of knowledge. As we have seen, Deleuze excludes revelation from the realm of expression—which alone has the potential of knowledge—as a confusing impression. The realm of knowledge, or expression, on the other hand, consists of all three types of knowledge, since each builds upon the others, from inadequate (first kind or imagination) to more adequate (second kind or reason), to the most adequate (third kind or intuition). As Deleuze himself acknowledges, there is a "certain occasional relation that explains the possibility of the leap from" the first to the second kind of knowledge, from imagination to reason. This is because "there is a necessary harmony between the properties of the imagination and those of the common notions [of the second kind of knowledge], such that the latter depends on the properties of the former," and, "insofar as they apply solely to existing bodies, the common notions have to do with things that can be imagined."[27] Imagination as the first kind of knowledge cannot be linked to revelation, since it is part of knowledge—in fact, a necessary part since adequate knowledge can be obtained only through inadequate knowledge. Put differently, imagination has always the potential of being recuperated as adequate knowledge, whereas, revelation never does. In short, contrary to Deleuze's equation of revelation with imagination, we have to conclude that Spinoza severs any knowledge—whose ideas, however inadequate, can always be recuperated within the cognitive process that leads to truth—from revelation and faith. The latter pertain to a status of thought other than that of knowledge.

We propose that Spinoza's distinction between the imaginary or the first kind of knowledge and faith in revelation reflects the psychoanalytic distinction between imagination and fantasy, or, in Laplanche and Pontalis words, "the faculty of imagining (the philosophers' Einbildungskraft)" and fantasy, "the German 'Phantasie.'" The latter initially "used to denote the imagination ... as the imaginary world and its contents, the imaginings or fantasies into which the poet or the neurotic so willingly withdraws." In this "opposition," which "antedates psychoanalysis by centuries," the faculty of imagination was considered to be a part of reality indispensable in attaining truth, whereas the fantastic world was defined in terms of what "the world of reality" is not.[28] According to this pre-psychoanalytic model, it would appear that, in Spinoza too, only the first kind of knowledge or imagination pertains to reality and partakes in the formation of truth, while faith and revelation are reducible to the purely negative category of reverie, whose sole redeemable value consists in inspiring obedience in the ignorant and superstitious masses. (It is this model that is effectively reflected in Deleuze's reading.) If everybody were enlightened, revelation and faith would be redundant and everybody would have direct access to truth.

However, we want to suggest that Spinoza's treatment of faith and revelation anticipates the psychoanalytic treatment of fantasy, in which, again in Laplanche and Pontalis' words, "the status of fantasy"— which constitutes "the fundamental object of psychoanalysis," that is, the "unconscious"—"cannot be found within the framework of the opposition reality-illusion (imaginary)" but rather pertains to "a third category, that of structure" or "the 'symbolic order' [as] defined by Lévi-Strauss and Lacan."[29] By this symbolic order is meant "an organization made of signifiers anteceding the effect of the event and the signified as a whole," a "pre-structure inaccessible to the subject"—in short a network of differential relations among empty or senseless values.[30] This nonsensical pre-structure is the structure of the unconscious itself, insofar as, in Lacan's words, "[w]hat is there ... when it is a question of the unconscious of the subject ... [consists of] irreducible, *non-sensical*—composed of non-meanings—signifying elements."[31] Here, we must draw the important distinction "between the original and the secondary fantasies (whether repressed or conscious)."[32] The pre-structure of the unconscious is the primary or original fantasy presupposed for any secondary fantasy, conscious or unconscious (i.e., repressed). In secondary fantasies, "the scenario is basically in the first person, and the subject's place clear and invariable. The organization is ... weighted by the ego."[33] By contrast, "the Urphantasien, primal (or original) fantasy," which can be recovered "beneath the diversity of individual fables," is "characterized by the absence of subjectivization, and the subject is present in the scene: The child, for instance, is one character amongst many in the fantasy 'a child is beaten.'"[34] The issue in being present in the scene beyond subjectivation is not simply a matter of "recogniz[ing] the equivalence" between active and passive, beating and being beaten, for "so long as there is some idea of a subject, even if playing a passive role," the protagonists persist and we cannot "reach the structure of deepest fantasy," as "a purely transcendental schema" that "provides the possibility of experience."[35] Since it is "impossible to determine whether the primal scene"—of one's own conception during the parent's sexual act—"is something truly experienced by the subject, or a fiction, we must in the last resort seek a foundation in something which transcends both individual experience and what is imagined"[36]—this foundation beyond both actual event in reality and fiction or secondary fantasy is what the deepest or primary fantasy provides.

Inversely put, primary fantasy or the pre-structure of the unconscious is something that needs to manifest itself both as reality or truth and as fiction (secondary fantasy). That is, the *truth* of the unconscious or of the primary fantasy needs to be told both as the truth about reality and as a fiction or secondary fantasy (a reaction engendered by the very same reality)—both as philosophical truth and as revelatory faith. That is, the pure or empty structurality of the primary fantasy is the standard of both itself (philosophy/knowledge) and the false (revelation/faith). Yet again, truth or the unconscious is the standard of both itself—(philosophical) truth—and of the false (faith).

Spinoza's secondary and primary fantasies

Already in the preface of his *Theologico-Political Treatise,* Spinoza introduces two individual types of subjects which are recurrently referenced throughout Spinoza's political texts—the "Philosophical Reader," who has seen the light of reason and is the intended audience of Spinoza's treatise, and the passion-driven member of the *vulgus* (*TTP* 11). The subject of reason "would keep most religiously to [his] compact in [his] desire for the chief good, namely, the preservation of the state, and would cherish good faith above all things," because he understands the law as eternal truth. By contrast, this is not possible for the superstitious commoner who, in his lack of reason, "is drawn away by his pleasure" and needs some form of master, feared or loved, to induce obedience in him (*TTP* 204). But, as we have seen Spinoza argue later in his treatise, the above difference is only one of perspective and motive, not of effect (obedience), which is also to say it is a subjective difference in precisely the sense of the subjectivity that characterizes the secondary fantasy. Were we to dissolve the ego in each fantasy—the ego of the philosophical reader and that of the superstitious commoner—we would discover that the one is the underside of the other, or what amounts to the same, that what appears as difference between two individuated subjects is in truth an internal split of subjectivity. In other words, the man of reason and the man of superstition are the protagonists of Spinoza's two interlaced secondary phantasies regarding the workings of power. And it is only at the level of the primary phantasy that the individuated subjective positions dissolve and reveal the internal split that is constitutive of subjectivity.

That Spinoza's subject of reason and subject of superstition are not two distinct individuals follows from Spinoza's conception of subjectivity, which, according to Étienne Balibar, replaces the individuality of the subject with "transindividuality, or a 'transindividual process of individuation.'"[37] The subject for Spinoza is a unity which "is composed of some parts" insofar as this unity "relates [the subject] to an infinite multiplicity of other individuals."[38] Subjects are not discrete entities but are always caught up in an immanent network in which they are actively further individuated or produced. It is in this sense that Balibar argues that "'substance' and 'individuality' are reciprocal concepts," that is, "'substance' (or God, or Nature) is an infinite process of production of multiple individuals, whereas 'individuals,' being all different and all causally dependent, are the necessary existence of the substance." This is exactly what it means when Spinoza asserts that substance is the "immanent, not the transitive, cause of all things": substance does not externally cause modes or individuals to exist but, rather, substance actualizes itself as these modes of empirical existence (*E* I, P18). In short, "'substance' is nothing other than the individuals."[39] In this way, the two dimensions of reason and superstition cannot, in Spinoza's own account of subjectivity, be separated but rather they reflect the two dimensions of a subject whose transindividual constitution determines it to be always split—reflecting the split between substance's two cardinal attributes (thought and extension), and further, the split between all other equivalents of the attributes such as the internal division in truth between what functions as truth and what as false and the split of political power between authority and resistance. From the perspective of eternity, or truth at the level of substance, the two aspects of subjectivity—reason and faith—are on equal footing, but, as the two ways in which truth narrates itself in time. The aspect on the side of the false is always considered to be inferior, which is why it is often misrecognized or entirely ignored (suppressed and even repressed).

Spinoza's secondary fantasies are generated out of his primary fantasy, according to which (transindividual) subjectivity always involves both reason and faith or superstition. Thus, while Spinoza makes a clear distinction between philosophy and revelation—"the sphere of reason is ... truth and wisdom; the sphere of theology is piety and obedience"—he also takes pains to show that these two domains essentially support, rather than oppose, one another (*TTP* 194). This endeavor consists primarily of two moves: first his persistence that, although reason and theology pertain to different domains (truth and obedience, respectively), nevertheless belief in theology should be accepted by reason; and, second, his persistence in recuperating as part of theology even those parts of Scripture to which reason would clearly object.

Beginning with the first move, Spinoza asks "[w]hy ... should we believe in ... the basis of theology"—"the doctrine that man may be saved by obedience alone"—even though it "cannot be proved by reason whether it be true or false" (*TTP* 195). Spinoza answers that "the only reason ... which we have for belief in Scripture or the writings of the prophets, is the doctrine we find therein, and"—it is important to add, particularly for the second move below—"the signs by which it is confirmed." This doctrine consists in "extol[ing] charity and justice above all" and in the prophets' conviction "that men might become blessed through obedience." This "morality [the prophets] teach is in evident agreement with reason, for it is no accidental coincidence that the Word of God which we find in the prophets coincides with the Word of God written in our hearts" by the natural light of reason. Both reason and the Scripture concur in "the Word of God," which is defined as "the scheme and manner of obedience, or the true dogmas of piety and faith." So, while theology "does not admit of mathematical proof, [it] may yet be accepted with the approval of our judgment"—the judgment of the philosophical reader—because both theology and reason convey the same "Word of God." It is for this reason that the "revelation was necessary." For if "the Word of God" could be told only through reason, then theology would "be proved by reason ... [and] become ... a part of philosophy" (*TTP* 195)—which also means that it could be contested by means of reason (it could be deconstructed, as we would say today), unlike faith, which by definition can neither be grounded on reason nor undermined by it. Which is why *"simple obedience is the path of salvation,"* that is, "it is enough for salvation or blessedness, that we should embrace the Divine decrees as laws or commands; there is no need to conceive them as eternal truths" (*TTP* 276, n. 25). In fact, if salvation were possible only through reason—that is, through the conception of law as eternal truth—the "salvation of nearly all men" would be impossible, which is why Spinoza considers "the utility and need for Holy Scripture or Revelation to be very great" and concludes that "the bible has brought a very great consolation to mankind" (*TTP* 198–99).

Turning to the second move, Spinoza begins with an inequivalence between Scripture and theology. Theology, he writes, is "revelation in so far as it indicates the object aimed at by Scripture—namely, the scheme and manner of obedience, or the true dogmas of piety and faith. This may truly be called the Word of God." Theology—that is, revelation or the Word of God—is not the same as Scripture; the former is the object aimed at by the latter, namely: the dogmas of piety and faith. Thus, Spinoza can initially avow that not everything in Scripture seems to serve this aim—there is also much in Scripture that is "repugnant to reason," such as the "signs and wonders" by which the doctrine is confirmed by the prophets (*TTP* 3). Yet, he continues, this "has … no bearing on theology or the Word of God," for, as we saw above, "if we regard its precepts or rules of life" and "if we look to its aim and object, [theology] will be seen to be in nowise repugnant" to reason but, rather, "will be found in accordance with reason" (*TTP* 195). Thus, whatever the signs by which the prophets confirm the Word of God, and however repugnant they may otherwise be to reason, they must nevertheless be accepted as conducive to conveying "the Word of God."

Interpretation on the levels of reason, faith, and primary fantasy, or, the inseparability of truth and master

The sovereignty of interpretation is so diffusive that it operates from within both conscious domains of thought, revelation and philosophy, being practiced by both the practitioners of each and their receivers—that is, by everybody involved in the multitude and in authority, that is, in both, since they are always intertwined. And because it operates in both, albeit as we shall see in different ways, it indicates certain affinities in their respective methodologies.

We turn first to philosophy, and specifically to Spinoza's own *Ethics*, as a case that, because of its geometrical method can lead to the impression that, as Alain Badiou has argued, it is reducible to mathematical logic and, hence, it does not involve interpretation. As Joe Hughes argues in the first volume of this collection, the method of proof in the *Ethics* exceeds the "merely logical proof" in that it acknowledges "an inescapable apprenticeship through which thought learns to create" ideas. Spinoza's proofs always necessitate something beyond mathematical formalism because true ideas "can only be discovered, in so far as they are invented."[40] If proof involves discovery, historicity, and the potential of radical retroactive reconstitution of sense, then truth (philosophical or political) cannot be reduced to mathematical logic (just as it cannot be reduced to objective knowledge or procedural operations). Truth is produced, created, or invented in a kind of interpretation that is intrinsic to its own process of invention—a dimension that, along with temporality, points to truth's affinities with revelation.

Revelation, too, involves the work of interpretation, for, as Spinoza states, "a prophet is one who interprets the revelations of God to those who are unable to attain to sure knowledge of the matters revealed" (*TTP* 13). But the interpretation involved in revelation, as Spinoza notes, works "not on the truth of passages, but solely on their meaning," that is, interprets Scripture "solely by means of the signification of the words, or by a reason acknowledging no foundation but Scripture" (*TTP* 101). Meaning can only be established in the context of a fiction; to exemplify this we turn to a famous scene in the Scripture. While Deleuze's reading of Spinoza's analysis of the primal fall is confined within the recognition that Adam mistakes God's eternal truth for a moral command, we would argue that Adam's problem is not that he is moralizing but that he needs a cause for action. God tells Adam that he will die if he eats the fruit, but nothing in this statement indicates whether Adam should prefer to live rather than die, and this preference in itself presupposes an end (to live) as better than another end (to die).[41] Many Spinozists tend to assume that self-preservation or survival is the evident referent of Spinoza's *conatus*, but *conatus* concerns not any preservation whatsoever but each thing's striving "to persevere in its being" (*E* III, P6). This, as argued elsewhere, entails that *conatus* encompasses the death drive, up to and including literal death.[42] In other words, the decision to die or live, to eat of the fruit or not, requires a *telos*, which itself can be established not on the basis of reason or truth but only on a fiction. It is only with this fiction that God's statement can begin to have any meaning, that is, to point to a specific action. The interpretation performed on the level of revelation deals exactly with this negotiation of (eternal) truth and *telos* or fiction in deriving meaning.

The above two rough sketches account for interpretation as it operates on the level of the true and the false, that is, within the two secondary fantasies: the one that functions as truth (philosophy), and the other that functions as false (revelation). And, as we know, these two have as their standard *truth*, which, as we have argued, is reflected only on the level of the primary fantasy. There, the two ostensibly opposite sides (true and false) are revealed as the inseparable two expressions (attributes) of the same substance, and hence as equally essential. We want now to turn once again to Spinoza's primary fantasy, so as to examine his method of interpretation on that level, where reason or truth and revelation or faith are equally essential.

Spinoza's method of scriptural interpretation may at first strike the reader as inconsistent, if not arbitrary. This becomes particularly evident in Spinoza's identification of close textual reading with contextual analysis, and, further, with his sliding between the two in ways that could give room for apparently arbitrary decisions as to when the supplementary contextual information is or is not needed. Let us follow Spinoza's line of reasoning. He first announces that his interpretational approach attempts at an immanent reading of scripture— where meaning is derived "from Scripture alone" (*TTP* 100). Then, Spinoza feels no contradiction in adding to this that often supplementary information from outside the text is also needed, such as "the life, the conduct, and the studies of the author of each book, who he was, what was the occasion, and the epoch of his writing, whom did he write for, and in what language." And, further, we "should inquire into the fate of each book," from "how it was first received" and its entire itinerary all the way up to "how all the books now universally accepted as sacred, were united into a single whole" (*TTP* 103). In short, in what we could call a proto-Derridian gesture of framing, Spinoza presents the "'history' of Scripture" as if it were part of Scripture itself, and proposes both that "[o]ur knowledge of Scripture must ... be looked for in Scripture only" and that the "universal rule ... in interpreting Scripture is ... [that] we examine it in the light of its history"—without, however, indicating any need to justify the apparent contradiction (*TTP* 100–101). Instead, Spinoza sees in need of justification the division between cases that require the examination of "history" or the context and those that do not. He proposes that a major criterion consists in that "matters which by their nature are easily perceived cannot be expressed so obscurely as to be unintelligible," such as in the case of Euclid who wrote of "matters very simple and easily understood ... [and therefore] we can follow his intention perfectly" (*TTP* 113). While geometry is evidently simple and easily understood, matters such as prophecies and miracles are not, as here "it is necessary to know the opinions of those who first related them ... and to distinguish such opinions from the actual impression made upon their senses, otherwise we shall confound ... actual events with symbolical and imaginary ones" (*TTP* 93).

However convincing or not this criterion may sound, Spinoza then turns to comparisons among prophets. There he makes a great distinction between the "prophecies of Moses and those of other prophets," on the basis of the claim that Moses' revelations were the "only instance of a real voice," as opposed to all other prophets who relied on signs of their own imagination (*TTP* 15). As evidence for this unique instance of God's real voice in revelation Spinoza initially seems to reference the Scripture, testifying to that "Moses found God ready to commune with him any time" and other passages where Moses' "face to face" conversations with God are detailed. By contrast, to prove that other prophets did not in fact hear the real voice of God, but had instead only imaginary hallucinations, Spinoza invokes the prophet's biographical context. For instance, as opposed to Moses, Samuel's prophecies can be inferred to have imaginary causes because the voice he attributed to God had a "resemblance to the voice of Eli, which Samuel was in the habit of hearing and therefore might easily imagine" (*TTP* 15–16). However, as it becomes clear in more than one chapters in the *Theologico-Political Treatise*, the authenticity of Moses' testimony is grounded not so much in the Scripture but in "history"—yet, unlike in Samuel's case, not just in Moses' biographical history but in the history of the Hebrew nation. Thus, both Spinoza's interpretation of Moses and that of Samuel *are* contextual, with the difference that Samuel's context is reduced to his individual psychological connections, whereas Moses' to broader historical exigencies. The Hebrew history postulates that Moses' words be taken as God's own words and truth—and this even as Spinoza elsewhere admits that "no one except Christ received the revelations of God without the aid of imagination, whether in words or vision" (*TTP* 19). What motivates Spinoza's apparently arbitrary interpretative decision to equate the voice of Moses purportedly hears with that of God, in blatant contradiction with his overall argument about prophets?

As opposed to the orthodoxy of Scriptural interpretation, which implies the "election of God" as the supernatural favoring of the Hebrew nation, Spinoza argues that "the Hebrew nation was not chosen by God in respect to its wisdom nor its tranquility of mind, but in respect to its social organization and the good fortune with which it obtained supremacy and kept it for so many years" (*TTP* 45 and 46). This social organization is made superior, not by supernatural miracle, but by the "law of Moses ... which was set up as a national standard of right"— Moses being the "the sole promulgator and interpreter of the Divine laws" (*TTP* 17). Here we have to recall that the sole divine law promulgated through revelation concerns the dogmas of piety and obedience, that is, it is the most human law insofar as it expresses "a plan of living which serves only to render life and the state secure." For Spinoza, however, it is crucial that the two (human and divine law) be inseparable—as long as they concern precisely nothing further than obedience and the security of life and the state. Thus, Spinoza adds that "although [the law of Moses] was not universal, but entirely adapted to the disposition and particular preservation of a single people, [it] may still yet be called the law of God or Divine law, inasmuch as we believe that it was ratified by prophetic insight"—ignoring that, according to his own argument, prophetic insight is based on imagination (*TTP* 61). Moreover, Moses' law which "God spoke Himself, having descended from heaven to Mount Sinai for the purpose ... only ordained that Jews should believe in [God's] existence and worship Him alone," which for Spinoza amounts to piety and obedience, and nothing else, including anything about God's supposed nature—if anything the law "forbade [the Hebrews] to invent or fashion any likeness of the Deity" (*TTP* 17). Now, it is evident in Scripture that Moses preached of a transcendent God and authority, but the reason for this is that the Hebrews, as "uncultivated and sunk in the most abject slavery," did not have "any sound notions about the Deity." Thus, Moses was forced to teach "the rule of right living [obedience] ... not like a philosopher ... but like a lawgiver compelling them to be moral by legal authority." This meant that for the Hebrews "the rule of right living, the worship and love of God, was to them rather a bondage than the true liberty, the gift and grace of the Deity"—but as long as the effect was obedience, this did not matter. It is not the means of revelation that matters—a transcendent God or authority—it is rather its function as a cultivator of obedience. This is what Spinoza means when he says that "we are only bound to believe in the prophetic writings, the object and substance of the revelation; with regard to the details, every one may believe or not, as he likes" (*TTP* 40–41). God's real voice, which imparted upon Moses the law for the Hebrew nation, only prescribed the theological-moral dictates of obedience and not the worship of a transcendent God. Thus, by interpreting Moses' revelation as conveying God's actual voice, Spinoza distances the religion of a transcendent God and authority from his conception of the Word of God or theology. This is the reasoning behind the apparent arbitrariness of Spinoza's interpretational method.

Behind Spinoza's ostensibly arbitrary moves in his scriptural interpretation, there is a simple criterion. The decisions he makes aim at securing a secular God that is not imbued with any personalistic or supernatural traits, but is instead only a "natural cause"—according to his thesis that "Nature is the power of God" (TTP 25)—and whose Word concerns no other matter but its efficacy in inciting piety and obedience. Translating this on the level of politics, Spinoza's interpretational method aims at ensuring that we conceive of authority not as transcendent but as pertaining to immanence. Far from entailing the absence of decision, this means that the entire field of power, from the multitude to supreme authority, is permeated by acts of decision—decisions that are ultimately motivated not by truth but by meaning, that is, by power's efficacy or lack thereof. Spinoza's scriptural interpretation performs the proof that gives the lie both to absolute immanentists and, in Zupančič's words, to "the 'democratic masters' … of the university discourse" whose rules demand "that all political decisions be grounded in objective knowledge and follow only from an insight into the factual state of things." Spinoza's method of interpretation points to the irreducibility of "the gap between S2 (the chain of reasons)"—philosophy—"and S1"—the position of mastery or power, which is occupied by anybody who engages in any interpretative act, whether in the realm of revelation or of reason. Spinoza's interpretation endeavors to make us "recognize that it is precisely this gap, on account of which no political decision can be *fully* absorbed into the chain of reasons." As Zupančič aptly puts it referring to a concrete political example, "if the reports about Iraqi nuclear weapons had in fact been true, would the decision to attack Iraq have been any less political? No, it would still be a political decision, and precisely as such it could be countered by a different political decision."[43] Similarly, had God's voice indeed spoken to Moses, Spinoza's decision to claim that it did so would be an equally political decision.

This is why the field of power cannot consist purely of reason or objective knowledge and is inherently intertwined with interpretational decisions, including decisions to legitimize means repugnant to reason if they are necessary for the efficacy of the meaning of revelation. These two aspects of power are equally necessary and inseparable, yet they must be kept separate through their irreducible gap.

Notes

1 Jacques Lacan, *Le Séminaire. Livre XVII: L'envers de la psychanalyse*, ed. Jacques-Alain Miller (Paris: Seuil, 1991), 34; Jacques Lacan, *Book VII. The Other Side of Psychoanalysis*, ed. by Jacques Alain-Miller and trans. by Russell Grigg (New York: W. W. Norton, 2007), 31.
2 See also A. Kiarina Kordela, "Spinoza's Biopolitics," in ed. by A. Kiarina Kordela and Dimitris Vardoulakis, *Spinoza's Authority, Volume 1: Power and Resistance in the Ethics* (London: Bloomsbury, 2017).

3 Alenka Zupančič, "When Surplus Enjoyment Meets Surplus Value," in ed. by Justin Clemens and Russell Grigg, *Jacques Lacan and the Other Side of Psychoanalysis: Reflections on Seminar XVII* (Durham and London: Duke University Press, 2006), 155–278, here 159.
4 Gilles Deleuze, *Expressionism and Philosophy: Spinoza* (New York: Zone Books, 1990), 181.
5 Deleuze, *Expressionism and Philosophy: Spinoza*, 181, 182. We use Deleuze's juxtaposition between "expression" or "reason"—which operates with "common notions"—and "imagination"— which operates by means of "signs"—as a heuristic device for the purpose of our argument rather than as a summation of the Deleuzean position on Spinoza's epistemology. This latter is considerably more nuanced, as passages such as the following indicate: "Considered … in their practical function, [common notions] apply only to thing that can be imagined. Thus they may themselves, in some respects, be likened to images. *The application of common notions implies, in general, a strange harmony between reason and imagination, between the laws of reason and those of imagination*" (Deleuze, *Expressionism and Philosophy: Spinoza*, 294). Nevertheless, there is evidence in Deleuze's otherwise brilliant reading of Spinoza toward a certain transcendentalism that would entail the inferiority of the modes and, consequently, of the sign, compared to the attributes and reason, respectively (see also A. Kiarina Kordela. "Spinoza's Biopolitics," in ed. by Dimitris Vardoulakis and A. Kiarina Kordela. Spinoza's Authority: Volume I: Power and Resistance in the Ethics, Cited from the manuscript (New York: Bloomsbury, 2017).
6 Antonio Negri, "Spinoza: A Different Power to Act," in ed. by A. Kiarina Kordela and Dimitris Vardoulakis, *Spinoza's Authority: Spinoza's Authority: Volume I: Power and Resistance in the Ethics* (London: Bloomsbury, 2016).
7 Carl Schmitt, *Political Theology: Four Chapters on the Concept of Sovereignty* (Cambridge: MIT Press, 1985), 48.
8 Schmitt, *Political Theology*, 46.
9 Schmitt, *Political Theology*, 32.
10 Deleuze, *Expressionism in Philosophy: Spinoza*, 182.
11 Deleuze, *Expressionism in Philosophy: Spinoza*, 180, 181.
12 Jim Hansen, "Formalism and Its Malcontents: Benjamin and De Man on the Function of Allegory," *New Literary History* 35.4 (2004), 675.
13 See also A. Kiarina Kordela, *Being, Time, Bios: Capitalism and Ontology* (Albany: State University of New York Press, 2013), 4.
14 Lacan Jacques, *Book XI. The Four Fundamental Concepts of Psychoanalysis*, ed. by Jacques-Alain Miller and trans. by Alan Sheridan (New York: W. W. Norton, 1981), 59.
15 Cesare Casarino, "Grammars of Conatus; or, On the Primacy of Resistance in Spinoza, Foucault, and Deleuze," in ed. by A. Kiarina Kordela and Dimitris

Vardoulakis, *Spinoza's Authority: Spinoza's Authority: Volume I: Power and Resistance in the Ethics* (London: Bloomsbury, 2017), 57–86.

16 Warren Montag, "Who's Afraid of the Multitude? Between the Individual and the State," *South Atlantic Quarterly* 104.4 (2005), 559.

17 With this metaphor, Spinoza sets up a correspondence between politics and ontology, with authority and multitude matching the attributes of thought and extension, respectively. This metaphor, however, should not be read in accordance with the classical tradition of political thought and its, in Balibar's words, "anthropomorphic illusion" of a transcendent sovereign-mind leading the political body, as in "Hobbes' *Mortal God*." Such a reading would contradict Spinoza's parallelism in which "the order and connection of ideas is the same as the order and connection of things," because its sets up a hierarchical relation that privileges the mind or authority as leading the body or multitude (*E* II, P7). As Balibar has argued, this metaphor should be read instead through the understanding that fundamental to Spinoza's ontology is a rethinking of the individual—a new conceptual framework of modal interaction which Balibar calls "trans-individuality." By revealing the structure of power as trans-individual, wherein authority and multitude are constituted in one and the same process and as one and the same "subject," Spinoza's "analysis of political phenomena is," in fact, "the crowning path of a critique of this illusion," and therefore a rejection of precisely such anthropomorphic prejudice in political philosophy (Étienne Balibar, "Potentia multitudinis, quae una veluti mente ducitur: Spinoza on the Body Politic," in ed. by Stephen H. Daniel, *Current Continental Theory and Modern Philosophy* (Evanston: Northwestern University Press, 2005), 94).

18 Marie-Hélène Brousse, "Common Markets and Segregation," in ed. by Justin Clemens and Russell Grigg, *Jacques Lacan and the Other Side of Psycho-analysis: Reflections on Seminar XVII* (Durham and London: Duke University Press, 2006), 259.

19 Michael Hardt and Antonio Negri, *Empire* (Cambridge: Harvard University Press, 2000), 13, 14.

20 Schmitt, *Political Theology*, 5 and 12.

21 Schmitt, *Political Theology*, 12.

22 Michel Foucault, "The Subject and Power," in ed. by Brian Wallis, Art *After Modernism* (New York and Boston: The New Museum of Contemporary Art and David R. Godine, Publisher, Inc., 1999), 428.

23 Note that the reference to the multitude's mind here and throughout the *Theologico-Political Treatise* does not in the least undermine—in fact, it does not even interfere with—the connection we have established between, on the one hand, the body and the multitude, and, on the other hand, mind and authority. This connection was established in the *Political Treatise*, where the word for mind is *mens*—the same as the word designating the one attribute of the substance in the *Ethics*—whereas in the *Theologico-Political Treatise* Spinoza speaks of the *animus*.

24 Robert Pfaller, "Negation and its Reliabilities: An Empty Subject for Ideology?" in ed. by Slavoj Žižek, *Cogito and the Unconscious* (Durham: Duke University Press, 1998), 238, 239; citing Slavoj Žižek, *Tarrying with the Negative: Kant, Hegel and the Critique of Ideology* (Durham: Duke University Press, 1933), 254, n. 39.
25 Pfaller, "Negation and Its Reliabilities," 239.
26 Deleuze, *Expressionism in Philosophy: Spinoza*, 181.
27 Gilles Deleuze, *Spinoza: Practical Philosophy* (San Francisco: City Lights, 1988), 83 and 58.
28 Jean Laplanche, and J. B. Pontalis, "Fantasy and the Origins of Sexuality," in ed. by Riccardo Steiner, *Unconscious Fantasy* (London: Karnac, 2003), 107, 143, here 108.
29 Laplanche and Pontalis, "Fantasy and the Origins of Sexuality," 118, 133, 134, and 122.
30 Laplanche and Pontalis, "Fantasy and the Origins of Sexuality," 122.
31 Lacan, *Book XI. The Four Fundamental Concepts of Psychoanalysis,* 250.
32 Laplanche and Pontalis, "Fantasy and the Origins of Sexuality," 134, 135.
33 Laplanche and Pontalis, "Fantasy and the Origins of Sexuality," 128.
34 Laplanche and Pontalis, "Fantasy and the Origins of Sexuality," 122 and 128.
35 Laplanche and Pontalis, "Fantasy and the Origins of Sexuality," 129 and 122, 123.
36 Laplanche and Pontalis, "Fantasy and the Origins of Sexuality," 121.
37 Étienne Balibar, *Spinoza: From Individuality to Transindividuality* (Delft: Eburon, 1997), 12.
38 Balibar, *Spinoza, From Individuality to Transindividuality,* 8 and 15.
39 Balibar, *Spinoza, From Individuality to Transindividuality,* 8.
40 Joe Hughes, "The Cold Quietness of the Stars: Proof, Rhetoric, and the Authority of Reason in the Ethics," in ed. by Dimitris Vardoulakis and A. Kiarina Kordela, *Spinoza's Authority Volume 1: Power and Resistance in the Ethics* (cited from the manuscript; New York: Bloomsbury, 2017), 10, 17 and 18.
41 See also A. Kiarina Kordela, *$urplus: Spinoza, Lacan* (Albany: State University of New York Press, 2007), 9 and 8.
42 See A. Kiarina Kordela, "A Thought beyond Dualisms, Creationist and Evolutionist Alike," in ed. by Dimitris Vardoulakis, *Spinoza Now* (Minneapolis: University of Minnesota Press, 2011), 321–50.
43 Zupančič, "When Surplus Enjoyment Meets Surplus Value," 176, 177.

Bibliography

Balibar, Étienne. *Spinoza: From Individuality to Transindividuality*. Delft: Eburon, 1997.
Brousse, Marie-Hélène. "Common Markets and Segregation," in ed. by Justin Clemens and Russell Grigg, *Jacques Lacan and the Other Side of Psycho-Analysis: Reflections on Seminar XVII*. Durham and London: Duke University Press, 2006, 245–62.

Casarino, Cesare. "Grammars of Conatus; or, On the Primacy of Resistance in Spinoza, Foucault, and Deleuze," in ed by. Dimitris Vardoulakis and A. Kiarina Kordela, *Spinoza's Authority* I: on the *Ethics*, Cited from the manuscript. New York: Bloomsbury, 2017.

Deleuze, Gilles. *Expressionism and Philosophy: Spinoza*. New York: Zone Books, 1990.

Deleuze, Gilles. *Spinoza, Practical Philosophy*. San Francisco: City Lights, 1988.

Foucault, Michel. "The Subject and Power," in ed. by Brain Wallis, *Art After Modernism*. New York and Boston: The New Museum of Contemporary Art and David R. Godine, Publisher, Inc., 1999, 417–33.

Hansen, Jim. "Formalism and Its Malcontents: Benjamin and De Man on the Function of Allegory," *New Literary History* 35.4 (2004), 663–83.

Hardt, Michael and Negri, Antonio. *Empire*. Cambridge: Harvard University Press, 2000.

Hughes, Joe. "The Cold Quietness of the Stars: Proof, Rhetoric, and the Authority of Reason in the Ethics," in ed. by Dimitris Vardoulakis and A. Kiarina Kordela, *Spinoza's Authority* I: on the *Ethics*, Cited from the manuscript. New York: Bloomsbury, 2017.

Kordela, A. Kiarina. *Being, Time, Bios: Capitalism and Ontology*. Albany: State University of New York Press, 2013.

Kordela, A. Kiarina. *$urplus: Spinoza, Lacan.* Albany: State University of New York Press, 2007.

Kordela, A. Kiarina. "A Thought beyond Dualisms, Creationist and Evolutionist Alike," in ed. by Dimitris Vardoulakis, *Spinoza Now*. University of Minnesota Press, 2011, 494–537.

Kordela, A. Kiarina. "Spinoza's Biopolitics," in ed. by Dimitris Vardoulakis and A. Kiarina Kordela, *Spinoza's Authority: Volume I: Power and Resistance in the Ethics*, Cited from the manuscript. New York: Bloomsbury, 2017.

Lacan, Jacques. 1981. *Book XI. The Four Fundamental Concepts of Psychoanalysis*, ed. by Jacques-Alain Miller and trans. by Alan Sheridan. New York: W. W. Norton.

Laplanche, Jean and Pontalis, J. B. "Fantasy and the Origins of Sexuality," in ed. by Riccardo Steiner, *Unconscious Fantasy*. London: Karnac, 2003, 107–43.

Montag, Warren. "Who's Afraid of the Multitude? Between the Individual and the State," *South Atlantic Quarterly* 104.4 (2005), 655–73.

Negri, Antonio. "Spinoza: A Different Power to Act," in ed. by Dimitris Vardoulakis and A. Kiarina Kordela. *Spinoza's Authority: Volume I: Resistance and Power in the Ethics*, Cited from the manuscript. New York: Bloomsbury Publishing, 2017.

Pfaller, Robert. "Negation and Its Reliabilities: An Empty Subject for Ideology?" in ed. by Slavoj Žižek, *Cogito and the Unconscious*. Durham: Duke University Press, 1998, 225–46.

Schmitt, Carl. *Political Theology: Four Chapters on the Concept of Sovereignty*. Cambridge: MIT, 1985.

Spinoza, Baruch/Benedict de. *The Collected Works of Spinoza*, ed. and trans. by Edwin Curley. Princeton: Princeton University Press, 1985.

Spinoza, Baruch/Benedict de. *A Theologico-Political Treatise and a Political Treatise*, trans. by R. H. M. Elwes. New York: Dover, 1951.

Zupančič, Alenka. "When Surplus Enjoyment Meets Surplus Value," in ed. by Justin Clemens and Grigg Russell, *Jacques Lacan and the Other Side of Psycho-Analysis: Reflections on Seminar XVII*. Durham and London: Duke University Press, 2006, 155–78.

7

Spinoza and Signs:
The Two Covenants and Authority in the *Theological-Political Treatise*

Gregg Lambert

In addition to being a philosopher of pure immanence, or even the "Christ of the philosophers," according to Deleuze, in the following chapter, I will argue that Spinoza should be recognized as the first and perhaps the greatest of modern semioticians and hermeneutic critics as well. Here, I agree with Todorov's assessment that the critical divergence between philosophy and logic on one side, and commentary and criticism on the other, first emerges in the analysis of the nature of signs in the *Theological-Political Treatise* where Spinoza draws a distinction between these two different matters, or *Sacherhalten*.[1] Whereas signs are interpreted, ideas of reason are purely expressed in themselves, since "substance is that which is conceived through itself and does not require another conception [e.g. a sign] to explicate it" (*E* I, D3). Henceforth, philosophy will be concerned with truth as object of the proposition and logic with the rules of accordance or *adequatio,* whereas criticism or commentary will no longer concerned with truth, but rather with the statement and its meaning. In other words, two very different regions of expression are posed which correspond to very different questions and procedures for finding a solution: the philosopher may ask "is it true?" in reference to an object that may even be pre- or extra-linguistic (e.g., in consciousness or nature), while the critic only has for her object only the statement as such and the question "what does it mean?"

Whether in scripture or in nature, however, the science of interpretation concerns only signs. "For as interpretation of Nature consists in the examination of the history of nature, and therein deducing definitions of natural phenomena on certain fixed axioms, so Scriptural interpretation proceeds by the examination of Scripture, and inferring the intention of its authors as a legitimate conclusion from its fundamental principles" (*TTP* 99). Therefore, the concept of interpretation outlined in the *Theological-Political Treatise* does not strictly follow this deductive principle, which would be more in keeping with the method of the *Ethics*, but rather concerns a special class of signs that determine moral experience and, thus, belong to a class of what Spinoza will call "confused ideas," since the material nature of the sign is a mixture of passion and imagination that reproduces in the mind the effect of an original passivity (*affectus*). In other words, for Spinoza, before constituting a *datum* of consciousness, the nature of the sign expresses the formal relations of power that causes consciousness to become either active or reactive. Moral interpretation, especially, is caused by the exteriority of the sign to the expression of the understanding, especially concerning the origin of the moral law, which often invokes the authority (*auctoritas*) of one who "augments" (*augeo*) the passive reception of the sign with the power of interpretation. In other words, to quote Deleuze's very succinct definition in *Spinoza: A Practical Philosophy*, "a sign is always an idea of an effect apprehended under the conditions that separate it from its causes."[2]

From the original Latin, the terms *superstitio* and *superstese*, as Emile Benveniste shows, the faculty of witnessing refers particularly to those things that are not naturally present, such as in the acts of divination or prophetic acts (e.g., hearing the voice of a God) and thus are rare and reserved for a special class of individuals. Thus, superstitious signs are different from conventional or indicative signs in that they represent nothing except the augmented vision of the one who appears as *superstese*, that is, in the role of a divine witness.[3] Consequently, the sole question of interpretation concerns the authority (*auctoritas*) of the one who commands, dictates (*dicere*), or who interprets the law in such a way that the sign of this authority becomes effective and causes obedience, which is different from agreement (*consensus*) or understanding (*intelligence*). As we will see, Spinoza's employment of the notion of a*uctoritas* in scriptural authority, particularly in the example of Moses, exclusively refers to the role of the *superstese*, as "the one who causes possession, as he who possesses the right," but also in the sense of *augeo*, as one who augments the simple right that belongs to every individual, which appears in the imagination as an increase of power (*potestas*). This can be classified as a "confused idea," in this case, the appearance of an additional attribute that belongs to this individual substance alone, causing an increase effect of power, an overpowering force, or even a form of domination that is *expressed* by the principle of sovereignty.

* * *

At this point, it may be useful to summarize Deleuze's indexical classification of signs in Spinoza's system. This classification in *Spinoza: Practical Philosophy* is particularly prevalent in his analysis of scripture in the *Theological-Political Treatise*. There are three classes of signs: indicative, imperative, and interpretive. The class of indicative signs are the effects of the mixture between ideas with the passions belonging to external bodies. These form the basis of conventional signs (or language), since they are fundamentally characterized by *equivocity*, that is, by the multiple and associative chains of signification that accrue over time and constitute a language. Second, the class of imperative signs is the effects of revelation in such a way that the sign is taken as the cause of the idea itself. As a primary example drawn from the argument of *Theological-Political Treatise*, the class of signs that determine the expression of law as either commanding or prohibiting are merely the effects ascribed to the presence of an external body or figure of sovereignty that pertains to this class of signs, in particular, effects which are motivated by fear and ignorance concerning the nature of right. It is for this reason that Spinoza argues that imperative signs simply require obedience, and not knowledge, and that they are mixed with the individual and collective passions of fear and hope (which is also an implicit reference to Hobbes' concept of law, to which I will return to later). Finally, the third class of signs, which are specifically the object of the *Theological-Political Treatise*, are interpretative signs, that is to say, the effects of "superstition" (the "*superstese*"). The problem with this class of signs, in particular, is that they project the original state of fear into language, accompanied by affects of confusion and ignorance, thereby coloring the indicative or conventional signs employed to express ideas of causality (especially in the case of sovereignty and power, as I will show). Finally, all these different classes of signs are neither static nor pure, but enter into different living mixtures and variable conventional uses that determine both a language and a distinctive culture (e.g., the Hebrew language, religion, culture, and politics).

The primary example that Spinoza offers—the sign that determines the concept of God or Nature (*Deus sive natura*)—is taken from the Hebrew word *ruagh* (translated in Latin as *spiritus*), which is shown to have multiple or indicative senses that accumulate through the passage of tradition and by the augmentation of the term through the distinctive and vivid imaginations of the prophets. Here, I will offer a truncated version of the longer passage from the first chapter of *Theological-Political Treatise*:

> The word *ruagh* in its literal sense means "wind," as noted, but it is very often used to refer to many other things, all of them, however, derived from "wind." It is used: to signify "breath," as in *Psalm* 135.17, "also there is no spirit in their

mouth"; "life" or "breathing." [...] Hence it is taken for "courage" and "strength," as at *Joshua* 2.11. [...] Hence it is taken for "ability" and "capacity," as at *Job* 32.8, [...] It can also denote a "sentiment" of the mind, as at *Numbers* 14.24. [...] Likewise *Proverbs* 1.23, "I will tell you my spirit" (i.e., "my mind"). In this sense it is used to signify "will" or "decision," "desire" and "movement of the mind." [...] Further, this word *ruagh*, in so far as it signifies "mind," serves to express all the passions of the mind and even its talents; for example, "a lofty spirit" serves to denote pride, "a lowly spirit" humility, "an evil spirit" hatred and melancholy, "a good spirit" kindness; we also find "a spirit of jealousy," "a spirit" (or appetite) "of fornication," and "a spirit of wisdom" (or "counsel" or "courage"), [...] also, "a spirit of benevolence," etc. [or] It denotes the mind or soul itself, as at *Ecclesiastes* 3.19. [...] Finally it can refer to the quarters of the world (because of the winds that blow from them), and also the sides of any thing which look toward those quarters: see *Ezekiel* 37.9, 42.16–19, etc. (*TTP* 31–35)

In compiling this exhaustive catalog of signs, Spinoza presents us here with a vivid example of the living mixture of all three classes of signs (indicative, or conventional; imperative, or revealed; and, finally, superstitious, or interpretive and imaginative), which are additionally all influenced by other factors such as: climate, geographical conditions, custom (*conuetudo*), habit (*habitudo*), and disposition (*dispositio*) that is unique or "peculiar" to a people or multitude (*multitudinus ingenium*), constituting the concrete arrangements of the common notions into a species of *conatus* (an individual, a group, a nation, etc.).

In many respects, Spinoza's theory of signs may also recall Nietzsche's genealogical interpretation of metaphor in "On Truth and Lies in a Nonmoral Sense," since there is no original distinction between literal or proper sense of the terms and their various figures or metaphorical equivalents, which might even appear to contradict the major proposition already found in the *Ethics* (also stated in the preface of the *Theological-Political Treatise*) that God or Nature does not express itself by means of signs. Consequently, in resolving this problem of expression that is caused by the equivocity of signs, Spinoza will apply a practical principle comparable to "Ockham's razor" by choosing the most simple and direct meaning: spirit is simply breath, or according to its secondary definition, "voice." But what is a voice? It is simply the living and breathing "sign" of expression. Nevertheless, it would be an error to determine the presence of the voice as the cause of understanding: "Certainly, when anyone says with his mouth, 'I understand,' we do not attribute understanding to the mouth but to the mind of the speaker" (*TTP* 16). Therefore, while the voice is the *sign of expression*, it is not expression itself, since it is also a body that is external to the moment of understanding and thus remains an arbitrary, indeterminate, and constant source of confusion. In other words, expression cannot be determined by the expressed, just as the statement "I understand" in no way resembles the expression of the idea in the mind of the speaker.

It is this confusion that will be employed in the interpretation of prophetic speech to characterize the voice of the prophet as being "the mouthpiece of God," within the semiotics of revelation developed in the chapter "On Prophecy." Here, the prophets constitute the modes or various modifications of God's expressions, and in this way, they could be represented as all the "voices" that filled his mind; however, these modifications were due to factors and dispositions peculiar to each prophet (personality, imagination, ethical disposition or piety, etc.). As in the example of *ruagh* above, each new attribute or mode of God was introduced by the creation of a distinctive sign, which was itself the manifestation of the prophet's particularly active imagination—even though Spinoza would define this activity not in terms of an active understanding, since the prophets often did not understand what they were saying, but rather as the passive state of affection (*affectus*), or simply, the emotional and bodily passions that conditioned the creation of new signs. Recalling the natural scarcity of this kind of individual, Spinoza also argues that this is restricted by natural selection to certain exceptional individuals who are identified as the prophets in scripture, but this finite grouping can even be further restricted to an indefinite moment of the individual prophet's life. As Spinoza writes: "Inasmuch as the imagination is fleeting and inconsistent, we find that the power of prophecy did not remain with prophet for long, nor manifest itself frequently, but was very rare; manifesting itself only in a few men, and in them not often" (*TTP* 26). Recalling the definition of the roles reserved for the *superstes* (or divine witness) discussed earlier, following Benveniste, "*auctoritas* is a rare gift reserved only for those individuals who cause something to surge forth and—literally—*to produce its existence.*"[4] Consequently, in the *Theological-Political Treatise*, it is Moses especially who represents this type of rare and gifted individual; and one who possess the right and authority to interpret the sense of the moral law, that is, literally, to bring forth its existence in the mind of the Hebrew people by means of an external voice that is also identified as the voice of the deity. For example, as Spinoza shows, it is clearly stated in the Torah that God spoke with Moses as if "face to face," even though this is later contradicted by another passage that has God's back to him, and thus Moses heard an external voice, whereas the later prophets such as Samuel and Elisha only heard imaginary voices. In other words, in the case of Moses, the sense of interpretation is more productive or active since Moses actually creates the moral law (and thus hears directly the voice of God), whereas the later prophets interpret the voice that is already mediated by the Mosaic covenant.

At first, Spinoza's interpretation might appear strained until we come to realize the different historical and teleological moments of the Hebrew Commonwealth that this distinction belongs to in accordance with the exceptional authoritative role of Moses himself, and the reason why Spinoza insists that in his case, and his case only, we are dealing with a real external voice and not an imaginary voice that occurs with the later prophets. In the first instance, the Hebrew (or *ipiru*, or wandering tribes) are not yet a people united under a sovereign principle and, as I will show, it is more of the fact that they assigned to Moses the *auctoritas* as the one who produces their existence, to create in the mind of the people the voice of God as commanding them to depart from a previous state of bondage and to live in obedience to God's law. Of course, this does not necessarily mean to come out of Egypt all at once in one great migration like the scene in De Mille's *Ten Commandments*, but rather simply refers to the decision to no longer submit or transfer their rights to an earlier form of sovereignty, a decision that could have actually evolved over many years and with numerous emigrations from Egypt. In the case of the prophets who come later, however, the Hebrew people already exist and the function of the prophets has changed, since they are not given the authority to create "a new God," but rather, to interpret the one that had already been given by Moses directly to the people *in his own voice*, which caused them to first come into existence as a people. In other words, later God only spoke indirectly to the prophets, and it was through the mouth of the prophets that he thus spoke indirectly to his people in order to chastise them for their wickedness; however, at no time did the people mistake the voices of the prophets themselves for the voice of God, as they originally did in the case of Moses. Moreover, nothing I am suggesting here should be construed as my own interpretation, but is clearly argued in the *Theological-Political Treatise*. Thus, Spinoza interprets the effect of this sign in the mind of the multitude as a sign of desire or hope, which is in reference to Hobbes argument in *Leviathan*, the hope that by transferring their separate and natural right to the sovereign authority of Moses as theocratic dictator, that they will escape from a state of warfare and fear of death and live in a state of relative peace and prosperity in the territory that a God also promises in exchange for the transfer of individual sovereignty.

In Chapter 17, "On the Hebrew Theocracy," Spinoza renarrates the original account from Exodus of the different bands of primitive *ipiru* from out of Egypt precisely in terms of the Hobbesian state of nature as the war of all against all, in which suddenly freed from horrible slavery, each individual entered into his natural right and was "bound by no covenant," and was free to either "retain this right, to give it up, or transfer it to another" (*TTP* 219). However, here we witness a fundamental distinction with Hobbes argument, since the state of nature in Spinoza's account is not ahistorical, nor prelapsarian, but rather a state that follows the first period of subjection and slavery. "Being then," he writes, "in the state of nature, they followed the advice of Moses, in whom they chiefly trusted, and decided to transfer their right to no master who was merely another animal like themselves, but only to the voice of God, which is to say, to the expression of Law" (*TTP* 219). In other words, it was their own experience in slavery under a sovereign who was an animal or a human being like themselves, that they mutually devise a new plan to avoid this form of sovereignty for themselves in the future as a means of also avoiding a form of absolute loss of their sovereignty as free individuals. As Spinoza writes, "it is because they believed that nothing but God's power could preserve them that they surrendered to God the natural power of self-preservation, which they formerly, perhaps thought they possessed, and consequently they surrendered at the same time all their natural right" (*TTP* 219).

Nevertheless, this statement already contains an implicit contradiction, which is hinted at in the phrase, "they surrendered what they thought they had formerly possessed," since this directly contradicts the principle proposition that heads this chapter, if not the entire treatise: "It is shown that no one can, or need, transfer all his rights to a sovereign power and still remain a human being" (*TTP* 214). Why is this so? First, because no individual substance actually possess such power of self-preservation absolutely in its own substance (i.e., the power of *conatus*), since this power is always conditioned by a relation to greater and lesser powers according the proportional law of nature that is argued in the draft of the *Ethics* that was written during the same period. Consequently, it is impossible to transfer a right that one does not possess to begin with, which is implied in the statement "perhaps, they thought they possessed." Second, an augmentation of an existing power is not a creation *ex nihilo* as will occur later in Christian doctrine. Therefore, God's dictate may have appeared suddenly in the voice of Moses, but according to Spinoza's theory of *conatus*, the power already exists in each individual mode and merely undergoes an augmentation through the unnatural power of the imagination accorded to signs. Consequently, this was already a confused idea of individual right, which the Hebrew people suddenly transferred onto the idea of God: it is this misapprehension of their own individual essence that becomes the basis for the misapprehension of the true nature of God as an image of sovereign—*in short, for the creation of religion and the idea of God as the sudden and miraculous augmentation of mere natural right into something supernatural in origin.* In a nutshell, I have just illustrated the entire argument of the *Theological-Political Treatise*, which responds to one question: how is it that the nature of power is misapprehended so as to appear in the image of the sovereign?

At the same time, Spinoza discovers within the very same "confused idea" of God or Nature, as well as in the peculiar nature of the Mosaic covenant with God, a primitive democratic principle of sovereignty that also distinguishes the Hebrew form of government from a Monarchy (*pace* Hobbes). As Spinoza writes:

> Inasmuch as the Hebrews did not transfer their rights to any other person but, as in a democracy, all surrendered their rights equally, and cried out with one voice, "Whatsoever God shall speak (no mediator or mouthpiece being named) that will we do," it follows that all were equally bound by the covenant, and they all had the equal right to consult the Deity, to accept and to interpret his laws, so all had an exactly equal share in the government. (*TTP* 220)

This is what Spinoza describes as the first covenant with God, the first Hebrew understanding of their freedom. It is precisely at this point where the Hebrew people are said to most resemble a universal form of *imperium* in which each individual has an exactly equal share in self-government and thus equal *auctoritas* in the interpretation of the laws by which they will choose to govern themselves. However, here Spinoza immediately recounts the return to a state of nature, which is to say an original state of fear that leads to the creation of a new superstition by which they shrink back before the abyss opened in the voice of an equality they could not understand, as a power they became fearful of in that they did not feel capable of possessing this power for themselves. "Full of fear, therefore, they went afresh to Moses, saying, lo, we have heard the voice of God ourselves speaking in the fire, and surely we will die and this fire will consume us" (*TTP* 220). As a result, they surrender their individual existence by speaking in one voice, but since the multitude is composed of many separate voices, they also surrendered their direct access to the deity and their own individual right to interpret God's ordinances, and therefore surrendered to Moses who alone possessed the right to interpret. As Spinoza writes, "They thus clearly abrogated their former covenant, and absolutely transferred to Moses their own right to consult God and to interpret his commands" (*TTP* 221). In other words, as Spinoza interprets it, the original covenant—the covenant that would have been more democratic in principle since it establishes a subjective principle of equality by investing the principle of sovereignty not in any human being, but in a voice that speaks in consensus in giving each individual access to the direct interpretation of the law and to a form of self-government—is thereby, owing to fear, transformed into the principle of sovereignty that replaces the democracy with a form of government identified as a Theocracy. As Spinoza argues,

> it is enough to have shown that after true death of Moses no one man wielded power of a sovereign; as affairs were not managed by one man [the form of monarchy], nor by a single council [the form of an aristocracy], nor by the popular vote [the form of democracy], but partly by one tribe, and partly by the rest in equal shares, it is most evident that the government after the death of Moses was neither monarchic, nor aristocratic, nor popular, but as we have said, Theocratic (*TTP* 225–26).

* * *

Ultimately, it is this failure of the democratic principle to fully incarnate itself in the minds of the people that leads to the later compromise formation in which the figure of sovereignty itself is split into two unequal halves: on the one hand, the monarchy or later the Davidic dynasty, as a king who enjoys sovereign right but not the right to interpret God's law; on the other hand, the one who represents God's *voice* to the people, as the interpreter of the law, embodied in the figure of the prophet. "For the right of interpreting laws was invested in one man, while the right and power of administering the state according to the laws thus interpreted was invested in another man" (*Numb.* 27:2). Again, here we have two sovereign powers, not one: an executive power of sovereignty and a juridical or interpretive authority reserved only for the prophets, which stem from these two separate covenants. For example, there are the Levites who represent the only tribe that does not sin and fashion golden idols in the wilderness (in other words, the only tribe not guilty of sedition against the divine sovereign) that are bestowed the power held by Moses to interpret the divine ordinances (under the pretext that it is only this tribe that found favor with God and was "clean of sin"), although, originally, this was an authority (*auctoritas*) that was first of all bestowed upon Moses by the tribes in order to unify them under one sovereign dictator. In the later incarnation of the Hebrew Commonwealth, it is the fact of the freedom of prophetic speech itself, which appears to be equal to the dictate of the King and often serves as its double, and becomes embodied as a representation of the voice of God in the popular and historical imagination of the Hebrew people. *Thus, it is a primitive principle of "popular resistance," later on expressing the freedom of thought and the spontaneous authority of the vox populi, which foreshadows Spinoza's argument concerning the perfection of democracy as the form of absolute imperium.*

Contrary to Hobbes' argument, the nature of sovereignty between the monarchic and aristocratic or feudal forms of power is shown in sharp relief. In its despotic form, the nature of right is understood as dominion, as the insuring of the mechanism of power to subjugate the people or the multitude under a single principle of sovereignty that is embodied in the person of the sovereign or in a separate class of intelligentsia. However, in democracy, the law only asserts the freedom of thought according to the constraints of the greatest equality, and thus equality itself becomes a critical or prophetic point of agonism against any form of sovereignty that restricts or limits this freedom in the name of the two primary virtues or common notions that pertain to democratic societies: justice and charity. Consequently, Spinoza finds the spirit of the law that belongs to democracy as a form of absolute imperium in the single moral teaching of Christ: "love your neighbor as yourself." This is the spirit of law that animates a democratic constitution of sovereignty, which is distinguished from both Machiavelli and Hobbes, whose theories of sovereign are still predicated on *dominion* as the source of civil security, and not on the democratic emotions of justice and charity, that is, emotions that will later be responsible for challenging inequality between subjects as well as the disproportionate distribution of wealth and power in modern democratic societies. In order to demonstrate this difference, we only need to recognize that the motives of equal rights to larger populace as well as the fair distribution of wealth would be viewed only strategically in the systems of Machiavelli and Hobbes, but would only be employed as a means of securing dominion over the multitude. In other words, even though they often appear as expressions of prudence (*prudentia*) in the discourse of the *Prince*, they are pure fictions—in fact, Machiavelli calls them lies and justifies their employment in the art of governing—in order to insure the security of the sovereign himself. Of course, it is this strategy of government that is later taken up by Marx and Engels (and in the contemporary moment by Foucault) and is shown to be purely a *stratagem* and thus not attached to any ideal end of the society, but rather to a means that realizes a completely opposite end and serves only the expansion of dominion, both temporally and territorially, since the power of dominion of the modern nation state was based on the expansion and diversity of its territories, including the diversity of the species and the populations that resided there. On the other hand, according to Spinoza's definition of the concept of right, neither justice nor injustice exist in a state of nature, just as religion is inconceivable since no one naturally understands his or her obedience to the principle of sovereignty, but only in a civil society bound by laws. Therefore, the possibility of justice or injustice is created by the utility of the laws themselves, which are also sometimes employed as a stratagem in order to alienate or deprive a subject of equality, power, and possession of right. Thus, "Justice is a fixed intention to assign to each person what belongs to them in accordance with civil law. Injustice is to take away from someone under the pretext of right, what belongs to them by correct interpretation of laws" (*TTP* 208).

To return to the second class of signs that include command and prohibition, here we also find the relation of law to the command or decree which conditioned the appearance of the voice in revelation as having a certain divine relation, and the determination of law itself as absolute and bound to the figure of the sovereign would no longer be valid. In fact, the argument even questions the validity of the concept of law in its earlier usage within an arrangement of democracy—that is, its concept is revealed to be inadequate to the relations of forces and affections that combine and express the common notions that belong to democratic organization. Rather, law becomes purely positive, no longer expressing the right of a dictator, but rather assent or agreement. Consequently, this concerns ultimately Spinoza's question concerning the division of positive laws and their exclusion from the realm of thinking or expression. At this point, the concept of law approaches the second determination that Spinoza accords it: that of expression which prepares the way for *conatus*, whereby Reason accedes to express a dominate affection or "common notion" by which the power of the social whole is formed. Here, the concept of sovereign right would be replaced by the notion of "contract" and by the practical procedures of jurisprudence— which has at its foundation the determination of expression in the "sign" of agreement, given that the problem of jurisprudence and interpretation of the law both have a precise corollary in the interpretation of the scriptures according to the principles of the *Theological-Political Treatise*.

Accordingly, if the *auctoritas* (or the "voice of God") are divine in origin, there could be neither hermeneutics (or the science of interpretation) nor jurisprudence (the science of right). Thus, *conatus* can no longer resemble the obligatory law or the absolute power of its first determination, or the articulations of the affective passions (fear and hope) that belonged to earlier forms. In the concept of democracy, however, monarchy has replaced the original state of nature that determines the affections of fear and hope, passivity and activity, sadness and joy or "happiness" (i.e., in a democracy there is the fear of remaining in the state of nature articulated by the domination of a tyrant, who is another animal, and the hope of emerging from it), since it substitutes the love of freedom and the fear of injustice as pure affections of reason. These democratic passions (or virtues) can be extended to address the modern movements in democratic societies, which express the same fear and hope—above all, as a principle of resistance to any transfer of right to a sovereign who is revealed, after all, to be another animal.

In conclusion, and to summarize my reading of the *Theological-Political Treatise*, the voice that corresponds to the sign of revelation expresses its relation to *conatus* only negatively or passively—that is, it "represents" the mind's self-affection as the "effect" expressed by another mind, or an external body acting upon the mind as cause of the idea of law. Consequently, the most serious error of moral interpretation consists precisely in its having disregarded and hidden the difference in nature between obeying and knowing, that is, in causing us to have taken the principles of obedience for models of knowledge. This forms the expressed argument of the *Theological-Political Treatise* that "Revelation and Philosophy stand on totally different footings." However, the true object of this dualism could be said to be the analysis of the articulation of the "law as expression," which correspond to the different arrangements of what Spinoza first defines as the "common notions" within monarchy, aristocracy, and democracy—e.g., freedom, generosity, piety, reason, the affective passions of fear and hope (c.f. *TTP* 119). As he develops more explicitly later on in the *Political Treatise*, Spinoza submits the concept of law to the analysis of its historical arrangements or "common notions" (which parallels, as above, the natural history of the concept of politics which is inferred from different arrangements of its fundamental principles) in order to demonstrate that the nature of the signs that express the idea of moral law understood as command or imperative is contingent upon its political expression in the form of the monarchic or despotic arrangement of the common notions. In the *Theological-Political Treatise*, Spinoza offers an explanation of how and why this arrangement is particular to the formation of the Hebrew State, which serves both as an historical example and as an allegory of the modern formation of sovereignty.

As a whole, the *Theological-Political Treatise* employs the Hebrew state as an allegory of the different articulations of political power: the Davidic dynasty corresponds to the arrangement of monarchy, which is succeeded by the construction of the temple and the rule of the Levites who represent the aristocracy or nobility (the feudal states), and finally, the Diaspora (the loss of the State and the destruction of the temple) corresponds to the formation of democracy (i.e., the dissolution of the State ruled by a king, the fundamental introduced into the analogy between natural violence and political domination (i.e., *potestas* can no longer be expressed as dominion), the rise of reason and love of charity and justice as the fundamental virtues, or common notions, that disposition of an ideal democratic state or absolute imperium. This forms the paradox that motivates Spinoza's inquiry: How is it that, in view of different combinations of the forces, which determine society and the expression of a nature that no longer resembles a tyrant, the concept of law is still determined by command, or injunction, and the "event" by a crisis—"since the people admire most what they comprehend least"—and, finally, expression by the passive relation to the revelatory "effects" of an *auctoritas* that deforms power (*potestas*) into a form of domination (*dominion*)?

Finally, the constitution and destiny of the Hebrew Commonwealth through the Mosaic covenant (as a treaty or contract of protection with the sovereign) will have important lessons as an allegory of the modern notion of sovereignty and right figured in the passage from the stages of monarchy to democracy, particularly in reference to the contemporary Dutch situation—i.e., like the Hebrew who just came out of bondage to a form of Monarchy, the Dutch are also in the perilous situation of choosing their own form of government, and thus the allegory of the Hebrew people who have the unique position of choosing something resembling a form of democracy, but then shrinking back out of fear to choose something resembling a form of Monarchy. This informs a somewhat pessimistic outlook that Spinoza has on the current state of Dutch politics and his own aspirations for a more radical democratic form, following the imprisonment and death of his close friend Koerbagh.[5] However, Spinoza's concept of democracy was not utopian, since any utopian forecasting of the arrangement of common notions with a theory of sovereignty could not be called empiricist, and Spinoza's historical theory of sovereignty must be understood as a unique form of rational empiricism. Therefore, I would hold that the famous incompletion of the *Political Treatise* is not owed to any interruption, but because such a utopian theory would be impossible according to the empirical nature of the study in which such a state must first exist and cannot be forecast or "revealed" by theoretical description, or utopian projection. In Spinoza's well-known letter in which he outlines the plan for the *Political Treatise*, we note that the "subjects of aristocratic and popular dominion," as well as "laws and other particular questions of politics" is the final chapter, and not a description of democracy as a final state in a teleological order of the forms of the state and civil society. Even the references to the democratic environment of Amsterdam that appear in the conclusion of the *Theological-Political Treatise* are interrupted by the new laws restricting the freedom of expression, followed by a period of schism, civil war, and foreign invasions—i.e., the Anglo-Dutch wars and the French invasion in 1672, the overthrow of the anti-Orangist regime in Holland, and finally, the murder of the Brothers De Witt. In this situation, therefore, it is a foregone conclusion that any systematic description of the democracy would be based on sound rational deduction of the principles outlined in his political philosophy, rather than on any expression of utopian idealism—in short, a conception of "men as they are [and not] as [one] would like them to be" (*TP* 1:1).

Notes

1 Tzvetan Todorov, *Critique de la critique* (Paris: Editions du Seuil, 1984), 32.
2 Gilles Deleuze, *Spinoza: A Practical Philosophy* (San Francisco: City Lights Publishers, 2001), 105.
3 Émile Benveniste, *Le Vocabulaire des institutions indo-européennes II: Pouvoir, droit, religion* Sommaires, tableau et index établis par Jean Lallot (Paris: Éditions Minuit, 1969), 278.
4 Benveniste, *Le Vocabulaire des institutions indo-européennes II*, 151, emphasis added.
5 See Steven Nadler, *A Book Forged in Hell: Spinoza's Scandalous Treatise and the Birth of the Secular Age* (Princeton: Princeton University Press, 2011).

Bibliography

Benveniste, Émile. *Le Vocabulaire des institutions indo-européennes II: Pouvoir, droit, religion*. Sommaires, tableau et index établis par Jean Lallot. Paris: Éditions Minuit, 1969.
Deleuze, Gilles. *Spinoza: A Practical Philosophy*. San Francisco: City Lights Publishers, 2001.
Deleuze, Gilles and Guattari, Felix. *What Is Philosophy?*, trans. by Hugh Tomlison and Graham Burchell. New York: Columbia University Press, 1994.
Nadler, Steven. *A Book Forged in Hell: Spinoza's Scandalous Treatise and the Birth of the Secular Age*. Princeton: Princeton University Press, 2011.
Spinoza, Baruch/Benedictus. *The Ethics*, trans. by Samuel Shirley, intro. and notes by Seymour Feldman. Indianapolis: Hackett, 1992.
Spinoza, Baruch/Benedictus. *Political Treatise*, trans. by Samuel Shirley, intro. and notes by Steven Barbone and Lee Rice. Indianapolis: Hackett, 2000.
Spinoza, Baruch/Benedictus. *Spinoza Opera*, 5 vols, ed. by Carl Gebhardt. Heidelberg: Carl Winters Verlag, [1925] 1972.
Spinoza, Baruch/Benedictus. *Theological-Political Treatise*, 2nd ed., trans. by Samuel Shirley. Indianapolis: Hackett, 2001.
Todorov, Tzvetan. *Critique de la critique*. Paris: Editions du Seuil, 1984.

8

Spinoza and the Hydraulic Discipline of Affects: From the Theologico-Political to the Economic Regime of Desire

Chiara Bottici and Miguel de Beistegui

Dilemmas of servitude

The fundamental problem for political philosophy today, Deleuze and Guattari claim in *Anti-Œdipus*,[1] remains the one that Spinoza saw so clearly when he raised the question of the conditions under which "human beings fight for their own servitude as if they were fighting for their deliverance, and will not think it humiliating but supremely glorious to spill their blood and sacrifice their lives for the glorification of one man" (*TTP* 7).[2] The question, in other words, is that of knowing how, independently of the exercise of physical force or coercion, subjects can desire their own servitude.[3]

Spinoza's answer to that question is summarized in the following statement, which he borrows from Curtius: "Nothing governs the multitude as effectively as superstition [*superstitio*]" (*TTP* 5).[4] By "superstition," we need to understand a specific art of government, which draws on the imagination and requires the disciplining of bodies. The reason why it is so effective a method of government is that it is able to capitalize on the fact that human beings, who are naturally governed by the relentless fluctuation of their affects, constantly oscillate between fear and hope (*TTP* 1). While seemingly opposed, fear and hope are actually two sides of the same coin. Fear, Spinoza tells us, is an inconstant *sadness*, which arises from the idea of a thing, the outcome of which we are in some doubt (*E* III, Def. of aff. 13). Hope, on the other hand, is a *joy*, which arises from the idea of a thing, the outcome of which we are also in some doubt (*E* III, Def. of aff. 12). Since we are doomed to live in a condition of uncertainty, in which we do not control our destiny, these two passions are inseparable. The only difference between them is that fear is a form of sadness, whereas hope is a form of joy. As Spinoza openly put it at the beginning of the *Theological-Political Treatise*:

> If men were always able to regulate their affairs with sure judgement, or if fortune always smiled upon them, they would not get caught up in any superstition. But since people are often reduced to such desperate straits that they cannot arrive at any solid judgement and as the good things of fortune for which they have a boundless desire are quite uncertain, they fluctuate wretchedly between hope and fear. (*TTP* 1)

And this, he adds immediately, is why most people are quite ready to believe anything, and why superstition is a particularly effective technology of government. The primary aim of the *Theological-Political Treatise*, which Spinoza wrote in haste and as a response to a specific historical and political context, is precisely to investigate the mechanisms of such a technology. As we know from his correspondence, in 1665 Spinoza interrupted the writing of the *Ethics* in order to write his *Treatise* (*Ep.* 30). The reason he did so was that, in the context of the fragile institutions of the Dutch Republic, he felt the threat of its overthrow by some active radical Calvinists who, like the ancient Hebrews described in the *Theological-Political Treatise*, perceived themselves as chosen by god and on the basis of such a prophecy aimed at installing a theocracy.[5]

In contrast to other Enlightenment thinkers, Spinoza does not simply dismiss superstition and prophecy as an error or an illusion. He is rather interested in understanding how it works, why it is so widespread, and the extent to which it is inevitable.[6] It is both a natural disposition and a technology of government. Spinoza is indeed clear about the fact that, while it is possible to elevate oneself beyond the realm of imagination at the individual level, the situation is quite different, and far more complex, at the political level. And while the *Ethics* reveals the path that allows us to liberate ourselves from servitude by turning the sadness of passive affects into the joy of active ones through adequate knowledge, the *Theological-Political Treatise* focuses on the situations in which, due to the intrinsic nature of the multitude, the liberation in question is not possible, or is at least far more difficult to achieve.[7] Given the essentially capricious and thus unstable nature of the multitude (*TTP* 210), there arises the need to organize, contain and channel the flow of human affects through a certain discipline of imagination. Every society is, to a certain degree at least, imaginary, and needs to rely on technologies of the imagination in order to tame the antagonistic and unpredictable nature of affects. The difference between pure superstition and other configurations of imagination becomes one of degree:[8] each configuration reveals a more or less adequate understanding of our condition, and, thus a different degree of power or *potentia*.[9]

At this point, it is important to recall that Spinoza defines affects firstly as the affections of the body by which the body's power to act (*potentia agendi*) is either increased or diminished, helped or hindered, and, second, as the ideas of those affections (*E* III, D3). Whereas the notion of affect points to the possibility of such an increase or decrease of our *potentia*, "desire" (*cupiditas*) is the more general ontological category with which Spinoza defines the essence of human nature (*E* III, Def. of aff. 1).[10] The reason why desire is the very essence of human beings is that, according Spinoza's ontology, everything, in so far as it is in itself (*quantum in se est*), endeavors to persevere in its being (*in sue esse perseverare conatur*) (*E* III, P6). Within this theory of the *conatus*, which applies for Spinoza to every single being, negativity and destruction can only come from external causes (*E* III, P4). The justification for this doctrine ultimately lies in Spinoza's ontology of unique substance, that is, from the fact that being comes before nonbeing, or better said, that there is something rather than nothing (*E* I, P11Pr2). And the fact that something *exists* also and by definition means that it endeavors to persevere in its being. Within this perspective, desire is appetite, or the *conatus* itself when related to both body and mind, together with the consciousness of that appetite (*E* III, P9). As such, it is the result of an ontological plenitude and the expression of one's own *potentia*, which, as we will see, can either be increased through active affects or diminished through passive ones.

Now, while knowledge enables us to transform our passive affects into active ones, thereby increasing our power or *potentia*, imagination, which is an inadequate form of knowledge, tends to generate passive affects, that is, affects that decrease our power. We will come back to Spinoza's distinction between activity and passivity, which is crucial in order to understand how liberation is possible. For the time being, it is sufficient to underline that, while reason, as grounded in common notions, unifies us, imagination brings discord.

As a result, human beings find themselves in a condition similar to that described by Hobbes in his state of nature (*TTP* 199–200). Insofar as that condition endangers their own survival, they subject themselves to a common power.[11] The structure of Spinoza's argument is very similar to Hobbes' justification of the sovereign state, but with a crucial difference: since desire is the very essence of human beings, no subject could ever deprive herself of the right to do whatever is in her power, that is, to renounce her own nature. And given that, for Spinoza, "right" is nothing but *potentia*, or power itself, the subject is perfectly within her right when she does something at a certain point in time and its opposite later on, according to the fluctuations of her affects (*TTP* 199–200).[12]

But since the particular instantiation of a mind and a body are, for Spinoza, just one mode seen from two different attributes of the same substance, there cannot be a discipline of the mind that is not also a discipline of the body. What we would like to call the hydraulic discipline of affects works at the point of encounter between the two attributes.[13] We cannot enter into a detailed discussion of Spinoza's ontology. But it is important to remember that, for Spinoza, there is only one, infinite substance that expresses itself through an infinity of modes, or affections of the substance (*E* I, D1, D5). This idea grounds Spinoza's radical monism, which lies at the heart of the issue we are concerned with here.

Within this radical monism, thought and extension are therefore simply two attributes of the substance, that is, two different ways in which the substance is perceived by the intellect (*E* 1, D4). As a consequence, a single body is just a mode of the unique substance in the attribute of extension, while a single mind is a mode of the very same substance in the attribute of thinking. There is therefore no body-mind dualism: although thought and extension are the two attributes that we, as finite modes, have access to, the substance is itself characterized by an infinite number of attributes (*E* 1, D6). As a consequence, a discipline of affects, that is, of affections of the body that are, at the same time, the ideas of those affections, is inseparable from a discipline of the mind. Conversely, as Spinoza fully explains in the course of the *Theological-Political Treatise*, affects can be captured and channeled only by the imagination itself, which, for Spinoza, is, in turn, just a form of bodily awareness.[14]

This point clearly emerges in Spinoza's puzzling analysis of political obedience (*TTP* 209). He establishes the principle of political obedience as necessary to the creation of a social order (*civitas*). But it is a principle that is intrinsically fragile, and constantly threatened, given that the transfer of natural rights from the individual body to the political body is only ever tentative, and could be withdrawn at any time. This is the reason why, given the essentially affective, and thus fickle and unpredictable nature of the multitude, the state needs to develop techniques of obedience, which the multitude will internalize, to the point of turning them into a second nature. In other words, in addition to the problem of sovereign power, and its legal solution, there is the problem of what, following Foucault, we would like to call "governmentality," or "the art of conducting conducts."[15] The problem for the state, then, is one of knowing how best to guarantee the stability of the transfer of rights that led to its creation in the first place; it is a question of knowing by what means subjects will continue to accept the supremacy of the state. Spinoza observes that this can happen through physical coercion: "One man has another in his power if he holds him in bonds, or has deprived him of the arms and means of self-defense or escape" (*TP* 2.10). But he also thinks that the same goal can be achieved through the instillation of certain affects, such as terror, or by forcing the other into feeling indebtedness, as a result of having conferred upon him some benefit or privilege. Of the two techniques, Spinoza argues, the second is far more effective, in that it takes hold not of the other's body, but of her mind. But we need to go even further, and acknowledge a form of power that, whilst drawing on passions, is yet more precise and effective: individuals are never more inclined to desire the desire of an other, and never more submissive, than when they embrace it *wholeheartedly*:

> Therefore he who wholeheartedly [*integro animo*] resolves to obey another in all his commands is fully under another's power [*sub alterius imperio est*], and consequently he who reigns over his subject's hearts holds the greatest power. ... [H]earts are to some degree under the control of the sovereign power, who has many means of inducing the majority to believe, love, hate what it wills. (*TTP* 202)

It is not only by instilling fear, by the threat of harm, or by depriving subjects of their freedom, but by winning over their hearts, that a sovereign power can chain its subjects to its own desire. Spinoza's conclusion is unequivocal: "In my opinion no more effective means can be devised to influence men's hearts, for nothing can so captivate the heart as joy springing from devotion, that is, love combined with admiration" (*TTP* 216).

The theological-political siphon

In order to disentangle such technologies of the heart we need to turn to Spinoza's analysis of the history of the Ancient Hebrews, which occupies most of the *Theological-Political Treatise*, providing the pretext for a more general reflection on the imaginary nature of society itself: every political body needs to construe itself around some pattern of imagination, through which the unstable character of the multitude is tamed, and their affects disciplined. To the extent that, in the long term, people tend not to tolerate pure coercion, but also fail to submit to the common power for rational reasons only, myths, rituals and other collective and bodily forms of government of the imagination become an essential ingredient of politics itself. Borrowing a term from Louis Althusser, we could say that, for Spinoza, every society needs its own "ideological state apparatus." The use of that term in this context is not accidental, insofar as Althusser explicitly says that it is by following Spinoza that he came to insist on the "material existence of ideology."[16] With this expression, he meant not only its material social *conditions*, that is, its connections with interests blinded by the imagination of a social group (ideology as false consciousness), but also the *materiality* of the very existence of ideology, the fact that, within a monistic framework such as Spinoza's, it does not make sense to counterpoise the ideal and the material or, for that matter, the mind and the body.

According to Spinoza's reconstruction, Moses was able to institute such a regime of the imagination, precisely by inserting the immanent, historical and contingent condition of his people within the framework of a more general *sacred* history, which transcended it. In his view, after the exodus from Egypt, the people of Israel fell again into a pure state of nature. It is in this context that Moses labeled the Hebrews the "chosen people," and employed the idea of *historia sacra* as a means of morally encouraging his people to subject themselves to a lawful condition. Spinoza is explicit on this point: "This is why Moses, with his virtue and by divine command, introduced religion into the commonwealth, so that people would do its duty more from devotion than from fear" (*TTP* 74).

Spinoza's analysis of the Hebrews' history displays thus a very peculiar view of political theology. While Carl Schmitt sustains in *Political Theology* that the most important (modern) political concepts are the result of a transposition of originally theological ideas into politics, Spinoza suggests in Chapter 3 of the *Theological-Political Treatise* exactly the opposite: concepts such as the omnipotent God as a lawgiver of monotheism are the religious transposition of specific political situations.[17] It is because the Hebrews had only recently left their slavery in Egypt and were therefore used to it that Moses had to present God as a supreme lawgiver and persuade them to subject themselves to the law. In the theological-political nexus, it is the political, and not the religious, which comes first. Despite its title, Spinoza's *Theological-Political Treatise* can thus be read as an attempt to bring political theology to an end, because it is an attempt to bring the transcendence of the sacred history back into the immanence of politics. On many occasions, Spinoza asserts that the purpose of religious ceremonies and of the sacred history that sustains them is the preservation of the state.[18]

The idea of a sacred history or a transcendent plane on which the Hebrews were playing a particular role serves thus as the pivot of a hydraulic system aimed at channeling the antagonistic passions of the multitude. The way in which the political-theological nexus works here is similar to the functioning of a siphon: it is by creating an artificial *lack*, a *void*, that desires are drained, siphoned off into a vortex. The belief in the sacred history becomes thus the ideal expression of a material regime of desire that shapes it in the form of a systematic lack: the lack of the fall from paradise, the lack of a Messiah, which is always to come, the lack of a plenitude which is always announced, but never fully there.

The Hebraic state was, from the point of view of obedience, and initially at least, a remarkable success, insofar as it managed to bring the desires of the Hebrews as a whole in line with the desire of God as interpreted by the Prophets, and then in line with Moses as God's privileged interlocutor and interpreter. In other words, it succeeded in gathering, channeling and funneling the desires of the Hebrew through the transcendence of the Law and the devotion inspired by prophecy. Its success was due primarily to its ability to create techniques of obedience, which shaped bodies and minds alike, and included love of country, religious fervor (combined with hatred for other religions and states), regular and precise rituals and ceremonies, holidays and traditions such as the jubilee, practices such as charity, and, of course, all the commandments and prohibitions prescribed by the Law (*TTP* 224). In sum,

> every single thing they had to do according to a specific prescript of the Law. They could not plough as and when they pleased, but could only do so at certain times and in particular years, and with one kind of beast at a time; they could sow and reap only in a certain way and at a particular time; their lives without exception were a continual *practice of obedience*. (*TTP* 224, emphasis ours)

And again:

> Three times in the year they feasted with God ... they had to cease from all work on the seventh day of the week and allow themselves to rest; and, besides these, other times were designated when honest enjoyment and feasting were not so much allowed as prescribed. I do not think that anything can be devised which is more effective than this for swaying men's minds. Nothing captivates minds more effectively than the cheerfulness arising from devotion, i.e. from love and wonder together. (*TTP* 225)

It is therefore through such a set of practices that affects were channeled, like in a hydraulic system where the flux is apparently free to flow, but only to end up within the boundaries of a carefully engineered system. We could refer to this set of rules, habits and codes, the aim of which is to discipline the mind and the body, as a "regime of desire" and, more specifically, as a technology of the heart.

We are using the notion of "regime" in a manifold sense, which ranges from the political to the medical, through the sexual and the dietary. What unifies them is the body, which, as we have seen, is the same as the mind for Spinoza's ontology, but expressed through a different attribute. The central role of the body is perhaps most visible in the passage on circumcision. According to Spinoza, this practice alone would have been sufficient to keep the Hebrew people separated from any other—so much so, Spinoza states with characteristic irony, that we could not exclude that, were the opportunity to present itself, "God will choose them again" (*TTP* 55). By writing the covenant with God in the body itself, circumcision simultaneously inscribes it deeply in the mind and thus becomes a most powerful and effective technique of government.

This is how, in the end, in the eyes of those wholly accustomed to this hydraulic discipline of desire, their situation "must have appeared to be freedom rather than slavery" (*TTP* 224). They ended up loving the Law, and desiring "only what was prescribed" (*TTP* 224). As a result of such practices of obedience, people end up seeing it as the expression of their own freedom, and are ready to fight for it, as if it were for their own deliverance. Furthermore, and more disturbingly, they enjoy obeying and desiring what is prescribed, which is another way of saying that they desire the desire of an Other (we will return to this specific logic of desire).

To be sure, the obsessive character of the Hebrew rituals was justified by their particular historical condition. But Spinoza clearly points out that the recourse to such a discipline is far from being a prerogative of the ancient Hebrews. Christian ceremonies, he observes, also "have [no] sanctity in them," and are only instituted with a view to preserving the political community within which they were established (*TTP* 75). Similarly, the Chinese "zealously retain a kind of topknot on their heads, by which they distinguish themselves" from other people (*TTP* 55). In sum, the character of such rituals may vary from one society to another, but all societies have to rely on them, because every society needs to manage and control the instability of our affects.

The economic-neoliberal siphon

This is the lesson that Spinoza, by looking at the example of the Ancient Hebrews, applied to his own political world, in which, as we have seen, many radical Calvinists also saw themselves as the "chosen people." With a move that is perhaps not in Spinoza's letter, but certainly in his spirit, we would like to apply now the previous considerations to our own time. What, if any, is the dominant configuration of desire in our western, late capitalist societies? The hypothesis we would like to put forward is that there is a deep analogy between the theologico-political hydraulics of desire, as described above, and the government of desire that characterize the market in contemporary capitalism. What we have called the siphon of desire works equally well, albeit differently, in the economic, and specifically neoliberal context. The similarity is, as we will see, structural and involves a lack that structures, orders and orients desire. The siphon of desire aims to produce a certain type of subject by shaping minds and generating habits, by encouraging one to *act* in a very specific way. It corresponds to a specific way of "conducting conducts" and "encouraging behaviours."[19] In other words, it is a technology of power, and one that has more features in common with the theocracy described in the *Theological-Political Treatise* than with the paradigm of a political sovereignty centered around natural right and symbolized by the sword.[20]

The problem of the liberal, and specifically neoliberal governmentality can be expressed in the following terms: How—through what techniques or technologies—can desire be enrolled and federated? How can we be *made to consent* and align our own desire with that of Capital? What better way than by drawing on the supreme motivation, or what is taken to be the supreme motivation, that is, pleasure, or, more precisely, the promise of enjoyment? The market, as a technology of government and a specific assemblage of desire, does not operate only—and, in the case of liberal governmentality, not primarily—through fear (at least in the coercive, vertical or classical sense), but through enjoyment, or the promise of enjoyment, in the broad sense of the term, that is, as the hope of recognition, reward, and even love.

To be sure, the technology in question required new mechanisms and techniques, an entire reorganization of desire and the production of new types of objects of desire, which differ from the theocracy that Spinoza's contemporaries aimed at installing, as much as the latter differed from that of the ancient Hebrews. But its ultimate aim is the same: It is to capture and govern human beings' desire, that is, their power to act. Otherwise stated, it is not a question of governing—whether oneself or others—*against* one's passions, of dominating, controlling or eradicating them, according to strategies that could be described as ascetic or materialist, but of governing oneself *with* and *through* one's passions. The market, we wish to argue, is the space in which desires are thus set free, but also funneled, channeled and captured, in short, siphoned off.

In this respect, the liberal political economy is the new superstition, which in the name of a supposed "rationality" introduces and justifies the existence of the market. Markets, which existed before the emergence of political economy, are, as Foucault rightly emphasizes, subjected to an epistemological transformation as a result of the emergence of that discipline. From a place of "jurisdiction," which bore the mark of the sovereign, and expressed his law, the market becomes a place of "veridiction," with laws that are now ascribed to human nature and to the market as a quasi-natural field, governed by human passions and interests: "Just as the physical world is ruled by the laws of movement," Helvetius writes, "no less is the moral universe ruled by the laws of interest."[21] Put in nutshell, whereas the superstition that governed the theologico-political nexus was that of the divine law, with its promise of a paradise to come, that governing the market are the supposed laws of human nature, with their promise of worldly pleasures and satisfactions.

Within this narrative, it would be unreasonable, therefore, and altogether pointless to seek to govern (whether oneself or others) by going against the laws of human nature. What is required, rather, is a proper and complete understanding of the laws in question, which alone can decide what will constitute good and bad government. Quite logically, good government will be seen as allowing the maximum amount of space for the free expression of those laws, which themselves, insofar they are laws of nature, *spontaneously* tend to produce a state of balance, equilibrium and happiness. And the market is precisely presented as the space in which this spontaneous order can unfold and human nature flourishes. This is how, in the words of Adam Smith, and once the idea of the "invisible hand" (or "Providence") has been adopted, it is possible to affirm that even the "natural selfishness and rapacity of the rich," with their "most frivolous desires," "their own vain and insatiable desires," actually contribute to the common good.[22] In other words, it can no longer be a question of governing oneself in spite of, or even *against* one's "frivolous" desires, but *with* them, or according to them.

In practical terms, this means that, in the economic, and specifically neoliberal regime, desires are governed, but in the sense of being *managed*. The central question is no longer one of knowing what it is legitimate (or not) to desire, but what can generate the highest degree of satisfaction for any *individual*, how to best govern not "subjects" or "citizens," but "individuals" who are naturally moved by their own desires, and who recognize as their true "sovereign" the principles of pleasure and pain. The problem of governmentality becomes thus an *economic* problem; and the "science" of economics, and the object it seeks to understand and predict, namely, the market, define the solution to that problem. Precisely to the extent that it is now invested with an efficiency and a rationality that is carried out, paradoxically, by individual interests, desires and passions, the market is seen as the principle, the model and the form of *good* government, and of the state itself. The market, therefore, so long as it is not interfered with directly, is perceived as a *spontaneous* producer of satisfaction, a natural vehicle for the increase of pleasure.

That is the reason why, in such a domain, defined by *sponte acta* and a natural course, governmental intervention must be kept to a minimum ("Be quiet!"). Governmental reason is now required to follow the laws of individual *interests* (interest is now a plural), of social utility and economic profit, of the balance of the market and the regime of public power. It is now caught up within what Foucault calls the "phenomenal republic of interests," and freedom is identified with the freedom to follow one's passions in the market place, the fundamental mechanism of which is *competition*.[23] In their Draft Statement of Aims, published in 1947, the founding fathers of neoliberalism, gathered in Switzerland at a place called Mont Pèlerin, made this connection very clearly:

> Individual freedom can be preserved only in a society in which an effective competitive market is the main agency for the direction of economic activity. Only the decentralization of control through private property in the means of production can prevent those concentrations of power which threaten individual freedom.[24]

It is no longer a matter of governing *because* of the market, and the situations of inequality it can generate, but *for* the market. Neoliberalism requires *both* this maximalist conception and practice of governmentality, for which the role of government is to accompany, support, facilitate, encourage the market economy, *and* this absolutely minimalist conception of the state. The state is to play no direct role in the economy itself; it is not an actor, or a decision maker in matters pertaining to the economy. But it plays a decisive role in providing the *conditions* for its exercise, and its expansion.

This general and constantly growing economic framing of desire has led to a transformation of the meaning of subjectivity itself, and the birth of the *homo economicus*. The *homo economicus* is the subject who has internalized the values of management and competition to the point of making it a principle of conduct of life itself, of his or her *own* life. In short, he has become the *entrepreneur* of his own self, or the self that produces itself through entrepreneurial techniques. The aim of the neoliberal technology of government is to allow each and everyone of us, every individual, to recognize and experience him or herself as a manager, albeit of him or herself, of his own home, property, family, body, and mind. The worker is no longer defined by his or her labor force, but by his or her "skills" and "human" capital, which now includes one's genetic inheritance ("genetic capital"), cultural background and education ("cultural capital"), and even looks ("erotic capital").[25] The idea of a labor-force, which needed to sell itself at the market price to a capital that would be invested in a firm, has been replaced by the idea of skills *as* capital, which receives an income in return for its services.

Through the figure of the entrepreneur, and the theory of human capital, it is precisely the difference between labor and capital that is erased. And, to quote a commentator, "the opposition between capitalist and worker had been effaced not by a transformation of the mode of production and distribution of wealth, but by the mode of subjection, a new production of subjectivity."[26] The worker is no longer compensated for a quantum of force that he or she expresses, but for an (essentially libidinal) investment that he or she made, and continues to make—for example, in education, now a service industry selling skills that are negotiable in the market economy, and in need of regular updating and upgrading. There is no longer anything like a pure salary: salaries themselves are viewed as income, and by that we need to understand a return on investment in human capital broadly defined. And insofar as the investor–consumer generates her own satisfaction or utility in that way, she is also a *producer*. Human capital, Schultz writes, is "*human* because it is embodied in man, and *capital* because it is a source of future satisfactions, or of future earnings, or of both."[27] In other words, "man" is the producer of his own enjoyment. Every worker is an agent or subject engaged in the same activity, that of the maximization of the utility function, and in that respect equivalent to any other activity.

Capitalism has proved remarkably adept at creating techniques and technologies to capture, channel, package and sell our libidinal energy, such as marketing, communication and advertising. Those techniques required a new discipline and effort, which Paul Mazur of Lehman Brothers once expressed very candidly, or perhaps cynically, in an article from 1927, published in the *Harvard Business Review*:

> We must shift America from a needs- to a desires-culture. People must be trained to desire, to want new things, even before the old have been entirely consumed. [...] Man's desires must overshadow his needs.[28]

Advertising was crucial in enacting that shift, in that, according to a specialist and former director of the General Motors Research Lab, it is nothing other than "the organised creation of dissatisfaction."[29] More recently, AIDA, an acronym for Attention, Interest, Desire, Action, was invented as a communication model used by firms to help them sell their products and services. But one also and increasingly thinks of the computer technology which uses and capitalizes on the extraordinary development of social networks, online videos, tweets, clickstreams and other "unstructured sources" by gathering, analyzing and ultimately selling to other companies what is referred to as "big data," and which a recent advertisement by IBM characterizes as the "data of desire."[30]

Yet if, through those new technologies, firms are able to understand, predict and anticipate the desires of their (actual or potential) clients, as well as generate new desires, desire also constitutes the internal mechanism or engine of the firm itself. It radiates through the firm as a whole, from its lowest echelons to its highest peak, and through the creation of new hierarchies and grades between those extreme poles (middle management, back office, intermediaries, etc.) to which corresponds a quasi-infinite list of titles (director, vice-president, president, CEO, CFO, etc.). As systems of desire, companies—and, increasingly, universities— also require the assistance of various techniques of "motivation" (such as seminars, conferences, trips, and social gatherings, aimed at encouraging and consolidating the corporate ethos), "reflection" (such as coaching, performance evaluations, self-evaluations, and targets, aimed at improving productivity and competitiveness), and "recognition" (such as promotions or symbolic gestures through which members of the corporation feel valued, and even loved).[31] The bipolarity of the old schema has been replaced by the infinitely more nuanced and wide spectrum of a single Desire, by a series of stages or steps that one climbs patiently, by the ladder of the unifying Desire—the desire to maximize one's potential, or to obtain a maximal return on one's investment, by following the natural laws of interest-seeking and competition that are said to govern our behavior. Finally, and as we already suggested, the model of the enterprise has been internalized and applied to life itself and as a whole: we are encouraged to comport and govern ourselves as units of capital, for which we are responsible, and which require a never ending cycle of investment and return. Capital now defines the very *being* of the *human* being; it is the new anthropological paradigm.

To be sure, such techniques of subjectivation are different from the disciplinary techniques of, say, the military, the prison, or even the school. In a sense, they are more effective—that is, more productive and "rational"—precisely to the extent that they achieve their goals through consent and a softer *dressage*. But let us not forget that, ultimately, it is a question of *dressage*, that is, of making the multitude behave in a certain way, or of conducting its conduct. Specifically, it is a matter of producing "individuals" through the realization and maximization of their capital, of generating skilled subjects able to compete on the global market place. On the surface, and through the market, it seems that desire was freed, and that the market is precisely the expression of the multiplicity, the infinity, even of human desires. But it is of the utmost importance that those desires all work in the same direction, that each step or stage be a cog of the same mechanism, the desire of a unique, infinitely differentiated Desire—the Capital-Desire. This is how, already in 1972, Deleuze and Guattari summarized it: "The wage earner's desire, the capitalist's desire, everything moves to the rhythm of one and the same desire, founded on the differential relation of flows having no assignable exterior limit, and where capitalism reproduces its immanent limits on an ever widening and more comprehensive scale."[32] In that respect, capitalism can be seen as the greatest apparatus of capture of desire ever invented, the greatest (and constantly evolving) force to have aligned the multiplicity of desires on a meta-desire. It is an apparatus that, following Lordon, we could characterize as "epithumosynthetic," in that it manages to gather, federate and organize the majority of desires. But insofar as it also generates or produces its desires, it is also "epithumogenetic."[33] At once federator and generator of desires, post-industrial capitalism has become something like the World Organization of Desire (WOD).

Spinoza's analysis of the dynamics of affects can help us to further disentangle how such a government of desires works. In the *Ethics*, he observes that, "if we imagine a thing like us, toward which we have had no affect, to be affected with some affect, we are thereby affected with a like affect" (*E* III, P27). This mimetic dimension of the dynamics of affects is crucial to account for the phenomenon of competition, as well as for the convergence and homogenization of desires. With regard to the former, Spinoza says the following: "If we imagine that someone loves, desires, or hates something that we ourselves love, desire, or hate, we shall thereby love, desire, or hate it with greater constancy" (*E* III, P31). Competition, therefore, does not only come from the mere desire to be different, but, more specifically, from the desire to be different within sameness. And, indeed, as Spinoza observes in the corollary of the proposition just quoted, "each of us strives, so far as he can, that everyone should love what he loves, and hate what he hates"(*E* III, P31C). Accordingly, we clearly see why the exercise of power through the imagination is the dominant form of government today, and why the so-called rationality of the economic discourse and the efficiency of markets presuppose this imaginary world. In other words, the practice of subjectivation through economic consent—a consent that results from precise and well-adapted techniques—is the contemporary face of servitude.

Paradoxically, we arrive at a situation that is the exact opposite of the one that is said to be the natural outcome of the market economy: the market, we recall, is supposed to be the place where pleasure and happiness are maximized. But the pleasure in question, and thus the form of desire it presupposes, is one that cannot and must not be satisfied. It *cannot* be satisfied, since, uncertain as we are about our future, we keep oscillating between fear and hope, in such a way that our relief from anxiety, and our enjoyment, can only be temporary. It *must* not be satisfied because it is precisely by fuelling such an uncertainty that the superstition of the market works, and its future is assured. Something like a Faustian pact is introduced through that form of power: the tap of desire is turned on and allowed to flow apparently freely, but only so long as its turbulent flow ends in the siphon of the master-desire, the desire as lack or void that can never be filled. By following the supposed natural laws of our human nature, we can reassure ourselves to be the new chosen people, who will one day be rewarded by income and happiness (if not salvation), but our promised land is one that is, by necessity, always "yet-to-come."

The question, as Deleuze and Guattari emphasize, thus becomes one of "organizing lack within the abundance of production," or "precipitating desire as a whole in the great fear of lacking."[34] Desire becomes, as Augustine would have it, "a land of want," and the economy its systematic organisation.[35] Yet, as we will now see, the morphology of desire as lack that underpins such a servitude is only an artificial construction, or superstition, if you want, which hides the fact that our capacity to desire is not the result of our constitutive lack, but rather the expression of our power (or *potentia*). Desire as lack must give way to desire as plenitude, or, to put it in more contemporary terms, the imaginary must give way to the real.

With Spinoza, toward a different morphology of desire

With his analysis of the mechanisms which led people to fight for their own servitude as if it were their own deliverance, Spinoza's conceptual apparatus allows us to both criticize the current regime of desire and move toward a different morphology. In fact, the critique of the morphology of desire as lack is possible because, as Spinoza shows by drawing from his theory of the *conatus*, and thus from his ontology, the morphology in question is an artificially introduced negativity that reverses the original movement of desire, which is not toward lack, but rather an expression of the plenitude of being.

Let us begin with the critique. As we have already mentioned, the fear that underpins the neoliberal regime is not that of the transcendence of God, as in the theologico-political nexus. It is a far more diffuse and atomized fear: the fear of lacking in goods and services that others possess, the fear of not performing or competing, the fear of falling behind in the race toward the ultimate reward, which is no longer eternal peace and bliss in the afterlife, but income and the maximization of one's potential. But it is equally a fear that is nothing but the other side of hope: the hope that, if we follow the laws, we will be ultimately rewarded. In both cases, the basic technique of siphoning off desire, that is, of creating a void or a lack from and toward which it can be oriented, is the same. The market is supposed to be the space in which men and women exercise their freedom, when, in fact, it aims to chain them to passions, to make them live (and think) like automata of production and consumption or, worse still, as entrepreneurs managing their "human capital." It is, therefore, primarily as a government of the imagination and of passions—of rivalry, jealousy, envy, fear, and ambition in particular—that the market "works" (like religion and politics); yet, this form of governmentality by the passions, we are told, spontaneously generates the maximum degree of rationality and utility. In a way, therefore, the neoliberal regime of desire is based on superstition even more than the theologico-political one described by Spinoza: The latter is based on the imperative "you shall have no other God before me," while the former adds to servitude the illusion of freedom. Yet, in both cases, we are actually obeying the imperative of desire as lack.

The crucial question, from a Spinozist point of view, is to know whether desire thus configured corresponds to activity, synonymous with a greater power or *potentia*, or to the reign of passivity, that is, of passions and inadequate ideas, under the hold of which one is less able or powerful. As should be clear at this point in the argument, the answer is negative. Along with much of the Western philosophical tradition, we tend to think that our ability to desire is the result of a primal and irreducible lack, constitutive of who we are. Within the Spinozist perspective, and as a consequence of his ontology, the opposite is the case: Lack can only be secondary, artificially created and thus illusory.

Siphoning and draining off our desire in the form of a lack means subjecting it to external forces and thus, ultimately, to powerlessness: under an "economic" regime, which requires lack and negativity in order to operate, desire is in fact weakened and diminished, and leads to the opposite of what it seeks naturally. Servitude is ignorant and blind desire, abandoned to itself in what it imagines to be its own spontaneity, but which is in fact only its submission to external forces.

The passivity of affective life along with the sadness and toxicity that usually accompanies it is thus a result that contradicts and frustrates the fundamental movement of desire, which is the pursuit of joy, or the increase of one's power to act. The economic "system" in which, for the most part, and increasingly, desire currently unfolds is based on the pursuit of a goal—a quantity—that is ontologically *unachievable*. As such, it leads to a joy that is only ever temporary and underpinned by sadness, one to which, remarkably, and as Spinoza makes clear, metaphysics seems to have resigned itself by saying that it is inevitable or, worse still, deserved.[36] But the goals of philosophy and adequate ideas are to convert sadness into real joy, dearth into excess, passion into action and to liberate life so that it can deploy its own freedom. Such is the meaning of Spinoza's *œuvre*, which rejects the morality of transcendent values and the metaphysics of powerlessness, and adopts instead an ethics of the joyful modes of existence.[37]

The project of liberation in question arises from within the analysis of affectivity itself, specifically from the point of view of *active* affects. It should therefore not be mistaken for a liberation from desire itself (an impossibility for Spinoza), but as the freedom from desire insofar as it is under the grip of imagination or, to be more specific, fantasy and superstition, as involving an inadequate idea.[38] It is not through free will (no such thing exists for Spinoza) that the mind can oppose the passions, but through desire itself. This means that it cannot be a question of dominating one's desires through exercising one's will, or through some ascetic practice (of which we can find many examples in the history of Western philosophy and spirituality), but through the sole *energy* of desire, remarkable in that it is able to *transform* itself (which does not mean *sublimate* itself). One desire can be confronted and overcome only by another, more powerful desire, which means by the idea of a greater joy associated with a fuller life. The transition from servitude to freedom is thus not the result of an appeal to transcendence or free will, but the fruit of a deepening of desire itself. The difference between the two lies in the ability to act, rather than receive life passively, that is, to live in the knowledge of its causes and the affirmation of its necessity. A bad regime of desire, that is, a regime based on superstition, fear and anxiety and which inevitably diminishes the power (*potentia*) of human beings, cannot be overcome through a negation of desire, but through a different regime based on an adequate knowledge. Such is the reason why superior types of knowledge, such as reason and intuitive science, can open the path to the highest "virtue." It can bring desire to its highest expression and its greatest joy. When, through knowledge, joy has reached such a state of freedom, autonomy and independence that it is possible to speak of "salvation" or "glory," it is known as "beatitude."³⁹ At that point, the individual feels a "sovereign and permanent joy" and enjoys in this enjoyment of being (*fruitio essendi*) a certain kind of eternity. This free relation of the individual to itself and the world is also known as the "intellectual love of God." That desire properly understood and realized ultimately coincides with love is perhaps the most beautiful lesson that can be drawn from Spinozism.

What are the consequences of this inversion for the dominant morphology of desire as we have defined it? First of all, desire is not defined by its object, but instead defines its object. There is no (transcendental or transcendent) object of desire that structures and defines desire. There is no noumenon behind the phenomenon of desire. There is only a *subject* of desire. What does this mean? It means, first of all, that the subject produces itself as a desiring subject, or that desire is constitutive of its essence. But it also means that the subject *produces* its own object: "We neither strive for, nor will, neither want, nor desire anything because we judge it to be good; on the contrary, we judge something to be good because we strive for it, will it, want it, and desire it" (*E* III, P9S). Spinoza replaces the logic of lack, loss, even intentionality and fulfillment, with a logic of production.

This means, as Deleuze insists, that, like consciousness, desire is not first and foremost, or primarily, desire *of* something, but that it *is* something: It is a transitive *act*, the manifestation of a *power*, the *expression* of an essence, and not a passion, or passivity itself.⁴⁰ There is a genesis of being (or of the object) through desire, and not a genesis of desire through a lack of being. This, in turn, confirms that lack is never primary, but always introduced artificially, constructed, imposed by external forces, as in the hydraulic system of a siphon. But it also means the following: there is no object that is good in and of itself; there are only objects (or subjects) in which we invest our desire. Consequently, the only question is one of knowing what those objects are, how they become invested in a particular way, and whether they indeed fulfill their goal, which is to increase one's power to be and act, and therefore one's joy, or whether they generate sad affects. If the latter is the case, then, according to the Scholium to Proposition 9 of Part III of the *Ethics*, the object of desire can easily be changed: There is no fixed, structural or transcendental object of desire, but only a dynamic of desire.

Second, if desire is not limited a priori and negatively by its missing or evasive object, it cannot be limited positively either: because desire, as signaling the unity of the substance and the essence of the human, produces its own object, there is no way of saying, in advance, how far it will go or what form it will take. To characterize desire as the distinctly human *conatus*, or as the specific effort to persevere in its own being, is not the same as to define it negatively, that is, in terms of what it is lacking in, as if it could aspire to be something other than what it is—other than the specific power and potentiality that it is.

To persevere in one's being simply means to realize one's essence or increase one's power to act. The real and only question is, up to what point? How far can desire go, given its own essence? How can it maximize its own power and, in so doing, increase its joyful affects? If the life of desire is not oriented toward an impossible object, it is not oriented toward homeostasis, or pure conservation either.[41] Because it cannot, even at its maximal degree of expansion, coincide with substance as such, the human *conatus* is not unlimited (hence the emphasis on the *quantum in se est* in the passage quoted above, which introduces Spinoza's theory of the conatus). Yet, because substance is not transcendence, but pure immanence, its modes—including human beings—are not signs of its degradation or fall, but an *expression* of its power and necessity.[42] Because substance is *expressed* (as opposed to imitated or emanated) in its attributes and its modes, the latter do not limit or diminish it. If substance is said of everything that is, including itself, it is said in one sense, and one sense only. There are, therefore, no degrees of separation from substance and no hierarchy within beings. Instead, we find something like a flattening or an anarchic leveling of beings; and where there is no chosen or superior being, there is no fallen or lesser being either. Difference must not be mistaken for distance, nor expression for degradation.

Finally, it follows from the two previous points that desire is not necessarily a passion, or essentially passive. As we have already mentioned, whereas desire is constitutive of our own essence, the notion of "affect" signals the ways in which the affections of our bodies and mind either increase or diminish our *conatus*, and thus our desire. In other words, affect (*affectus*) is not something that happens to an already constituted subject, but that through which the subject constitutes itself. Furthermore, this process of affection (*affectio*) translates into a more or less sad or joyful state, according to the degrees of passivity or activity involved. When we are affected in a purely passive way, we fall prey to the sadness of passions that diminish our *potentia*, and thus our desire. By contrast, active affects increase our *conatus*, and thus our desire. As the essence of the human being, desire is the very expression of the connection between the attributes of thought and extension.

However, this also means that desire is not opposed to reason, and need not, contrary to what an entire philosophical, spiritual and moral tradition has asserted, come *under* the rule of reason. Reason cannot be an instrument to tame desire, because it is desire itself or, even better, an active affect that increases our *potentia* and thus our desire. This is essential to understand the ethics of the *Ethics*, and the idea that knowledge/thought is an ethical enterprise. There is no doubt that, from the point of view of the perpetuation of our own existence, knowledge has a crucial role to play. This, however, does not mean that human beings desire in order to know, or even, as Aristotle and the entire philosophical tradition after him have claimed, that they desire to know *by nature*.[43] Rather, they seek to know in order to realize their desire. It is because knowledge increases human beings' power to act and to be that they desire to know. Desire is essentially a desire *to be*, and not to possess. Such is the reason why, in Spinoza, the ascetic *morality* of desires, which can be traced back to Greek and Roman antiquity, gives way to a *right* or an *ethics* of desire understood as "power" or "virtue."

Conclusion

In conclusion, let's return to the quotation from Curtius we mentioned at the very beginning. We hope to have shown why "nothing governs the multitude as effectively as superstition." But we also hope to have shown why, in Spinoza's own words, "it is easy for people to be captivated by a superstition, but difficult to ensure that they remain loyal to it" (*TTP* 5). Whilst the first proposition speaks to the ease with which we allow ourselves to be governed by our imagination, rather than our reason, the second proposition speaks to the necessity of inventing and sustaining technologies of affects that tame their instability. But we also showed that the two forms of government of desire we analyzed are fundamentally based on an artificially generated lack, which we referred to as the siphon of desire: it is by creating a void that drains off our desire that both the theologico-political and the economic-neoliberal regime of desire can govern.

However, if Spinoza is right in asserting that the desire that is constitutive of our very essence is not one of a lack, but one of abundance, there is no reason to believe that the flow of desire can ever be captured entirely. Ultimately, this is the reason why, where there is power, there is also resistance: the organization of lack by a transcendent form of power, however secure and totalizing it may seem, is fundamentally vulnerable. Every apparatus of power is an apparatus capable of capturing desire; every form of governmentality corresponds to an investment of desire. But the flow of desire can take directions that we cannot predict and that power structures themselves cannot control. In other words, as long as it continues to flow, no siphon, however effective, will ever be able to absorb it completely.

Notes

1 Gilles Deleuze and Félix Guattari, *Anti-Oedipus*, trans. by R. Hurley, M. Seem, and Helen R. Lane (London and New York: Continuum, 2000), 31.
2 We have used the following editions of Spinoza's works. For Spinoza's Latin works, see Benedict de Spinoza, *Opera*, ed. by Carl Gebhardt (Heidelberg: Winter, 1925), 4 vols. For the English translations, see *Theological-Political Treatise*, trans. by Michael Silverstone and Jonathan Israel (Cambridge: Cambridge University Press, 2007); *Ethics*, trans. by Edwin Curley in *The Collected Works of Spinoza* (Princeton: Princeton University Press, 1985); *A Political Treatise*, in *A Theologico-Political Treatise, and A Political Treatise*, trans. by R.H.M. Elwes (New York: Cosimo Classics, 2005); *Spinoza: The Letters*, trans. by Samuel Shirley (Indianapolis: Hackett Publishing Company, 1995).
3 Along with an old tradition associated with La Boetie and anarchist writers, one could summarize this dilemma with the concept of "voluntary servitude," but we prefer to avoid such a formulation since for Spinoza there is not such a thing as the will. Note, on the other hand, that in the very first sentence of the Preface of the *Ethics*, Spinoza defines servitude as a form of impotence, or a lack of power (*impotentia*). Part IV of the *Ethics* later goes on to demonstrate how servitude is impotence as such, and impotence the inability to control (*moderandis*) and contain (*coërcendis*) one's affects (*affectibus*).
4 Quintus Curtius, *History of Alexander the Great*, trans. by John C. Rolfe (Cambridge, MA: Harvard University Press, 1946), Book 4, 10.
5 On this point we are indebted to Michael A. Rosenthal, "Why Spinoza Chose the Hebrews: The Exemplary Function of Prophecy in the *Theological-Political Treatise*," in ed. by Genevieve Lloyd, *Spinoza: Critical Assessments* (London: Routledge, 2001), Vol. III, 245–81.
6 Thomas Hippler, "Spinoza et l'histoire," *Studia Spinozana* 16 (2008), 155.
7 On the definition of the multitude and its political relevance, see Etienne Balibar, *Spinoza and Politics*, trans. by Snowdon (London: Verso, 2000); Michael Hardt and Antonio Negri, *Empire* (Cambridge, MA: Harvard University Press, 2004), *Multitude: War and Democracy in the Age of Empire* (New York: Penguin, 2001); Martin Saar, "Multitude," in ed. by Mark Bevir, *Encyclopedia of Political Theory* (Thousand Oaks, CA: Sage, 2010), Vol. 2, 912–14.
8 As Bove emphasizes, a certain reliance on the imaginary is necessary because it is vital, that is, born of our effort to persevere in our being: to be accepted, the chaotic and threatening reality that we experience immediately requires its own image, its own code, which we then take to be reality itself, precisely because it is able to introduce order and meaning in the world. So, as Bove says, what is negative and objectionable from the point of view of Reason plays an important role from the

point of view of life's effort to perpetuate itself. This, however, does not mean that all codes are equally illusory and poisonous. See Laurent Bove, *La stratégie du conatus. Affirmation et résistance chez Spinoza* (Paris: Vrin, 1996), Chapter 7.

9 As a consequence, as Hippler notes, historical knowledge can indeed play an important ethical role, insofar as it can enable us to increase our collective power by distinguishing between different historical interpretations and making them accessible to free consent ("Spinoza et l'histoire," 158).

10 Among those who have insisted on this aspect of Spinoza's notion of affect, see Hasana Sharp, *Spinoza and the Politics of Renaturalisation* (Chicago: Chicago University Press, 2011).

11 The latter is therefore chosen as the lesser evil, as we will see later on (*TTP* 200).

12 This argument is also the basis of Spinoza's justification for democracy insofar as is not a simple form of government, but the very constitution of the society itself, so much so that a total alienation of natural right, such as the one described by Hobbes, is for Spinoza impossible. See the opening of Chapter 17 of the *Theological-Political Treatise*, where Spinoza claims that even the democratic transfer of natural rights described in his previous chapter is merely "theoretical" because no one will ever be able to transfer his power and consequently her right to another person in such a way that she ceases to be a human being.

13 This hydraulic metaphor seems to us particularly appropriate given the centrality of the dynamics of fluids in Spinoza's project as it emerges in the so-called "little treatise on physics" that appears in Part II of the *Ethics*.

14 On Spinoza's definition of imagination, see Moira Gatens and Genevieve Llyod, *Collective Imaginings: Spinoza, Past and Present* (London: Routledge, 1999), 12; Thomas Hippler, "The Politics of Imagination: Spinoza and the Origins of Critical Theory," *The Politics of Imagination* (New York: Routledge, 2011), 55–72; Chiara Bottici, "Another Enlightenment: Spinoza on Myth and Imagination." *Constellations* 19.4 (2012), 1–19.

15 Michel Foucault, *Abnormal: Lectures at the Collège de France, 1974–1975*, trans. by Graham Burchell (New York: Picador, 2003), 49.

16 Louis Althusser, "Spinoza," ed. by W. Montag and T. Stolze, *The New Spinoza* (Minneapolis: University of Minnesota Press, 1997), 8. For the sake of completeness, we note that Althusser also mentions Pascal on this point. On the notion of ideological state apparatuses, the obvious reference is Louis Althusser, "Ideology and Ideological State Apparatuses," *Lenin and Philosophy and other Essays* (New York: Monthly Review Press, 1971), 127–86.

17 Carl Schmitt, *Political Theology* (Cambridge, MA: MIT Press, 1985).

18 See in particular Chapter 5 of the *Theological-Political Treatise*. On Spinoza and the secularization of the notion of sacred history, see Yirmiyahu Yovel, "Spinoza on History and Its Secularization," *Graduate Faculty Philosophy Journal* 34. 1 (2013), 97–109.

19 Michel Foucault, "Deux essais sur le sujet et le pouvoir," in ed. by Hubert Dreyfus and Paul Rabinow, *Michel Foucault: Un parcours philosophique* (Paris: Gallimard, 1984). Another source of inspiration in what follows is Frédéric Lordon's *Capitalisme, désir et servitude. Marx et Spinoza* (Paris: La fabrique éditions, 2010), which describes the market, and specifically the world of enterprise, in terms of a specific government of affects.

20 See Michel Foucault, *The History of Sexuality* (New York: Vintage Books, 1990), Vol. I, 136. Foucault uses the same expression (and develops exactly the same argument) in *Society Must Be Defended*, trans. by David Macey (London: Penguin, 2004), 240. In contrast to what Foucault seems to suggest, we do not believe that there has ever been a time in history where sovereignty expressed itself only as a pure power of the sword, but for our purposes it is sufficient to distinguish between the two paradigms as ideal types.

21 Claude Adrien Helvétius, *De l'Esprit* (1758–59) (Paris: diffusion Inter-forum, 1973), 60.

22 Adam Smith, *The Theory of Moral Sentiments*, ed. by D. D. Raphael and A. L. Macfie (Oxford: Oxford University Press, 1976), IV. 1. 9 and 10.

23 Michel Foucault, *The Birth of Biopolitics: Lectures at the Collège de France*, trans. by Graham Burchell (New York: Palgrave Macmillan, 2008), 48.

24 From the Draft Statement of Aims of the Mont Pèlerin Society. Cited in Philip Mirowski and Dieter Plehwe, eds., *The Road From Mont Pèlerin: The Making of the Neoliberal Thought Collective* (Cambridge, MA: Harvard University Press, 2009), 22, 23.

25 Although the idea of "human capital" first appears in 1902 in Gabriel Tarde's sociology, it is usually attributed to Theodore W. Schultz. See, for example, his *Investment in Human Capital: The Role of Education and of Research* (New York: Free Press, 1971) and *Human Resources* (New York: National Bureau of Economic Research, 1972). Another strong proponent of the theory of human capital, also from the Chicago School, is Gary Becker, *Human Capital* (Chicago: The University of Chicago Press, 1993).

26 Jason Read, "A Genealogy of Homo Economicus," *Foucault Studies* 6 (2009), 33.

27 Schultz, *Investment in Human Capital*, 48.

28 Paul Mazur as cited by Norbert Häring and Niall Douglas in *Economists and the Powerful: Convenient Theories, Distorted Facts, Ample Rewards* (London: Anthem Press, 2012), 17. In a book published a year after his article, he expressed the same idea, before adding that human nature "very conveniently presents a variety of strings upon which an appreciative sales manager can play fortissimo"—strings such as "threats, fear, beauty, sparkle." Paul Mazur, *American Prosperity: Its Causes and Consequences* (New York: Viking Press, 1928), 44 and 47.

29 See Juliet Schor, *The Overworked American: The Unexpected Decline of Leisure* (New York, Basic Books, 1991), 120.

30 See "From Details to Desire: The Power of Big Data," *Financial Times* May 4–5, 2013.
31 For a more detailed description of those techniques, see Lordon, *Capitalisme, désir et servitude*, 127–30.
32 Deleuze and Guattari, *Anti-Oedipus*, 259.
33 See Lordon, *Capitalisme, désir et servitude*, 75.
34 G. Deleuze and F. Guattari, *Capitalisme et schizophrénie. L'Anti Œdipe* (Paris: Minuit, 1972), 36.
35 His is the expression used by Augustine to describe his own concupiscence as an adolescent: "I slid away from thee, and I went astray [*defluxi abs te ego et erravi*], O my God, from thee my Stay, in these days of my youth, and I became to myself a land of want [*et factus sum mihi regio egestatis*]"; from Augustine, *Confessions*, trans. by William Watts (Cambridge, MA: Loeb Classical Library, 1919), Book II, Ch. X, 95.
36 See, in particular, the opening page of Part III of the *Ethics*.
37 As Gilles Deleuze rightly emphasizes in Chapter 2 of *Spinoza: Philosophie pratique* (Paris: Les Éditions de Minuit, 1981).
38 Although for Spinoza imagination is clearly the only source of errors and passions, it is not necessarily false. He goes so far as to say that the mind can increase its own potentia by imagining in a more or less powerful way (*E* III, P12). For a more general discussion of the possible contribution of imagination to the liberation and human freedom, see Hippler, "The Politics of Imagination" and Bottici, "Another Enlightenment."
39 This Glory (*Gloria*), which is that of God himself, should be distinguished from the personal, ambitious and proud glory that Spinoza characterizes as a sad passion. This is the name that the Sacred Scriptures gave, not without reason, to "the constant and eternal love of God and God's love for men" (*E* V, P36S).
40 See Gilles Deleuze, *Cinema 1: The Movement Image*, trans. by Hugh Tomlinson and Barbara Habberjam (London: Athlone, 1992), 56.
41 Beyond conservation, life seeks what we could call health, that is, a process of overcoming and expansion. This means that life—including human life—is not the result of a primordial lack, but of an abundance, is not reactive, but active and creative: it invents solutions to problems that arise; beyond its ability to adapt, that is, to modify its relation to its environment (in a way that a machine can), it displays an ability to transform itself from within, by inventing new structures and introducing itself entirely within the axiomatic of vital (and by that we also mean social and political) problems.
42 Gilles Deleuze, *Expressionism in Philosophy: Spinoza*, trans. by Martin Joughin (New York: Zone Books, 1992), Introduction.
43 See Aristotle, *Metaphysics*, 980a21.

Bibliography

Althusser, Louis. "The Only Materialist Tradition, Part I: Spinoza," in ed. by W. Montag and T. Stolze, *The New Spinoza*. Minneapolis: University of Minnesota Press, 1997, pp. 3–19.

Althusser, Louis. "Ideology and Ideological State Apparatuses," *Lenin and Philosophy and other Essays*, trans. by Ben Brewster. New York: Monthly Review Press, 1971, 127–86.

Aristotle, *Metaphysics* ++add edition.

Augustine, *Confessions*, trans. by William Watts. Cambridge, MA: Loeb Classical Library, 1919.

Balibar, Etienne. *Spinoza and Politics*, trans. by Peter Snowdon. London: Verso, 2000.

Becker, Gary. *Human Capital*. Chicago: The University of Chicago Press, 1993.

Bottici, Chiara. "Another Enlightenment: Spinoza on Myth and Imagination," *Constellations* 19.4 (2012), 1–19.

Bove, Laurent. *La stratégie du conatus. Affirmation et résistance chez Spinoza*. Paris: Vrin, 1996.

Curtius, *History of Alexander the Great*. Cambridge, MA: Harvard University Press, 1946, Book 4, 10.

Deleuze, Gilles. *Cinema 1: The Movement Image*, trans. by Hugh Tomlinson and Barbara Habberjam. London: Athlone, 1992, 56.

Deleuze, Gilles. *Expressionism in Philosophy: Spinoza*, trans. by Martin Joughin. New York: Zone Books, 1992, Introduction.

Deleuze, Gilles. *Spinoza: Philosophie pratique*. Paris: Les Éditions de Minuit, 1981.

Deleuze, Gilles and Guattari, Félix. *Anti-Oedipus*, trans. by R. Hurley, M. Seem and Helen R. Lane. London and New York: Continuum, 2000, 31.

Foucault, Michel. *Abnormal: Lectures at the Collège de France, 1974–1975*, trans. by Graham Burchell. New York: Picador, 2003.

Foucault, Michel. *The Birth of Biopolitics: Lectures at the Collège de France*, trans. by Graham Burchell. New York: Palgrave Macmillan, 2008.

Foucault, Michel. "Deux essais sur le sujet et le pouvoir," in ed. by Hubert Dreyfus and Paul Rabinow, *Michel Foucault: Un parcours philosophique*. Paris: Gallimard, 1984.

Foucault, Michel. *The History of Sexuality*. New York: Vintage Books, 1990, Vol. I.

Foucault, Michel. *Society Must Be Defended*, trans. by David Macey. London: Penguin, 2004.

"From Details to Desire: The Power of Big Data," *Financial Times* May 4–5, 2013.

Gatens, Moira and Llyod, Genevieve. *Collective Imaginings: Spinoza, Past and Present*. London: Routledge, 1999.

Hardt, Michael and Negri, Antonio. *Empire*. Cambridge, MA: Harvard University Press, 2004.

Hardt, Michael and Negri, Antonio. *Multitude: War and Democracy in the Age of Empire*. New York: Penguin, 2001.

Häring, Norbert and Douglas, Niall. *Economists and the Powerful: Convenient Theories, Distorted Facts, Ample Rewards*. London: Anthem Press, 2012.

Helvétius, Claude Adrien. *De l'Esprit* (1758–59). Paris: diffusion Inter-forum, 1973, 60.
Hippler, Thomas. *The Politics of Imagination*. New York: Routledge, 2011.
Hippler, Thomas. "Spinoza et l'histoire," *Studia Spinozana* 16 (2008), 155.
Lordon's, Frédéric. *Capitalisme, désir et servitude. Marx et Spinoza*. Paris: La fabrique éditions, 2010.
Mazur, Paul. *American Prosperity: Its Causes and Consequences*. New York: Viking Press, 1928.
Mirowski, Philip and Plehwe, Dieter, eds., *The Road from Mont Pèlerin: The Making of the Neoliberal Thought Collective*. Cambridge, MA: Harvard University Press, 2009.
Read, Jason. "A Genealogy of Homo Economicus," *Foucault Studies* 6 (2009), 33.
Rosenthal, Michael A., "Why Spinoza Chose the Hebrews: The Exemplary Function of Prophecy in the *Theological-Political Treatise*," in ed. by Genevieve Lloyd, *Spinoza: Critical Assessments*. London: Routledge, 2001, Vol. III, 245–81.
Saar, Martin. "Multitude," in ed. by Mark Bevir, *Encyclopedia of Political Theory*. Thousand Oaks, CA: Sage, 2010, Vol. 2, 912–14.
Schmitt, Carl. *Political Theology*. Cambridge, MA: MIT Press, 1985.
Schor, Juliet. *The Overworked American: The Unexpected Decline of Leisure*. New York: Basic Books, 1991.
Schultz, Theodore W. *Human Resources*. New York: National Bureau of Economic Research, 1972.
Schultz, Theodore W. *Investment in Human Capital: The Role of Education and of Research*. New York: Free Press, 1971.
Sharp, Hasana. *Spinoza and the Politics of Renaturalisation*. Chicago: Chicago University Press, 2011.
Smith, Adam. *The Theory of Moral Sentiments*, ed. by D. D. Raphael and A. L. Macfie. Oxford: Oxford University Press, 1976.
Spinoza, Baruch. *Ethics*, trans. by Edwin Curley in *The Collected Works of Spinoza*. Princeton: Princeton University Press, 1985.
Spinoza, Baruch. *Opera*, ed. by Carl Gebhardt. Heidelberg: Winter, 1925.
Spinoza, Baruch. "A Political Treatise," in trans. by R. H. M. Elwes, *A Theologico-Political Treatise, and A Political Treatise*. New York: Cosimo Classics, 2005.
Spinoza, Baruch. *Spinoza: The Letters*, trans. by Samuel Shirley. Indianapolis: Hackett Publishing Company, 1995.
Spinoza, Baruch. *Theological-Political Treatise*, trans. by Michael Silverstone and Jonathan Israel. Cambridge: Cambridge University Press, 2007.
Yovel, Yirmiyahu. "Spinoza on History and Its Secularization," *Graduate Faculty Philosophy Journal* 34.1 (2013), 97–109.

Biographical Notes

Miguel de Beistegui is Professor of Philosophy at the University of Warwick. His publications include *Heidegger and the Political: Dystopias* (1998); *Thinking with Heidegger: Displacements* (2003); *Truth and Genesis: Philosophy as Differential Ontology* (2004); *The New Heidegger* (2005); *Immanence and Philosophy: Deleuze* (2010); *Proust as Philosopher: The Art of Metaphor* (2012); and *Aesthetics after Metaphysics: From Mimesis to Metaphor* (2012).

Joseph Bermas-Dawes graduated in 2017 from Macalester College in St. Paul, Minnesota, with a major in philosophy and a concentration in critical theory. In 2015, he received a research grant from the Andrew W. Mellon Foundation that offered him the opportunity to spend the summer doing research on Spinoza.

Siarhei Biareishyk is a Post-doctoral Research Associate at the Center for Literary and Cultural Research (ZfL) in Berlin. He received his PhD in Comparative Literature at New York University with the dissertation *Spinozan Mediations: The Limits of Materialist Thought in Novalis and His Contemporaries*. Working in the Spinozan materialist tradition, his current research concerns the encounters between literary theory and political philosophy in German Romanticism, Russian Formalism and Soviet Marxism. He has published articles on Hegel-Kojève and Stalinism as well as on psychoanalysis and the avant-garde.

Chiara Bottici is Associate Professor of Philosophy at the New School for Social Research in New York. She is the author of *Imaginal Politics: Images beyond Imagination and The Imaginary* (Columbia University Press, 2014); *A Philosophy of Political Myth* (Cambridge University Press, 2007); and *Uomini e stati. Percorsi di un'analogia* (ETS, 2004), which was published in English as *Men and States* (Palgrave, 2009). She is also co-author, with Benoit Challand, of *Imagining Europe: Myth, Memory, Identity* published by Cambridge University Press in 2013 and *The Myth of the Clash of Civilizations* (Routledge, 2010). With Benoit Challand, she also co-edited a collection of essays entitled *The Politics of Imagination* (Routledge, 2011).

Filippo Del Lucchese is Senior Lecturer in History of Political Thought at Brunel University, London, Senior Research Associate, University of Johannesburg, and chair at the Collège International de Philosophie in Paris. His research interests are in the early modern period (from the Renaissance to the Enlightenment), history of philosophy and Marxism. He has been a Marie Curie fellow, and holds degrees from the universities of Pisa and Paris IV (Sorbonne). He is the author of *Conflict, Power and Multitude in Machiavelli and Spinoza* (Continuum Press, 2009, published in French by Éditions Amsterdam) and *The Political Philosophy of Niccolò Machiavelli* (Edinburgh University Press, 2015). He has also published articles on the history of early modern philosophy and political theory in journals such as *History of Political Thought, European Journal of Political Theory, Dialogue, International Studies in Philosophy, Differences*.

A. Kiarina Kordela is a professor of German and Director of the Critical Theory Program at Macalester College and honorary adjunct professor at the University of Western Sydney, Australia. She is the author of *$urplus: Spinoza, Lacan* (SUNY Press, 2007), *Being, Time, Bios: Capitalism and Ontology* (SUNY Press, 2013), and *Epistemontology in Spinoza-Marx-Freud-Lacan: The (Bio) Power of Structure* (Routledge, 2018). She is also the coeditor of *Freedom and Confinement in Modernity: Kafka's Cages* (Palgrave-Macmillan, 2011). Her work on a wide range of theoretical fields has been published in several collections and journals, including *Angelaki, Cultural Critique, Differences, History of Human Sciences, Parallax, Philosophy Today, Political Theory, Rethinking Marxism* and *Umbr(a)*. Her forthcoming work includes essays on "Spinoza," "psychoanalysis," and "biopolitics" for critical companions to theory, Marx and psychoanalytic politics, respectively.

Gregg Lambert is Dean's Professor of the Humanities at Syracuse University, New York, and Senior Research Fellow in Philosophy at Western Sydney University (Sydney, Australia). Professor Lambert has published several books with Bloomsbury, including *The Non-Philosophy of Gilles Deleuze* (2002), *The Return of the Baroque in Modern Culture* (2004) and *Who's Afraid of Deleuze and Guattari?* (2006). His most recent books are *Return Statements: The Return of Religion in Contemporary Philosophy* (2016) and *Philosophy After Friendship: Deleuze's Conceptual Personae* (2017).

James Martel teaches political theory at the department of political science at San Francisco State University. His focus is on the intersection of critical legal theory, political theology, comparative literature and postcolonial studies. He is the author most recently of *The Misinterpellated Subject* (Duke University Press, 2017). Prior to that his books include a trilogy of books on Walter Benjamin, the most recent of which was *The One and Only Law: Walter Benjamin and the Second Commandment* (Michigan, 2014). He is currently working on a book entitled *Unburied Bodies: the Subversive Power of the Corpse* which is under review at Amherst College Press.

Vittorio Morfino is Associate Professor in the History of Philosophy at the Università di Milano-Bicocca and Chair at the Collège International de Philosophie. He was visiting professor at the Universidade de São Paulo, the Université Paris 1 Panthéon-Sorbonne, the Université Bordeaux-Montaigne and l'Universidad Nacional de Cordoba. He is the author of *Il tempo e l'occasione. L'incontro Spinoza Machiavelli* (Milano, 2002; Paris, 2012), *Incursioni spinoziste* (Milano, 2002), *Il tempo della moltitudine* (Roma, 2005; Paris, 2010; Madrid, 2013; Santiago, 2015), *Plural Temporality. Transindividuality and the Aleatory between Spinoza and Althusser* (Leiden, 2014) and *Genealogia di un pregiudizio. L'immagine di Spinoza in Germania da Leibniz a Marx* (Hildesheim 2016). He is an editor of *Quaderni materialisti* and of *Décalages*.

Dimitris Vardoulakis is deputy chair of Philosophy at the Western Sydney University and director of *Thinking Out Loud: The Sydney Lectures in Philosophy and Society*. His books include *The Doppelgänger: Literature's Philosophy* (Fordham University Press, 2010), *Sovereignty and Its Other: Toward the Dejustification of Violence* (Fordham University Press, 2013), *Freedom from the Free Will: On Kafka's Laughter* (Albany, NY: SUNY, 2016), and *Stasis before the State: Nine Theses on Agonistic Democracy* (Fordham University Press, 2017). He is also the editor of *Spinoza Now* (University of Minnesota Press, 2011) and, with Andrew Benjamin, of *Sparks Will Fly: Walter Benjamin and Martin Heidegger* (SUNY Press, 2015).

Index

Note: Page references with letter 'n' followed by locators denote note numbers.

Agamben, Giorgio, 128
Albiac, Gabriel, 65 n.12
Althusser, Louis, 4, 18, 25 n.9, 30–1, 40 n.13, 101–2, 112–17, 120 n.18, 120 nn.21–2, 120 nn.26–30, 120 n.32, 121 n.33, 121 n.35, 122 nn.36–7, 136, 172, 188 n.16
Arendt, Hannah, 27–8, 37, 39–40 nn.1–3, 63–4 n.3
Aristotle, 30, 71–2, 186, 190 n.43
Augustine, 57, 64, 181, 190 n.35
Averroes, 12

Badiou, Alain, 121 n.34, 142
Becker, Gary, 189 n.25
Beistegui, Miguel de, 6
Benjamin, Walter, 129
Benveniste, Emile, 154, 157, 166 nn.3–4
Bermas-Dawes, Joseph, 5
Biareishyk, Siarhei, 4
Blyenbergh, William van, 38, 54, 57
Bodin, Jean, 84, 99 n.32
Bottici, Chiara, 6, 167, 188 n.14, 190 n.38
Bové, Laurent, 28, 36, 40 n.5, 42 n.33, 187–8 n.8
Boyle, Robert, 28, 40 n.7
Brousse, Marie-Hélène, 148 n.18

Canguilhem, Georges, 101, 111, 118 n.2
Caporali, Riccardo, 24, 25 n.13
Casarino, Cesare, 131, 147 n.15
Celani Inesi, Anna Maria, 42 n.40
Cicero, 63 n.2
Cristfolini, Paolo, 25 n.12
Cunaeus, Petrus, 84, 96 n.7, 99 n.32
Curley, Edwin, 36, 95 n.2

Del Lucchese, Filippo, 3, 24 n.1, 25 n.6, 40 n.5
Deleuze, Gilles, 5, 38, 42 n.39, 43, 54, 55, 64–5 nn.11–12, 121 n.34, 127–9, 131, 136–7, 142, 147 nn.4–5, 147 nn.10–11, 149 nn.26–7, 153–5, 166 n.2, 167, 180–1, 184, 187 n.1, 190 n.32, 190 n.34, 190 n.37, 190 n.40, 190 n.42
Derrida, Jacques, 60, 62, 65 n.16, 143
Descartes, René, 34–5, 37–8, 65 n.14, 95 n.2, 111
Dolar, Mladen, 121 n.34

Elliott, Gregory, 121 n.33
Epicurious, 121 n.34
Erasistratus, 39
Escher, Maurits Cornelis, 40 n.7
Euclid, 143

Fausti, Daniela, 42 n.40
Foucault, Michel, 101, 111, 118–19 nn.3–4, 120 n.14, 134, 148 n.22, 162, 170, 176–7, 188 n.15, 189 nn.19–20, 189 n.23
Freud, Sigmund, 101–2, 112

Gainza, Mariana de, 41 n.15
Galen, 39, 42 n.41
Garver, Eugene, 95 n.1, 99
Gatens, Moira, 188 n.14
Grotius, 84
Guattari, Félix, 167, 180, 181, 187 n.1, 190 n.32, 190 n.34

Hammill, Graham, 64 n.7
Hansen, Jim, 147 n.12
Hardt, Michael, 128, 132, 148 n.19
Hegel, Georg Wilhelm Friedrich, 120 n.17
Helvétius, Claude Adrien, 176, 189 n.21
Hippler, Thomas, 187 n.6, 188 n.9, 188 n.14, 190 n.38
Hippocrates, 39
Hobbes, Thomas, 4, 24, 25 n.7, 35, 37, 41 n.18, 58, 67–87, 89–95, 95–6 n.2,

96 nn.5–6, 97 nn.9–19, 97 nn.23–4, 98 n.26, 99 nn.34–9, 148 n.17, 155, 158–60, 162, 169, 188 n.12
Hofstadter, Douglas R., 40 n.7
Hughes, Joe, 142, 149 n.40

Ilyenkov, Evald, 103, 119 n.5

Johnston, David, 97 n.10

Kahn, Victoria, 97 n.10
Kavka, Gregory S., 96 n.3
Kilbanksy, Raymond, 65 n.15
Kordela, Kiarina, 5, 64–5 n.11, 120 n.14, 146 n.2, 147 n.5, 147 n.13, 149 nn.41–2

Lacan, Jacques, 102, 112–14, 120 n.20, 126, 129–30, 137, 146 n.1, 147 n.14, 149 n.31
Lambert, Gregg, 5
Laplanche, Jean, 137, 149 nn.28–36
Lebrun, Gérard, 25 n.7
Levene, Nancy, 55, 65 n.13, 96 n.6, 98 n.27
Lévi-Strauss, Claude, 137
Lordon, Frédéric, 180, 189 n.19, 190 n.31, 190 n.33
Lucretius, 121 n.34

Macherey, Pierre, 111, 120 nn.15–17
Machiavelli, Niccolò, 3, 7, 9–14, 16, 18–21, 23–4, 25 nn.3–4, 25 n.10, 30–1, 52, 54, 64 nn.8–9, 162
Maimonides, 55, 78
Martel, James R., 4
Martinich, Aloysius Patrick, 96 n.6
Marx, Karl, 27, 113–14, 120 nn.23–5, 121 n.34, 162
Matheron, Alexandre, 24, 25 n.14, 40 n.10
Mirowski, Philip, 189 n.24
Momigliano, Arnaldo, 40 n.4
Montag, Warren, 112, 120 n.19, 131, 148 n.16
Moreau, Pierre-François, 36
Morfino, Vittorio, 3, 25 n.6, 30–1, 40 n.11

Nadler, Steven, 166 n.5
Negri, Antonio, 40–1 nn.14–15, 96 n.4, 128, 132, 147 n.6, 148 n.19, 187 n.7

Nelson, Eric, 64 n.7, 84, 98–9 nn.30–3, 121 n.33
Nietzsche, Friedrich, 156

Panofsky, Erwin, 65 n.15
Pautrat, Bernard, 36, 41 n.20
Pfaller, Robert, 136, 149 nn.24–5
Plato, 12, 18, 80
Plehwe, Dieter, 189 n.24
Pocock, J. G. A., 96 n.6
Pontalis, Jean-Bertrand, 137, 149 nn.28–36
Preus, J. Samuel, 77, 94, 96 n.6

Read, Jason, 189 n.26
Rosenthal, Michael A., 97 n.11, 97 nn.20–2, 98 n.26, 99 n.42, 187 n.5

Saar, Martin, 187 n.7
Sacksteder, William, 95 n.2
Salemme Haas, Maria Antonietta, 42 n.40
Sartre, Jean-Paul, 129
Saxl, Fritz, 65 n.15
Schmitt, 5, 128, 132–3, 135, 147 nn.7–9, 148 nn.20–1, 172, 188 n.17
Schultz, Theodore W., 178, 189 n.25, 189 n.27
Selden, John, 84
Sharp, Hasana, 41 n.16, 55, 64 n.6, 65 n.13, 188 n.10
Skinner, Quentin, 97 n.10
Smith, Adam, 176, 189 n.22
Smith, Steve B., 93, 96 n.6, 99 n.41
Springborg, Patricia, 96 n.6
Strong, Tracy, 96 n.6

Tarde, Gabriel, 189 n.25
Tocqueville, de Alexis, 82
Todorov, Tzvetan, 153, 166 n.1
Totaro, Giuseppina, 25 n.8
Tuck, Richard, 96 n.3

Vardoulakis, Dimitris, 3–4, 41 n.17, 65 n.17, 119 n.12
Veneziani, Marcello, 25 n.8
Verbeek, Theo, 96 n.6

Yovel, Yirmiyahu, 188 n.18

Zourabichvili, Francois, 40 n.9
Zupančič, Alenka, 126, 146, 147 n.3, 149 n.43